I0755417

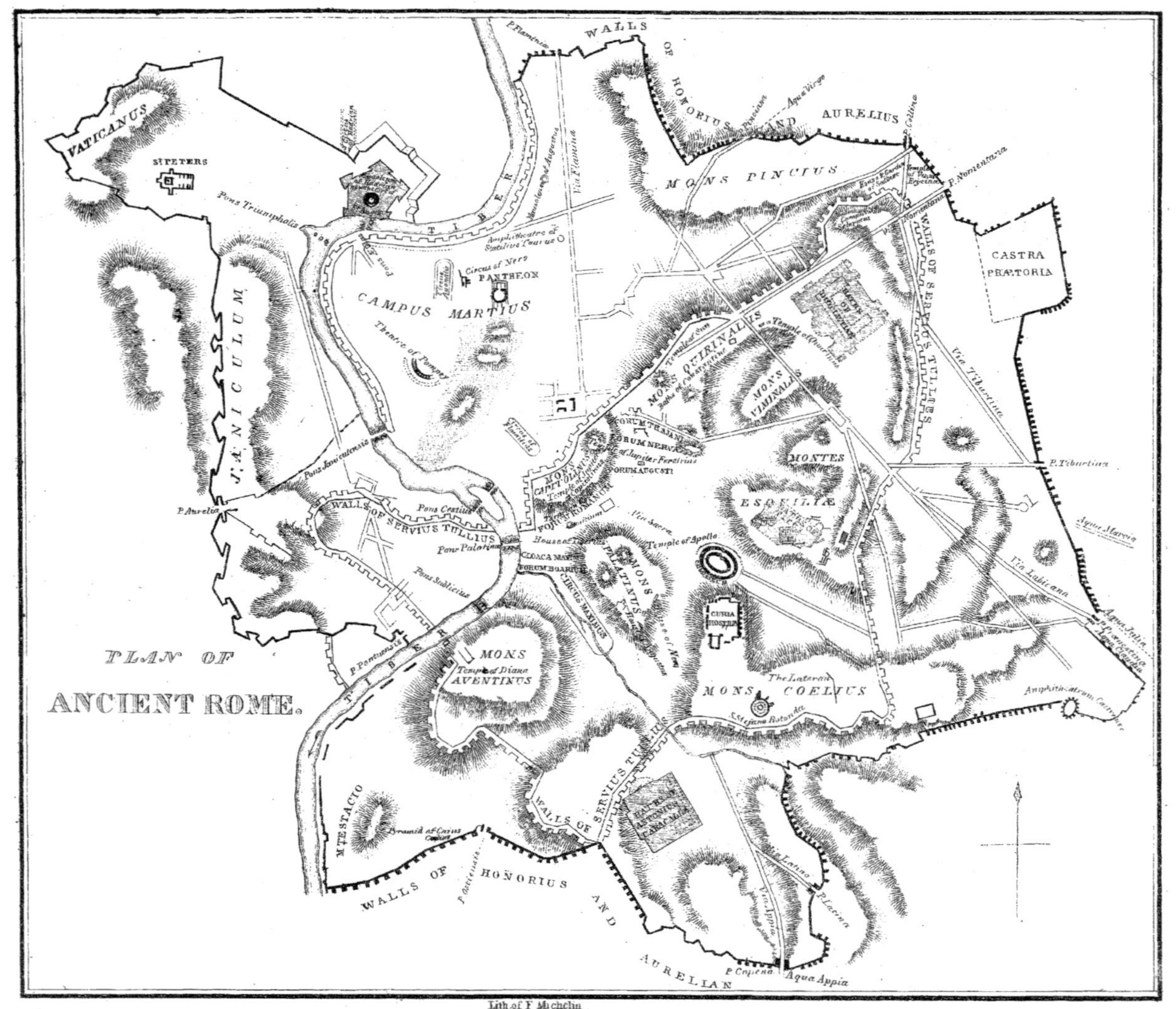

Lith of F Michelin

SIGHTS AND SCENES

IN

Europe:

A SERIES OF LETTERS

FROM

ENGLAND, FRANCE, GERMANY, SWITZERLAND AND ITALY,

IN 1850.

BY MRS. A. T. J. BULLARD.

ST. LOUIS, MO.:
CHAMBERS & KNAPP, PRINTERS AND BINDERS.
1852.

TO THE LADIES

OF THE

FIRST PRESBYTERIAN CHURCH, ST. LOUIS, MO.

THIS VOLUME IS

AFFECTIONATELY DEDICATED.

PREFACE.

The following letters appeared in the Missouri Republican, St. Louis, Mo. At the earnest request of many friends, the writer has been persuaded to issue them in a more permanent form. If they afford amusement and information to the reader, especially to the young, and serve in any measure as a guide and directory to other travelers, who may follow in her footsteps abroad, the highest wish and fondest hope of the author, will be realized.

A. T. J. B.

CONTENTS.

LETTER NO. IX.

LETTER NO. X.

LETTER NO. XI.

LETTER NO. XII.

LETTER NO. XIII.

LETTER NO. XIV.

LETTER NO. XV.

LETTER NO. XVI.

LETTER NO. XVII.

LETTER NO. XVIII.

LETTER NO. XIX.

LETTER NO. XX.

LETTER NO. XXI.

LETTER NO. XXII.

LETTER NO. XXIII.

LETTER NO. XXXII.

LETTER NO. XXXIII.

SIGHTS AND SCENES IN EUROPE.

LETTER NO. I.

BOSTON, June 29, 1850.

To one who has traversed our western rivers in "auld lang syne," the change which has been wrought in the facility and mode of transportation is *marvelous*. A passenger in the steamer "Fashion," at the present day, can scarcely comprehend the weariness and discomfort of the traveler, who descended the Mississippi in 1817 in a flat-boat, or even the small, incommodious steamers of a later date. Nor can the student of the geographies of our country in early times fail to be amused, as he compares the hopes and prospects of the sanguine men of those days, with the daily realization of travelers now. Morse, in his "Universal Geography," published in Boston, 1812, says, vol. 1, page 437: "It is found, by late experiments, that sails are used to great advantage against the current of the Ohio, and it is worthy of observation, that steamboats are found to do great service in all our extensive river navigation." The "great service" hoped from them, is explained on page 595, where he gives his ideas of our western commerce. "The difficulty of ascending the Mississippi has, in a great measure, cut off New Orleans from supplying the western States with foreign merchandize. Hitherto, it has been found cheaper to purchase articles in New York and Philadelphia and carry them *by land* to Pittsburgh, at the forks of the Ohio, and thence down that river to the various towns on its banks, than to transport them up the Mississippi and the Ohio. The experiment of the steamboat is trying in the western waters. If boats of that description, sufficiently strong to resist the *sawyers*, *planters*, *sleeping-sawyers* and *wooden islands*, which abound in the Mississippi, can be made to ascend it with loads of merchandize, at the rate of *three or four miles* an hour, and to travel safely by *night* as well as by day, New Orleans may bid defiance to the efforts of Montreal, New York and Philadelphia to engross the foreign trade of the whole western country. Should the experiment fail, most of the commerce she would obtain and enjoy will probably be divided between these three cities, and it will fall, of course, chiefly to the one which can supply foreign goods at the lowest prices." He says, also: "The canal of three hundred miles in length, on an inclined plane, proposed to be opened between Lake Erie and the Hudson, in order to divert the trade of the western country from Montreal to New York, has heretofore been mentioned. There appears little probability that this grand project can be carried into execution; at least, before the commercial connection and intercourse between the Ohio and the St. Lawrence have become so settled that it will be difficult to shake them." What would this good man think, could he open his eyes upon our telegraphic operations, our railroads, and our mammoth steamers?

We left St. Louis, June 17th, at 5 o'clock, the *time announced* for the boat's departure. A blessed period have we lived to see, when steamboat Captains keep their engagements, and boats are "off" at the hour. Formerly, the poor, helpless traveler with his baggage and body on board, and his temper at "boiling point," must wait, perhaps a day or two after the public announcement of the time of departure, afraid to go on shore lest he should be left, and feeling himself to be a sort of amphibious animal, with no privileges on land or water. The "Fashion" is truly a fine boat, with large cabins, commodious state-rooms, sofas, ottomans and rocking-chairs in abundance; in short, with every convenience, comfort and luxury—and last and not least, with an obliging *chambermaid*. This last appendage is more necessary to the comfort of passengers than is often supposed.

A disobliging chambermaid will do much to render a boat unpopular. I remember, once in particular, a snappish chambermaid, a colored woman, destroyed the comfort of the ladies' cabin completely, notwithstanding the efforts of the gentlemanly officers of the boat to make every thing pleasant.

In those days, one wash-bowl, one towel, one comb and brush, were deemed sufficient to accommodate the whole cabin. A tumbler of water, a candle, wash-bowl, or towel, was a superfluity in any state-room, which the chambermaid positively refused. Every favor was resolutely denied. She seemed to feel her province was to *rule*, and the passengers' duty was to *submit*. She made herself exceedingly odious, till a little incident occurred, which turned the tide of feeling in another direction, and, in our mirth, we forgot our annoyances. There was but one rocking-chair in the cabin, and that belonged to an invalid. When not occupied by the owner, it found many friends among the ladies. The chambermaid felt it her duty to set matters right in regard to this chair. She requested the ladies not to use it any more, as it did not belong to the boat, but was owned by a sick lady on board, "*who had a spine in her back*." We all laughed at the unfortunate lot of this woman, in the chambermaid's imagination.

We had one hundred and ten passengers, many of whom were the residents of St. Louis—a very agreeable company. As this is a passenger boat, and not heavily laden with freight, she makes speedy trips. The "Fashion" is deservedly one of the most popular boats on the western waters. It has but one fault; it allows *gambling*. We reached Cairo Tuesday morning, early, and Louisville, or rather the port below it at the canal, Thursday morn. A messenger was dispatched to engage state-rooms for the St. Louis company, but a crowd from the southern boats had monopolized every state-room but one in the ladies' cabin, and the best rooms in the other. We found ourselves very uncomfortably accommodated in consequence; but as it is the part of wisdom when one is *in* trouble, from which he cannot extricate himself, to sit down contentedly as possible, I resolved not only to *enjoy* my own sorrows, but to look about and *amuse* myself with other people's misfortunes. And this is by far a more interesting employment than one would imagine. As my position was nearly the centre of the gentlemen's cabin, I had a fine opportunity to observe. It seemed as if "every tribe, people, nation and kindred under heaven" was represented in the moving throng that rushed upon the Telegraph No. 2, the mail boat from Louisville to Cincinnati. It was quite amusing to notice with what eagerness each passenger sought out the number of his state-room, and peeped into his "Pandora's box," and then to listen to his exclamations of dissatisfaction, and see the grimaces and wry faces displayed at his lot. The ladies and servants were hunting up the bewildered children, gathering them like chickens, and putting each brood into its new nest. The servants were a curiosity in themselves—of all colors, from milk and molasses up to the darkest Egyptian marble—and the negresses from the South, moving about with steeples and topknots of the most fantastic shapes and colors imaginable. Not the least of my amusement was to see how many tumbled over the spittoons, which were arranged throughout the cabin evidently for the purpose of entrapping the unwary; they were of no use whatever otherwise, as every body spit upon the carpet. In the bustle and hurry and confusion of leaving shore, and being settled down in our new circumstances, it seemed as if the world either had come to an end, or was on the eve of dissolution, we could scarcely determine which.

After awhile the confusion abated, and a new operation commenced. A table was spread with napkins, and two mulattoes employed themselves in preparing them for dinner, and I became initiated in the mystery of folding doylies into the most fantastic shapes; this is quite an art. But the process of getting up a dinner for three hundred people, and clearing it away, which occupied three hours, quite absorbed my attention. This was the most elaborate performance of the kind I ever witnessed. The automaton-like movements of the waiters, as they walked up and down with measured step in single file, with the clatter of dishes, knives and forks, and the tinkling of spoons, and finally their regular and simultaneous movements in placing dinner upon the table, brought back vividly to my mind the evolutions of our old-fashioned militia—"Make ready—take aim—fire!"—and down came the dishes and off went the covers with such magical power, I almost feared an "open sesame" would come next, to wind up the scene, and we find ourselves in some fairy land involved in one general catastrophe.

I was pleased to see, in the cabin, framed printed notices to this effect: "Gambling for money prohibited on this boat." I expressed my pleasure to a gentleman present, who replied: "There is as much gambling on this boat as on others, but it is managed in an evasive way. A pile of *coffee kernels*, or something else, is substituted for money. Each kernel is counted for a dime or a dollar, as the parties may agree, and when the result of the game is known, matters are settled in the state-rooms." He told me many a young man was duped and fleeced by the professed gamblers who abound on our western rivers. The gambler selects his victim at an early stage of his journey, and by special attention, perhaps, if he is a young, inexperienced traveler, wins his confidence; when time passes wearily, he proposes to play a game of cards for *amusement*. This he consents to do, and is allowed at first to win. After a while the gambler declares the game insipid, and proposes to play for a *drink*. The young man often demurs, but finally, lest he should be thought mean, consents; and when he becomes excited with liquor, he is easily led on to other games, and soon begins to lose. He often loses all his money, and is fairly started on the highway to ruin before his trip is over.

We came to a little town on the river where we stopped to take on an old lady as a passenger. A stranger near me inquired of the porter the name of the place. He replied, waggishly, it was "Bethlehem of Judea." "And is that," retorted the passenger, pointing to the old lady who had just come on board, "the *star* of Bethlehem?"

We had one case of cholera on board while our boat lay at Louisville. A young man who came from St. Louis was seized very violently as soon as he came on to the "Telegraph." He had been unwell previously, and walking about the city in the hot sun developed the disease. Dr. M., of St. Louis, and some friends of the gentleman, came to his aid, and carried him off the boat to a place where he could receive every attention.

The weather was excessively warm all the way to Cincinnati, and being huddled together in such numbers, and occupying state-rooms so uncomfortable that we could scarcely breathe the fresh air, we were very glad when we arrived at Cincinnati, at half past 6 on Friday morning, the 21st. We breakfasted at the Burnett House. This is a magnificent hotel, inside and out. Everything is arranged in princely style. Princes and nabobs only can afford to patronize it. Many of our company breakfasted and dined here. Their bill was two dollars each. At half past 2 o'clock, we took the cars to Sandusky. Sixty passengers went from the Burnett House alone. We rode all night, and found it wearisome enough. This railroad is certainly an improvement on the old-fashioned "*rail*"-roads or "*corduroys*" of twenty years ago that abounded in Indiana and Illinois, but surely can claim to be nothing more than a *caricature* of an Eastern railroad. The seats for night passengers are very uncomfortable. There is a place to rest your head, such as you find in a daguerreotype chair, and I felt as if I had been sitting for my daguerreotype all night. We passed a very pleasant Sabbath at Buffalo, at the "Phelps House." This hotel is kept by Rogers, formerly of the "Delavan House," Albany. Travelers who wish every comfort and attention at reasonable prices, I would recommend to this hotel. We heard Dr. Thompson preach. His theme was the recent disaster on the Lake, and a most excellent discourse it was. We passed the wreck of the ill-fated "Griffith" on our way from Sandusky to Buffalo. The chimneys and one of the wheels were above the water. This was truly a most deplorable disaster, and is rendered more melancholy from the fact that it happened so *near* the shore, and in sight of so many homes. As I stood gazing at the wreck, I discovered a young woman near me who seemed deeply affected. She was sister of the pilot who was lost on that boat. She said her brother was one of the most expert swimmers on the Lake. He had often told his wife she need not fear that he would ever be *drowned*, "for," said he, "if the boat was on *fire* even, I could swim ten miles." He was the first to discover the smoke, and directed the engineer's attention to it. Finding it on fire, the engineer returned to him and told him "to stick to the wheel to the last." This he promised to do; and when completely enveloped in smoke and flame, and he found he could be of no farther use, he stripped off his coat and jumped overboard. But he was seized upon by the struggling mass and was drowned. He was the individual drawn up by the grappling-hooks with eight bodies attached to him. So little do we know the manner of our death! And so little, by any foresight or precaution of our own, can we prevent death's approach in his own way.

As our route from Buffalo to Albany by Niagara Falls and Lake Ontario to Oswego, taking the cars at that place to Syracuse and on, would be less fatiguing, less monotonous, and part of it novel and cheaper than the other, giving us four hours' time at the Falls, we took the cars to Lewiston. We found this a pleasant route, giving us a good night's rest on the splendid steamer Cataract to Oswego.

You will hear from me again at New York.

LETTER NO. II.

NEW YORK, July 8, 1850.

We found Niagara thronged with visitors. It was a splendid day, and we saw the "Falls" in their greatest beauty. But no human pen can justly describe this wonder of God's wonderful works. The eye alone can give a true impression of their magnificence. Three or four days will scarcely suffice a traveler to take a glimpse of all the interesting features of this place. You must go down the stairs to the foot of the American Fall, to have an idea of the vast height from which this cataract pours. There are five hundred and eighty steps, down and up again. If you choose, you can take an almost perpendicular ride, by means of pulleys, down the cliff. We wandered about Goat Island, which is almost as beautiful a spot as the picture my imagination has drawn of the garden of Eden. We saw the very spot where Charles Addington and the little girl went over the Falls, last June. She fell in about twenty feet above the "Fall." The stone was pointed out to us on which Mr. A.'s foot slipped, as he stepped to rescue the child, whom his ill-timed joke was about to destroy. We passed over the bridge where Mrs. Miller tied her shawl and bonnet, last year, to create a supposition of her suicide, and by the place where Sam Patch made his two successful leaps from a platform, raised on a ladder ninety-six feet above the water's edge. The Whirlpool, the Suspension Bridge, the Caves, the Battle Grounds in the vicinity of Niagara, Table Rock, the Burning Spring, and the Museum and Repositories of Indian works and curiosities, are all places of great interest, and wile away much time as you gaze and admire and are riveted to these enchanting spots. We found groups of squaws engaged at bead-work in the woods, and surrounded by many samples of their ingenuity and industry, which they dispose of to passers-by. I was quite amused at the Indian fashion of "tending a baby," and putting a "papoose" to sleep. One of the squaws had a very pretty infant, which was strapped into a shallow trough by a very beautiful piece of bead-work, a quarter of a yard wide—only the baby's head could be seen. This trough stood upright in the mother's lap, and she see-sawed it from side to side, till the baby was fast asleep—a more fatiguing process than the old-fashioned way of rocking a cradle.

We took the steamer Cataract on Lake Ontario; this is a very fine boat. We were about twelve hours from Niagara to Oswego. At Oswego, we took the cars to Syracuse, and reached Albany at 3 o'clock on Tuesday, 25th June.

I think, of all places I ever visited, there is none in which a traveler is more annoyed, on his arrival, than at Albany. Long before we reached the city, steamboat and hotel runners poured into the cars. By the time we were fairly landed, we were almost compelled to believe "Bedlam had broke loose," so like a pack of wolves did they rush upon us. While waiting to check our baggage, two of these runners besieged us in the most furious manner, determined to contest the point to the very last extremity. One was a pleader for the steamer Isaac Newton, and the other for the Manhattan. The fare in the former to New York was fifty cents, their printed card stated, and fifty cents for a berth. In the latter, fare twenty-five cents; berth in a state-room fifty cents. Both talked and coaxed, and we were compelled to hear both sides at once, for, wedged in the crowd, there was no way of escape. Finally, "Isaac Newton" said he would take us for twelve and a half cents each. "*He lies*," said Manhattan, "and you'll find you are awfully cheated, if you go on that boat." "*I don't lie*," said Isaac Newton, "and to prove it, if you will give me thirty-seven and a half cents for your company of three, I will give you three tickets on the spot." As the Isaac Newton is one of the finest boats on the North River, we concluded to take him up; and, with our tickets and baggage, proceeded to the steamer.

But our persecution did not end here. Like Bunyan's Poor Pilgrim in the "Valley of the Shadow of Death," we were followed by these satyrs and hobgoblins in human shape, springing up on every side, and shouting in our ears, some one thing and some another, till, like Christian, afraid of losing his "Roll," we feared we should lose our earthly possessions in the way of baggage, and, perchance, be carried off "*bodyaciously*" besides, as a *Hoosier* would say. "Will you go on the Manhattan?" said one man, very coaxingly. "No *respectable* people go on that boat," screamed out another. A colored man joined in the chorus, and offered to show us to the Isaac Newton. "Don't pay any attention to that nigger!" bellowed out the opposition. Sure enough, when we called for our berths on the Isaac Newton, we were charged three dollars besides our tickets, making three dollars and thirty-seven and a half cents; and on the Manhattan, for a very good state-room, fare and all, one dollar and seventy-five cents. So we changed to the last named boat. This is but a specimen of the outrages and imposition that meet you on every side.

Arrived at New York June 26th; dined at the Rev. H. Beecher's, of Brooklyn. His new church, just completed, is built on the site occupied by Dr. Cox's old church, formerly. It is a very large, unostentatious edifice. The front is plain, to a fault, I think, but I admire the interior very much. It will seat more than two thousand people, and although the aisles are filled with seats, crowds often go away. A pastor's study and reception room, with a lecture and two Bible class rooms, are in the rear of the church below, and above there is a Sabbath school room and two beautiful parlors, with folding doors, elegantly furnished with Brussels carpets, stuffed chairs, handsome sofas, a chandelier, &c., at the end of which are a gentlemen's and a ladies' dressing room attached. These rooms are for the accommodation of the Sewing Circle and the social gatherings of the congregation. They meet alternately every other Tuesday. These social parties are found necessary in so large a congregation, where the requisite visiting to promote the acquaintance desirable between a pastor and his people would be impracticable. Mr. Beecher's salary is $3,500, and he has lately received a very handsome horse and carriage as a gift from his people.

At 5 o'clock, we took the steamer Empire State to Fall River, where we arrived at 5 in the morning, and taking the cars to the "City of Notions," arrived in Boston to breakfast. They have an excellent arrangement on the Empire State, which it would be well for our western steamers to adopt—viz: A little door, about eight inches by six, in the top of the pillar or narrow panel between every two state-rooms. This door was locked. About dusk, a servant came with a torch, and unlocking the little door, unclosed a small lamp in a glass box of triangular shape, through which the light could shine into each state-room. As soon as the lamp was lighted, the little door was locked, the servant walking off with the key. In this way, without danger to the boat, each state-room was lighted all night, (a great accommodation, certainly, to those who have children traveling with them,) and a little red curtain was provided to shade the light, if necessary. I suppose there was an aperture in the top of the box for the smoke of the lamp to escape.

Dr. Webster's case, of course, forms one of the important topics of conversation in Boston. There are several rumors afloat concerning him, which may or may not be true. One is, that an idiot son died some time since, with striking evidences of having been poisoned, and that the Doctor was unwilling to have a *post mortem* examination, &c. As you and your readers will hear much in Dr. Webster's case of the doings of the Governor and Council, and as the Governor's Council is peculiar to Massachusetts, it may be well to say, that it stands in relation to the Governor much as the Senate does in other States. In Massachusetts, all the appointments and official acts of the Governor are by and with the advice and consent of the Council. The Council not only confirms and vetoes the acts and appointments of the Governor, but advises with him concerning them; in this respect, occupying the place of the Cabinet officers and Senate of the United States.

In constructing the government of Massachusetts, there was manifested a jealous care to keep each department separate and independent.

Dr. Webster has effectually destroyed all confidence in his veracity. His confession has come too late; and after such solemn appeals to the "Searcher of hearts" for the truth of his declarations of innocence in killing Dr. Parkman, as we find in his first petition to the Governor, April 24th, his present statement of the circumstances of his murder will have little weight. *Then* he asserts, in an awfully solemn manner, that he "did *not* kill Dr. Parkman"—"that he is a victim of a foul conspiracy or of circumstances." *Now* he confesses that he then perjured himself, by stating that he *did* kill him and attempted to secrete his body. *Now*, too, he appeals to the same omniscient Being, and affirms he tells the truth, when he asserts that he killed Dr. P. by *one* blow with a piece of *grape vine*, in a fit of passion, induced by great provocation on Dr. P.'s part. And that this *one* blow was so effectual that life was extinguished in ten minutes!

Surgeons in this part of the country are, I believe, unanimous in the opinion, that life could not *thus* be taken away in so brief a period. They say that death might be effectually *secured* by one blow, but that life would not be extinguished in ten minutes, were even the skull broken.

For the benefit of your traveling readers, Mr. Editor, I will give you the expense of the popular route we came from St. Louis, to Boston:

From St. Louis to Louisville	$7.00
" Louisville to Cincinnati	2.50
" Cincinnati to Buffalo	10.00
" Buffalo to Oswego	5.00
" Oswego to Albany	4.25
" Albany to New York	.75
" New York to Boston, by Falls river	4.00
	$33.50

By taking a boat *through* to Cincinnati from St. Louis, $1.50 might be saved, besides porterage and conveyance from the foot of the canal to Louisville. Also, by paying railroad fare to Sandusky *simply*, instead of Buffalo, one or two dollars' expense might be avoided, and a better boat secured in the opposition line. They had one excellent arrangement on the cars from Cincinnati to Sandusky; it was peculiarly grateful in a hot day. Every hour a man passed through the cars with a pail of cold water and a tumbler. On some routes it is exceedingly difficult, sometimes, to obtain water at all, and on others you are obliged to buy it.

In the Worcester depot, Boston, we found the following curious printed notice:

"*Insurance against steamboat and railroad accidents.*—The Franklin Health Assurance Company of Boston, Mass., especially empowered to insure against accidents! Capital $50,000. President, Hon. Sherman Leland; Vice President, Gen. H. A. S. Dearborn, &c. This Company insures travelers at the following rates:

Terms, 6 hours..	Premium 6 cents.
" 12 "	" 12 "
" 24 "	" 15 "

"Persons *employed* on railroads and steamboats are insured against accidents at the following rates, viz:

Engineers, firemen, brakemen, and other operatives,	3 months....	$3.00
Conductors, baggage masters, and express men........	3 "	2.00

"*Conditions of Policy.*—Any accident by railroad or steamboat resulting in the injury of any passenger holding a policy in this company, entitles the party insured to receive $200, if detained ten days; and $400 if any of his bones are broken by such accident, or if he shall be so far injured as to be incapable of attending to any business for the space of two months next succeeding such accident or injury."

The following certificate is from W. E. Richardson, conductor of the Worcester and Norwich railroad:

"On the 8th of April last, being a conductor on the Worcester and Norwich railroad, I purchased of the Agent of the Franklin Health Assurance Company, at the depot in this city, a policy of insurance against accidents on railroads, for which I paid fifteen cents. On the same evening, the cars fell through the bridge at Fisherville, and I was so much injured that I was detained from my business about fifteen days. I presented my claim to the Secretary of the Franklin Health Assurance Company, and he promptly paid me the sum of two hundred dollars, being the amount guaranteed to me by the policy I had purchased."

What will not be insured next?

We have spent one Sabbath in New York. Were roused at a very early hour by an incessant cry of *radishes* or *vegetables*, as on other days, I thought. I found afterwards it was the *news boys* who are employed in selling the Sunday papers. It is really a serious infringement on the quiet of the Sabbath and the morality of the people. Heard Dr. Stiles in the morning, successor to Dr. Skinner, Mercer street. He does not use notes; but his fluency and earnestness render him a very interesting speaker. His church is one of the most wealthy Presbyterian churches in the city; probably there are more men of influence and wealth congregated in this church than in any other of this denomination. We attended the Church of the Epiphany in the afternoon—Rev. Lot Jones, Rector. He is an indefatigable student, and a very laborious and successful shepherd. From a very small beginning, he has, in a few years, built up a large and flourishing church.

In the evening, we heard the Rev. Henry Beecher, of Brooklyn. His church, when lighted in the evening, is certainly one of the finest I have seen anywhere. The organ and the choir are in the rear of the pulpit, and the gallery, including the orchestra, forms a circle around the church. The effect is very fine. The house was filled. There are four aisles in the body of the church, and a gentleman stations himself in every aisle, and, with the utmost courtesy, seats every stranger. No one is made to feel here that he is trespassing on the rights of others, but, on the contrary, is most heartily welcomed even to the best seats; quite a contrast to the surly, selfish conduct often witnessed in our churches. Mr. Beecher's text was in 1st Pet. 5: 8, 9; "Be sober, be vigilant: because your adversary, the devil, as a roaring lion, walketh about, seeking whom he may devour," &c. It was the best sermon on Satanic agency I ever heard. Mr. Beecher has a fine voice, of great compass. He is exceedingly graphic and life-like in description, and his knowledge of men and things he shows up with great effect.

We expect to sail for Liverpool to-morrow, July 9th, at 12 o'clock, M., in the large and elegant packet New World, Capt. Knight. The captain is a very gentlemanly man, and a member of Mr. Beecher's congregation, Brooklyn. He limits his number of cabin passengers to eighteen. The following persons have engaged state-rooms: Judge Willard and lady, Troy; Rev. Mr. Sayres and lady, (Baptists,) Brooklyn; Rev. Mr. Chapin, Universalist minister, and Mr. B. B. Muzzy, Boston; Mr. Lyman Scott, and Rev. A. Bullard, St. Louis. I presume we shall have rare discussions on Baptism, Universalism, and Presbyterianism, and what other *isms* we can dish up by the way. We have been down to look at our transient home on the deep. Our state-room is very comfortable and capacious—twelve feet long and eight feet wide—affording a double berth and a single one on the same side. As to sea-sickness, the captain seems to think it is a sheer piece of nonsense, which no rational person will tolerate more than twenty-four hours. He recommends a strict diet for two or three days before sailing, and promises, if we follow his directions, that we shall only have a touch of it at any rate. I am afraid we have not as much "*spunk*" as the captain expects, and that we shall not be very successful in resisting the attacks of this monster, but you shall have our experience in due time.

LETTER NO. III.

LIVERPOOL, July 31, 1850.

On the 9th of July, at noon, the passengers of the "New World" were all assembled on the pier, waiting for a steamer to take them to the ship, which lay anchored at some distance from the city. Just as we left, another ship arrived, crowded from stem to stern with emigrants; she looked like a white rose covered with bugs. Every man, woman and child were straining their eyes for a first view of the land of their adoption, while we were taking a *last* look, perchance, of our native country.

The departure of a ship is a very different thing from that of a steamer. The ship was not rigged till just before the tow-boats left us at Sandy Hook, so we had a fine opportunity to see the whole process of unfurling the sails, and of learning the a-b-c of sea-life.

The "New World" is a splendid vessel, of fifteen hundred tons, built about three years since, and is differently constructed in many particulars from the sailing packets of former times. It has an upper deck, occupying about one-third the width of the vessel; affording quite a long promenade and a fine position for viewing the coast as we sailed out of the harbor.

We were towed by two steamers, one on each side, for several miles, when one of them returned, bearing away from us many of our friends, who had come down to the ship to accompany us a short distance on our way. In the course of the afternoon, it was found that four steerage passengers had been smuggled on board, and one was actually detected in robbing a fellow-passenger. He was driven over the side of the vessel in double quick time with a rope's end, and leaped on the steamer which still remained at our side. The captain told us that on his last trip from Liverpool to New York, among seven hundred passengers, he found that seven had been smuggled on board, but it was discovered too late to set them adrift. Sometimes a man is headed up in a barrel—he has known a man to be put in a sack and filled around with potatoes, and sometimes done up in feather beds and other luggage. Whenever he sees any suspicious looking bundles on board, he sends a man with a long stick that has two or three prongs to it, to stick into the luggage, and ascertain if it contains a piece of humanity.

So occupied were we with gazing at the scenery on the coast, and scanning the countenances and watching the movements of our fellow-passengers, both cabin and steerage, (for all were scattered about the decks on the look-out,) and witnessing the movements of the sailors, and listening to their songs, that we remained on deck till 10 o'clock at night, long after our last tow-boat had disappeared, and till the last faint glimpse of the lighthouse on Sandy Hook had vanished, and we began to feel that we were *at sea*, and that a long, long time would elapse before our eyes would again be blessed with the sweet vision of land.

Our passengers promised to be extremely pleasant companions; our captain was exceedingly affable and communicative, our accommodations were comfortable, and in the novelty of our situations we found every thing to amuse and interest us. So far, I was quite delighted with our prospects. I had learned that in all we had two hundred and three souls on board. The officers and crew numbered forty-two; there were twenty-seven cabin, twenty second cabin, and one hundred and fourteen steerage passengers. There were six clergymen, three lawyers, one physician, one surgeon, five ladies and four children. George Folsom, Esq., U. S. Charge d'Affaires at the Court of the Netherlands, lady, children and servants; Rev. Henry Ward Beecher, of Brooklyn; Dr. McFarlane, Superintendent of the New Hampshire Insane Asylum, and James Edwards, Esq., and lady, of Albany, were among our number. Five of our passengers were Delegates to the Peace Congress, at Frankfort, Germany.

I began to think a ship was a world in itself, and that there were pleasures on sea as well as on land, and with many pleasant thoughts I fell asleep. But in the morning all my bright visions of enjoyment had fled. Almost every passenger, as well as myself, was prostrated by sea-sickness for two or three days.

On Saturday, those of us who were able to make our appearance on deck, had come unanimously and decidedly to the conclusion that we understood more fully the theory of the "interior life" than we had ever done before. Such a crest-fallen, subdued set of mortals it has seldom been my lot to see. Some of the gentlemen were stretched on coils of rope, with cloaks for their pillows, and their faces upturned to the sky. One had cradled himself in one of the boats swung over the side of the vessel, where he had made quite a respectable nest, with a sail stretched over him as a shelter from the sun, and was the envy and admiration of the rest for his ingenuity and ability to make himself so comfortable. Others were pacing the decks "with measured strides and slow," and with a look of resolution and defiance which, in other circūmstances, would certainly have excited a smile. As for the ladies, they were all passive, gentle and silent, if not amiable. We had head winds ever after we left New York, and had made very little progress, which was no alleviation of our discomfort. Saturday night, while in the Gulf stream, it thundered and lightened for several hours, and the thunder boomed over the waters with a sound we never heard on land. Suddenly a terrific squall came up, and before the sails could be taken in the vessel was thrown on her side; three of the sails were carried away and one torn into ribbons, and the jib-boom (a beam more than a foot in diameter) was snapped in two like a pipe-stem. The pitchers and tumblers and chairs and baggage rolled about in glorious confusion—a couple of buckets full of ocean's brine poured into our window, while a greater quantity came splashing down the companion-way, deluging the cabin floor, and pouring into our state-room beneath the door. The captain's voice was heard in loud and hurried tones, the sailors ran to and fro, and the pulleys creaked as they furled their sails, the passengers flew out of their state-rooms, and to add to the general uproar, a knife-basket sitting on the cabin table was thrown with violence against the state-room, and the knives and forks, in a terrible clatter, flew into every corner of the cabin. This lasted only about twenty minutes, and was the only unpleasant occurrence during the whole voyage. While crossing the Banks of Newfoundland, we had some foggy days, as is always the case. We hoped to have had a glimpse of some of the fishermen and their vessels, but on account of the dense fog we did not distinguish one. Every few minutes, a signal bell was rung on our ship as a warning to any one who might be near us unseen.

As the passengers recovered from sea-sickness, sociability returned, and a committee was appointed to make arrangements for some intellectual treats. How much we missed the daily news! How we longed to know what was going on in the great world, to which we seemed no longer to belong! The only event of any importance that occurred among us, was an occasional visit from some of Mother Carey's chickens, which afforded a topic of conversation and wonder how they could stand upon the water, where they came from, why they were never seen near land, and where they made their nests—all of which questions nobody yet has been able to answer; or the sight of a shoal of porpoises which occasionally followed the vessel, and, in a most obliging and comical manner, performed a wallopade for our amusement. Several lectures were delivered, which were very useful and interesting. The Captain lectured on the "Ocean," giving us many important items of information, and stating many facts which were altogether new to some of us land lubbers. Dr. McFarlane lectured one evening on "Insanity." Mr. Bullard gave a lecture on "The West." The Captain spent another evening in giving us the details of the burning of the Ocean Monarch, two years since, not far from Liverpool. The New World rescued sixty of the passengers from the wreck. One of the Captain's crew was "Jerome," about whom so much was said at the time. Rev. Mr. Chapin delivered a first rate lecture on Intemperance, and Rev. Mr. Beecher gave an address on another occasion, &c. Then our table talk, if not interesting enough to give to the world, was so exceedingly pleasant to ourselves, that on more than one occasion, tea time found us all grouped around the table, unmoved, just as dinner left us. Stories, wild and tame, were told; discussions, hot and cold, took place. The political affairs of the old and the new world were all brought on to the carpet and *settled* by prophesy, if in no other way, to the satisfaction of all concerned. All the movements of the present day were canvassed, and either approved or condemned. Men and measures were handled without mittens, and sometimes without mercy. What else could be expected of so many idle lawyers, doctors, judges and ministers, without any causes to plead or criminals to condemn! There was a regular wordy contest, too, about all the isms and pathys of the age; and we had some very warm disputants, especially in favor of homœopathy and hydropathy. When tired of the cabin, we sat on deck. We had our amusements, too; the principal of which was a game of shovel-cove, played with blocks, squares and numbers being marked on the deck with chalk. Twelve, or more, could play at once. This game is a fine exercise, as well as amusement. One day, we became quite interested in the trial of a steerage passenger. Considerable excitement was raised on the forward deck by the conduct of one of the passengers, who had passed a counterfeit two dollar bill on a poor woman on board. When she ascertained it was a counterfeit, he refused to exchange it. The steerage passengers took it up. After consulting our lawyers and our judge, they put the man on trial in a regular way, summoning a jury and witnesses. The matter was tried; the man was found guilty, and sentenced to be ducked once an hour, day and night, in a hogshead of water, till he made reparation. Just before the first hour was out, he took back the bill, and forked over another.

As we approached a higher latitude, the weather, of course, became colder, and the nights shorter. Some days, it was really so cold that winter clothing was necessary; it was not dark till ten o'clock, and was day-break at a little past two in the morning. It seemed wonderful to me, that in the midst of the pathless ocean we could tell just where we were, and by throwing out the log, we could ascertain just how many miles we were going in an hour.

I cannot describe the joy with which our eyes first greeted Cape Clear. We had a fine view of the coast of the Emerald Isle — saw the place where the Albion was wrecked, near thirty years ago. Twelve of our party had resolved to land at Cork, and, taking a trip to the Lakes of Killarney, and from thence to Dublin, and down to Liverpool, calculated to reach the latter place almost as soon as the ship itself. But the wind would not allow us to land. We had head winds again in St. George's channel, and crept along slowly, but the weather was pleasant, and we saw the most beautiful sunsets imaginable. It is almost worth the trouble of a voyage to see a sunrise and a sunset at sea. As we began to draw nearer land, our attention was arrested by numerous vessels of all descriptions, unlike our own. This was peculiarly striking as we came into the river Mersey. The steamboats, tugboats, and smaller vessels are all painted black, with edges or stripes of white. The pipes of the steamers are painted, one-quarter of their height perhaps in black, one-quarter in vermillion color, then white, and topped with black, giving them a very gay appearance. The small sailing vessels, instead of white sails, had nearly all sails of brick or chocolate color. Several miles from Liverpool we took on board a pilot, and were towed up the river by a tugboat, as there was very little wind. Our delight at being so near land can scarcely be conceived by any who have not been at sea. Soon after our arrival at the bar was telegraphed, we were enabled to get hold of some English newspapers, from which we learned the death of Sir Robert Peel; and the first American news that greeted us as we came in sight of Liverpool was the sad intelligence of President Taylor's death. Owing to low tide, we were compelled to anchor out in the stream, and here were visited by custom-house officers. The steerage was first examined, and one man was detected in stowing away large plugs of tobacco about his person. On examination fourteen large plugs were found upon him, and in his chest a bag of plugs was found, weighing a great many pounds. It was taken from him, and he held in arrest, liable to a fine of £100 or $500. The examination on board ship was very rigid. Several men with lanterns searched every state-room, although it was broad day-light;

they looked under the berths, lifted up the matresses, looked between the bed-clothes, and in every nook and corner. The baggage of the passengers, however, was reserved for inspection at the custom-house, but the ship was faithfully searched. At length, a steamer took us from the ship, and with three cheers, long and loud, which it seemed must startle old John Bull, we bade adieu to the "New World,' and turned our faces to the beautiful city of Liverpool, which loomed up to our view. At 12 o'clock, July 30th, just twenty days from the time we left New York, we arrived at this place; "and so it came to pass, we escaped all safe to land."

LETTER NO. IV.

LONDON, August 17, 1850.

We arrived in London late in the evening, and stopped at Morley's Hotel. In the morning, when I raised my curtain and threw up my window, I was delighted with the scenes presented to my view. Morley's Hotel is opposite Trafalgar Square, with the Strand on one side and Pall Mall on the other. Two beautiful "jets d'eau" were playing in front; at my right was an equestrian statue of George IV., and at my left a monument to Lord Nelson. "The National Gallery" was also in full view.

We had hastened to London, by the advice of friends, as it had been announced that the Queen would prorogue Parliament in person, and as the sporting season commences

3

the 12th of August, the city would soon be deserted by the nobility.

There are so many objects of curiosity to a traveler in this great and wonderful city, that many weeks would scarcely suffice to obtain a glimpse of its wonders. We have, however, been very busy and have visited several of the most prominent points of interest. Taking a steamer at the Suspension Bridge, we proceeded down the Thames to the Tunnel, having a fine view of the city on each side, as this river winds through its centre. There are several bridges thrown across the Thames, and in passing under them the steamers are obliged to lower their chimneys. It is a curious sight to see the chimneys toppling over, on hinges, as you reach the bridges, and then to see them rise up again after you have passed. The Thames Tunnel is a stupendous work. By several pairs of winding stairs you descend into the Tunnel, which you find whitewashed and lighted well, with stalls, fitted up on one side for the sale of toys, books or confectionary. In the Tunnel, for the first time in my life, I heard music performed by *steam*. On one side of the Tunnel is a ball-room, in which I was assured people often have very merry times. I could not but wonder at the design and successful completion of this gigantic work, nor could I divest myself of the idea that a river was rolling over my head, and might, perchance, come bursting down upon me. I was glad once more to find myself in upper regions. The Tower and Tower Hill one cannot visit without deep interest. The area of the Tower, within the walls, is more than twelve acres. William the Conqueror, in 1076, is supposed to have commenced the building of this great pile, to which additions have been made by William Rufus, Henry I., Henry III., Edward IV., Richard III., Henry VIII., and new buildings are now being added to repair the ruins of a late fire. This place has been occupied as a palace by many of the sovereigns of Great Britain. And oh! how many scenes of blood have been enacted here. We saw the very spot where Anna Boleyn and Catharine of Arragon, and Lady Jane Grey, and hosts of others were beheaded; and saw the very instruments with which their heads were severed from their bodies, and the block on which so many heads have been laid, that it is covered with cuts and indentures like a butcher's block. The stones on the spot where these executions took place are for several yards so discolored, while all the pavement about is white, that it seemed as if they must be stained with blood.

We went into the chapel and stood upon the very spot where the bones of Anna Boleyn and the Lady Jane Grey now moulder, and saw the marble images of the Earl of Dudley and Lady Jane, as at full length they lay, side by side, sculptured within the chapel wall. We went into the cell where Sir Walter Raleigh was confined, and read some of the inscriptions cut by unfortunate prisoners on its walls. We also saw a thumb screw and saw it applied. The "Bloody Tower" was shown us, where, among other atrocities, it is said, "the Innocents" were smothered by their uncle, Richard III.; the room also where Anna Boleyn was imprisoned, and where Guy Fawkes was tried—and the tower, or rather the remains of the tower, where it is said the Duke of Clarence was drowned in a butt of malmsey. The Hall of Knights is full of interest. Here are knights, looking as if they were alive, and their eyes flashing fire, mounted upon their pawing steeds, in full armor—not only in the exact style of the various periods in which they lived, but in the very armor which was worn. The weight of their armor was enormous. And we were told that the little sprigs of nobility, from their earliest years, were trained to wear it. A boy of five years could wear armor that would weigh twenty-five pounds. It was fitted to his age and size, and a part of a child's daily discipline was, for a certain period, to wear his armor and accustom himself to its weight.

We were then shown the Queen's Regalia, some of which was to be taken out next day for her public appearance in Parliament. Here was Queen Victoria's crown, valued at £1,000,000, or $5,000,000. The crown which Anna Boleyn wore is here also, as is that of George the Fourth; the baptismal font of gold and the Royal communion service, consisting of a golden plate, elaborately wrought, two feet in diameter, and two golden flagons, &c. These are all enclosed in a glass case in the centre of the room, around which is an iron frame work to keep the precious jewels safe. The entire value of the Regalia is £3,000,000, or $15,000,000.

Through the politeness of Mr. Richard Cobden, we were shown over the House of Parliament, which is an immense building, and will be a splendid one when it is completed, and the ruins of the fire are wholly repaired. It is as intricate as a rabbit-warren, and we almost lost ourselves in its labyrinths. Ladies are not permitted to enter the House of Commons, but he took me to the entrance-door, the upper part of which is glass, shaded with so slight a curtain that I could distinctly observe all the proceedings without being seen myself. I saw the Speaker of the House with his great grey wig on, Lord John Russell, who was on the floor, &c. The House of Commons is very plain, but the House of Lords is most magnificent. We have nothing to compare with it in America.

I was indebted also to Mr. R. Cobden for a ticket of admission to the House of Lords to see the Queen prorogue Parliament. This, for an opportunity to see all the nobility, is fully equal to a presentation to the Queen. A ticket of admission is obtained only from the Lord Chamberlain through a Peer. My ticket of admission ran thus:

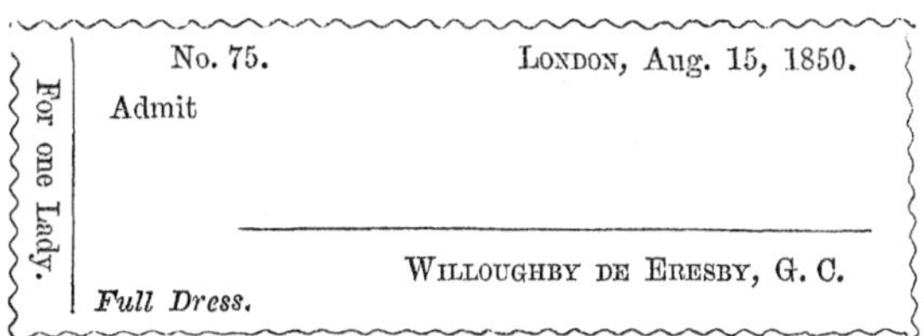

For one Lady.

No. 75. LONDON, Aug. 15, 1850.

Admit

WILLOUGHBY DE ERESBY, G. C.

Full Dress.

On the back of the card—

"No lady admitted except in full dress."

The streets were lined with people to see the Queen pass. I understand it is three years since she has prorogued Parliament in person. Temporary seats, three tiers or more, were built up on each side, for which some persons paid three shillings (or seventy-five cents) each.

No gentlemen are admitted to the floor of the House of Lords except peers, Bishops, and Ambassadors, and there are seats for only about two hundred ladies. It was announced that the Queen would arrive at 2 o'clock, and to be in season I took a carriage at half-past eleven. There were about fifteen carriages in advance of mine, and as the House was not opened until 12 o'clock, the ladies must of course sit in their carriages until their turn came to be admitted. Precisely at twelve the door was opened, and when all the carriages before me were emptied and my turn came, I was allowed to pass in, but without the escort of any gentleman. Only about thirty ladies were seated before me, and I was shown one of the most desirable places for observation in the room, near the Queen, and for two hours and a half I had an admirable opportunity to scan the novel scenes before me.

The House of Lords is a most gorgeous place. The ceiling is magnificently gilded in raised figures, and the galleries are formed of very open iron-work, also gilded. The

Queen's throne, or chair of State, her canopy, &c., have also all the appearance of the most elegant carved work, covered with gold. The seats, arranged lengthwise of the room in four rows, were without backs and covered with crimson morocco. One of the most beautiful young ladies in the rooms at at my right hand, and, very fortunately for me, she was agreeable and communicative, and pointed out many persons of rank, whom I could not have recognized but for her politeness. In answer to one of my inquiries, whether such a lady was a Peeress, my companion replied, "Oh, yes, we are *all Peeresses*, you know." I smiled, but did not undeceive her, thinking, as it was the first and last time I should ever pass for a Peeress, I would enjoy my rank.

The Duke of Wellington came early; he walked about, shaking hands and talking with all the ladies he knew, and I had a very fine opportunity both to see him and to hear him talk. He greeted our Minister, Mr. Lawrence, with great cordiality and respect. The Countess of Somers and some of the Dutchess Dowagers sat directly in front of me. The Bishops occupied a short front seat at the right of the Queen's chair of State; the Ambassadors were seated behind them. The Nepaulese and Turkish Ministers alone sat with their heads covered. The Nepaulese Ambassador wore a cap covered with jewels, which it would have been a great pity not to display; he seems to be quite "a lion" here at this time. Crowds follow him, if in the street, attracted, I suppose, mostly by the exceeding splendor of his costume. The front seat on each side beyond the Bishops was occupied by the Peers, in crimson robes, striped crosswise with ermine; and each had a black bow on his left shoulder, a badge of mourning, I was told, for the late Duke of Cambridge, the Queen's uncle. In the gallery, opposite the Queen's chair, the front seat was occupied by reporters, and behind were a few gentlemen and ladies. In the side galleries were about fifty ladies. In the centre of the room was a large table covered with documents and writing materials, behind which sat four gentlemen in grey wigs. All the Judges and lawyers wear such comical looking wigs that I can scarcely preserve my gravity when looking at them. The tip-top ones have long ears to them, like the tabs of a lady's cap, and they look woolly as if they were cut out of a sheep's hide and colored grey; I do not know what they are made of. Some wear wigs, shaped to the head, with three or four rows of tight curls and two little queues hanging down behind. When every thing seemed ready, and the time had nearly arrived for the ceremony, it was whispered about that the *Queen's speech could not be found.* I was at first disposed to be amused at the idea that the Queen *had lost her speech;* but, upon second thought, my selfishness suggested that it was no laughable matter, as in that case I should not hear it *delivered*, and so I joined in the general sympathy. At length, the Lord Chancellor, preceded by the mace, entered and took his seat. Prayers were read before her Majesty's arrival by the Bishop of Hereford. The prayers offered for the Queen are truly excellent; allusion is made, briefly, to "Prince Albert, Albert, Prince of Wales, and all the royal family." We then sat a few moments in silence. I can give you no idea of the splendor of the scene before me. I never saw so brilliant a display of jewels before; such costly array and such magnificent head-dresses, composed of feathers, flowers, pearls, diamonds and brilliants of every description. The room had the appearance of a flower garden, so varied and beautiful were the hues of the ladies' dresses. One of the prettiest young ladies I saw was Lady Constance, youngest daughter of the Dutchess of Sutherland. She was in mourning.

Some were dressed in rose-colored satin, with lace dresses over, flounced with very elegant Brussels lace a quarter of a yard wide, three rows. Two sisters wore very light blue silks with five flounces, pinked, and a white drooping feather on each side of their back hair, tipped with blue. White brocade silks with broad Brussels flounces, straw-colored, with black lace flounces, and the richest brocades of all colors, and plain changeable silks were worn. One lady was beautifully dressed in a very light delicate green silk, with flounces. She was very fair, had dark hair, and wore white plumes. Nearly all wore their hair twisted or braided very low behind. I saw very few French twists. Some wore cable twists. Their dresses are shorter waisted than with us, and they wear them so low in the neck, especially some of the old ladies, that I was quite scandalized, and scarcely knew whether to laugh or cry at the sight. At length, the report of cannons announced the Queen's approach, and a flourish of trumpets preceded her up the stairs. She stepped into her robing chamber before she entered and put on her robe of State. Then the door was thrown open and the Royal Procession was ushered in by the heralds—the officers of the Royal household followed. The Duke of Wellington bore the sword of State. The Marquis of Lansdown carried the crown on a crimson velvet cushion, which he held during the whole ceremony. This crown the Queen never wears. The Lord Chancellor carried the great seal.

Queen Victoria came next, leaning on Prince Albert's arm, wearing over her dress a crimson velvet robe, trimmed with jewels, her train being borne by the Lord and Lady in waiting, the Dutchess of Sutherland and two pages. She ascended the steps to the throne with peculiar grace and dignity, and her crimson robe was gently withdrawn. The Lord and Lady in waiting and the pages withdrew behind her chair. The Dutchess of Sutherland, a fine looking woman, in mourning, stood one step below the Queen at her left hand, the Duke of Wellington next her, and Prince Albert sat near him. The Marquis of Winchester, the Lord Chancellor and the Marquis of Lansdown stood at th Queen's right hand. The Queen is too small in stature, but she has a pleasing face and was dressed magnificently, and she is remarkably easy, graceful and dignified in all her movements. She wore a dress of gold and silver tissue, and her tiara, stomacher and necklace were all composed of diamonds. Every time she moved, even slightly, her jewels glistened in the most dazzling manner. Prince Albert wore a Field Marshal's uniform, with a band of black crape on his left arm. He is quite a handsome man. Of course, every body rose as the Queen entered and did not resume their seats till she sat down. I imagined she colored a little under the deep gaze of so many eyes and so many glasses as were cocked at her Majesty. The Queen then dispatched an usher to summon "the Commons," who were in waiting outside the House of Lords. They came in a body and formed behind a railing underneath the gallery and opposite her Majesty. The Speaker of the House of Commons addressed the Queen at some length. Two of the gentlemen who sat at the table then rose, and making very low bows to the Queen, one repeated the title of a bill to which her Royal assent was requested. The other turned round to the House of Commons, and said, "*La Reine le veut.*" "The Queen approves or assents." He then turned towards the Queen, and both the "wigs" bowed low again. This form was repeated a dozen or more times, till her assent to all the bills in question was made known. If the Queen does not approve the bill, he says, "*La Reine s'avisera.*" "The Queen will consider of it," which is understood to be a delicate way of expressing her disapprobation. Her Ma-

3*

jesty then proceeded to read her speech, which had been found, and was presented to her by the Lord Chancellor, kneeling. Her speech was written on foolscap, which she rested on her lap as she read, sitting. She is a beautiful reader. Her enunciation was slow and distinct—her manner calm, dignified and self-possessed. To republican eyes it was a strange sight to see such a body of men standing grouped before a lady to receive orders, and it sounded strangely to hear her say: "My Lords and Gentlemen, I have the satisfaction of being able to release you from the duties of a laborious session," &c. But she said it with wonderful grace and dignity as well as authority. Her speech was short; every word of it was heard distinctly by every person present.

The Lord Chancellor then received the copy of the speech from her Majesty, kneeling, and her commands in regard to the prorogation. Then rising, he turned to the House and said, "My Lords and Gentlemen, it is her Majesty's will and pleasure that Parliament be prorogued till the 15th of October next." The Queen then rose and retired as she entered. Her State carriage is as magnificent as her attire. It glittered with gold, and was drawn by eight cream-colored horses in gilt trappings. The life-guards walked on each side of the carriage, and the horse-guards rode behind. Thus ended this day's pageantry.

On Monday, 19th, the Delegation to the Peace Congress leave London for Dover and Calais, in company. The names of four or five hundred are already enrolled, and extra accommodations are provided.

LETTER NO. V.

At 4 o'clock, P. M., August 19th, we left London for Dover, by railroad, on our way to Frankfort, Germany, five hundred and eight miles. Four hundred and sixty-five names had been enrolled on the list of Delegates to the Peace Convention which was to assemble on the 22d. About 8 o'clock in the evening, we reached Dover. The streets and wharf were lined with people, who had swarmed thither out of curiosity to see the crowd of members to the Peace Congress. With the greatest difficulty we made our way through the multitude, and covered the steamer. It is only twenty-two miles to Calais, and as it was a beautiful moonlight evening, and would take but two hours to land us on the other side of the Straits of Dover, the majority of the company preferred remaining on deck. But there was quite a stiff breeze, and in a few minutes the vessel rolled and pitched, and the water splashed over our vessel's side, driving the passengers from stem to stern. They tumbled over the baggage and over one another, and were drenched in water; and, to add to all this, nearly every one became very sea-sick, while wedged in with the crowd they could not move. Oh, how much some suffered! To those who were so fortunate as not to experience any sea-sickness, the scene afforded the greatest amusement. They laughed most heartily, while the poor, miserable objects of their mirth wondered how any body *could* laugh at the misfortunes of others. It was a long two hours, but it had an end, and we hurried off the boat to the Custom House. Our train was an extra, fitted out especially to accommodate the members of the Peace Congress, and the friends of the cause who should go with them; and an arrangement had been made by the London Committee, with the officers of the different governments, to allow them to pass without examination of passports and baggage. Each one, however, had a large card, of the size of a small sheet of letter paper, done up in an envelop, signed, sealed and numbered by the committee, to show that he belonged to the company. They were allowed to go to Frankfort and return the next week, for the usual price of one way, which was about fifteen dollars in the second class cars, and a third more in the first. When we had all passed the Custom House in single file, showing our certificates, we seated ourselves in the cars and were soon whirled away, traveling all night. When you once get in a car, either in England or on the Continent, you are *in* and cannot get out, for the conductor passes from car to car and locks every door, and there you must stay till he sees fit to let you out. You see none of the popping in and out that prevails in America. Police men are stationed throughout the railroad routes in sight of each other, flag in hand, to notify in case of danger, and I have been much impressed with the care and watchfulness manifested every where. It is very seldom that any railroad accident occurs in these countries. You find no notices like the following, seen in our own country—"Look out for the engine while the bell rings"—but every avenue leading to the railroad is closed by a gate, or a policeman is at hand when the cars are expected, and the road undergoes a special review before the train arrives, by the numerous railroad police.

After such a siege of sea-sickness as we experienced the evening before, traveling all night, and eating nothing since 3 o'clock the day before, you may imagine that an appetite for a comfortable breakfast was not wanting; but, as if we were on an errand of life and death, we were not allowed to stop long enough to obtain refreshments till 11 o'clock in the forenoon, and then only ten minutes. The moment the doors were unlocked, the famished passengers set out on a full run to the nearest eating establishments, and, losing sight of their peace principles, there ensued a general skirmish for hot coffee and rolls. The stoutest and fiercest, of course, conquered; and the vanquished had to hush the gnawings of hunger till 1 o'clock, and then a dinner prepared for a hundred, perhaps, afforded a fit oscasion for another battle among the four hundred distinguished combatants.

To Ghent, we found the country level, and highly cultivated in small patches. No fences or walls marred the scene, but it was all like one large, beautiful garden. Some of the country seemed like our prairies, well tilled. Cows were drawing the plough, and we were surprised at the rudeness of the agricultural tools. Ghent was, perhaps, the largest and most populous city of Europe, in the time of Charles V., containing one hundred and seventy-five thousand inhabitants; now, it has only ninety-seven thousand.

From Liege, a city of seventy-five thousand inhabitants, to some distance beyond Aix la Chapelle, the scenery was mountainous and beautiful—beyond that, to Cologne, the land was level and poor. We saw women sawing wood, carrying coal, reaping, mowing, and engaged in all kinds of out-door work. Wheat, rye, oats, barley, beans, hemp, grass and clover, seemed to be the chief productions of the soil on our route. We saw very little corn, and that small. The houses were low and uncomfortable.

Aix la Chapelle contains, perhaps, forty-eight thousand inhabitants. It is a fine city, and is famous as the birth and burial place of Charlemagne, to whom it owes its eminence. In the Cathedral here, they profess to show you some wonderful relics, among which are the skull and arm-bone of Charlemagne; though it is affirmed by some, whose knowledge of anatomy leaves no room for a doubt, that the bone is no *arm* at all, but a *leg* bone. This arm is enclosed in a case, made for it by order of Louis XI., of France. They also show a lock of the Virgin Mary's hair, a piece of the true cross, a nail of the cross, the sponge which was filled with vinegar, some of the blood and bones of St. Stephen, some of the manna from the wilderness, and some bits of Aaron's rod. It was upon these relics that the Emperor of Germany swore at his coronation!

The "Grandes Reliques" are shown only once in seven years, from the 15th to 17th of July. The next exhibition will take place in 1853. So highly has the privilege of obtaining a glimpse at these relics been esteemed in former times, that no fewer than one hundred and fifty thousand pilgrims have resorted to this spot on the occasion; and in 1846, the last anniversary, the number exceeded one hundred and eighty thousand!

Some of these relics are as follows: The robe worn by the Virgin at the nativity—it is of cotton, five feet long. The swaddling clothes in which Christ was wrapped; they are of cloth, coarse as sacking, of a yellow color. The cloth on which the head of John the Baptist was laid. The scarf worn by our Saviour at the Crucifixion, stained with blood, &c.

We spent the night at Cologne. This city is the largest and wealthiest city on the Rhine; its population is eighty-five thousand. Here is one of the most beautiful Gothic Cathedrals in Europe; it is, however, like very many of the most elegant and costly churches on the Continent, unfinished. We did not reach Cologne till evening, and it was rather a difficult matter to dispose of nearly five hundred visitors. Our accommodations were miserable. It was a warm night in August, and my bed consisted of a huge feather bed, a large feather pillow to put my feet upon, and two pillows for my head, with a feather bed to cover over all. They use none but single bedsteads in Germany, either in hotels or private houses. I ought, in justice, to say that, except in one other instance, we have found excellent beds in Germany. They generally have a comforter of down, which you can use or not, for an outer covering; but only among the lower class do you find the huge feather beds to smother you in, which I have named above. We found, almost invariably, excellent matresses and clean beds throughout Germany and Switzerland.

In the morning, we took a steamer to Mayence; and in the beautiful scenery which burst upon us after we left Bonn, a city of fifteen thousand inhabitants, we forgot all the discomforts and annoyances of the preceding day and nights. Within twenty-four hours, we were in four different kingdoms — England, France, Belgium and Prussia.

Bonn is famous for its University, and a huge palace built for the Electors of Cologne in 1730, nearly half a mile long, serves to contain the University. Prince Albert was a student here. Beethoven, the composer, was born here in 1770.

The banks of the Rhine, even to the summits of the highest hills, are in a state of the greatest cultivation. Every little strip of land, even amidst the rocks and almost inaccessible places, apparently, seemed to be filled with grape vines. In some spots, where the hills were steep, they build up terraces. The vines are trained on poles, three, four, or five feet high, like hops, and require an immense amount of labor. The old castles, too, on each side of the stream, presenting every few miles their moss-covered ruins to our view, kept our curiosity alive. I did not count the castles we passed on the Rhine, but I think there must have been thirty or forty, perhaps more — all ruins — speaking of the past, telling of the dead — and in such meagre traditions as only to create mystery, excite imagination, and awaken melancholy.

Mayence is a beautiful city, with thirty-six thousand inhabitants, and has eight thousand soldiers stationed in it—half Prussian and half Austrian. It seemed, as we walked this city, that we were in a camp, surrounded with soldiers. The Cathedral is an object of interest. A part of it has been built nine hundred years. The tower suffered from the Prussian bombardment in 1793, and is just as they left it.

From Mayence to Frankfort, we had a few miles of railroad. We passed large fields of poppies, and a great abundance of plums. Hemp and flax fields, too, lined the road side.

We arrived at Frankfort on the morning of the 22d of August, where we spent one week. A committee to provide places for those who should attend the Peace Congress, assigned us lodgings in a family, the head of which is connected with the Post Office Department. They only assigned *places;* every member defrayed his own expenses.

LETTER VI.

Thursday morning, August 22d, the Peace Congress convened in St. Paul's Church, Frankfort, which was two years since given up to the German Congress, and has never been used since that time till it was opened for the Peace Convention. It is a very large building; the seats are circular, with two galleries, and it will contain five thousand people. It was well filled during the three days' session, and the meetings were exceedingly interesting. Most of the countries of Europe were represented there, and we had speeches in German, French, English and Italian. The same speaker sometimes addressed the assembly in three different languages. Mr. Jaup, late Prime Minister of Hesse Darmstadt, was in the chair. I cannot begin to give you an account of the many thrilling speeches that were made and translated, nor even give you a list of the many distinguished men of all nations, present. Cobden and Gerardin were decidedly the greatest lions there, as far as speeches are concerned. It was a delightful meeting, and will be productive, no doubt, of happy results.

A letter was read from the Archbishop of Paris, approving the meeting, &c. As near as I could learn, thirty-five American Delegates were present. I presume before this you have received, in the German newspapers, a full account of the meetings. I intended to have sent you an extra, published in English, if it had been out in time; but it was not issued till the day after we left. We visited many places of interest in Frankfort, among which were the Cathedral, (a building of the thirteenth century,) in which forty-six Emperors have been chosen and crowned before the altar; and the Banqueting Hall, in the Town House, where the festivities succeeding the coronation were celebrated. Here are the portraits of fifty-two Emperors, from Conrad I. to Francis II. In the Dom Platz, we saw the house in which Luther resided, and the window from which he addressed the people. Under it is his bust on the wall. We saw some very fine paintings also, among the best of which was a large painting of "Huss before the Council of Constance," an admirable picture, and a child of Rubens, painted by himself, which was all but alive.

The most curious place we saw was "Juden Gasse," the Jews' street, where the Rothschilds were born and lived, and where the old lady, not long since, died. I think I never saw a darker, more dirty, or forlorn looking place. I could think of nothing, as I looked into the long, dark, time-eaten halls of the houses in this quarter, but looking into the byways that lead to the bottomless pit. But black, old and gloomy as the place is, the old lady Rothschild could never be prevailed upon to leave the home of her youth and live in the palaces of her sons.

We visited, also, the house where the poet Goethe was born. This is a beautiful residence. Some of the streets and houses in the new portions of Frankfort are very handsome. The Cemetery at Frankfort is well worth visiting. It is unlike any other repository of the dead I have ever seen. The Old Cemetery, as it is called, is full; and as you enter a large and massive gateway, your eye meets one unbroken array of white marble gravestones, in the form of a cross. Trees, shrubbery and flowers surround the immense plat of graves. Bursting upon me unexpectedly, as it did, I felt for the moment that an army of the shrouded dead were waiting to receive us as we entered.

Bordering on this large square, among the trees, are many very beautiful tombs, fine walks and rare flowers. Fresh flowers were lying on almost every grave, and wreaths of fresh flowers garnished every tomb.

Among the monuments here was a chapel in gothic style, erected by one of the late Dukes of Hesse to the memory of the wife whom he married with his *left hand*. It cost an immense number of florins—I dare not say how many. On asking an explanation of a left-hand marriage, I was told that the Duke was allowed to marry two wives—a wife from the nobility, whom he married with the *right hand*, and a wife from the people, who could be married only with the *left*. That they were equally recognised and legal marriages, but the children only of the *noble* wife could inherit the titles and honors of the Ducal family. The Duke intended to have been buried in the tomb of the left-hand wife, but, as he made no *will* to that effect, when he died his remains were buried with his ancestors. He married another wife from the people after the death of his first left-hand wife, and his *noble wife* and the last left-hand wife are still living. I was quite incredulous about this matter, but was informed by four different intelligent Germans, natives of Frankfort, that it was even so.

The streets of the old part of the city are exceedingly narrow, and the upper stories of the houses in some of them jut over the street so far that you can almost shake hands with your opposite neighbors. The streets are altogether paved with large flat stones, the old ones having no sidewalks. Very many respectable families live in tiers or layers, one family living in the lower story, another in the second, and so on to the fifth, and sometimes higher. At the front door you will find five bell-knobs perhaps, one above the other, numbered one, two, three, and so on; you must ring the bell of the story in which your friend lives. Of course, the kitchen, &c., are all in the story occupied by each family.

We were greatly harassed for a few days with the currency—florins, groschens, silver groschens, kreutzers, and so on; and speaking no German, and but little French, we had marvelous times when we undertook to do any shopping.

We found here, as in Mayence, several thousand soldiers stationed, half Austrians, and the other half Prussians. The citizens of Frankfort and other prominent places in the vicinity are exceedingly restive under the burdens and restraints now laid upon them. The presence of foreign troops wounds their pride, and embitters their feelings toward their rulers. In speaking of these soldiers, as we passed some of them in the streets of Frankfort, a very intelligent, wealthy citizen remarked to us, that he hoped soon to have a chance to exchange shots with some of them. The Prince of Prussia, who is very far from being popular among the people of Frankfort, reviewed the Prussian troops the morning before we left the city. A respectable committee was deputed to call on him with a petition from the citizens, praying that the number of troops in that city might be diminished. We were informed that he replied, "You come from the discontented to complain, do you? I will give you cause to complain. The number of troops shall be increased." Many were greatly enraged by this reply. It is not easy to predict whereunto these things will grow. The standing armies, now employed in most parts of the continent to keep the people under, are a grievous burden—a burden which cannot long be endured. Nearly half the vigorous, able-bodied men are now in the army. As a consequence, the women in great numbers are forced into the fields, to do the hard labor that should be done by those who are wasting their time and strength in burnishing their weapons of war. If man forsakes his home for the army, and woman leaves it for the field, what becomes of the careful training of children, and who is to make bright and cheerful the fireside, and cultivate the dear delights of home?

LETTER VII.

On the twenty-eighth day of August we left Frankfort for Heidelberg by railroad, a distance of fifty-six miles. The country was level and uninteresting till we reached Darmstadt. This is the capital of the Grand Duchy of Hesse, and the Grand Duke resides here. Population thirty thousand. From Darmstadt to Heidelberg the scenery is beautiful. We had a view of the highest peak of the Odenwald chain of hills, the *Melibocus*, from the top of which you can see sixty miles. On our route to Heidelberg we had a view of the Castles of Auerberg, the Abbey of Lorsch, Starkenberg Castle, and the ruined Castle of Strahlenberg. Heidelberg and its vicinity are beautiful. From the terrace, facing the river Neckar, on which it stands, we had a magnificent view of the town and the majestic hills behind it. The castle has the most imposing front of any that I have yet seen. This was for many years the residence of the Electors Palatine. It is said very few towns in Europe have experienced the horrors of war more frequently than this city. It has been five times bombarded, twice burnt, and three times taken by assault and pillaged. Its castle would seem from its situation and strength to be impregnable; but one of the towers was undermined by the French, and half of it, instead of crumbling to pieces in the fall, has slid down in one solid mass into the ditch.

In the cellar we saw the famous *tuns* built to hold the wine used at the castle. One (the *small* one, as the guide called it) was built in 1662, and holds ten thousand gallons, or sixty thousand bottles. But it seems this did not begin to meet the necessities of the noble family, and another was built in 1751 which holds forty-six thousand gallons; it took six months to empty it. It is thirty-two feet long and twenty-four feet high, and cost eighty thousand florins, or thirty-two thousand dollars. After taking a look at its dimensions behind and before, and on each side, which were amazing, we walked up quite a flight of stairs to the top; over it is built a platform with a railing around it. Upon this platform the guide said it was customary to have a dance whenever the tun was newly filled. It has not been filled since 1769.

We visited St. Peter's Church and saw the door on which Jerome of Prague attached his celebrated theses, and the place where he expounded his doctrines to the multitude in the neighboring church-yard. The inscriptions, in the part of the church-yard which we saw, were altogether in Hebrew, and have stood many, many years.

The University of Heidelberg is one of the oldest in Germany—was founded in 1386. It has now six hundred students. We visited the library, which contains an immense number of books, and were shown some very great literary curiosities; among which were Luther's manuscript translation of Isaiah, in a state of excellent preservation—the manuscripts of Thucydides and Plutarch, of the 10th and 11th centuries—a copy of the Heidelberg Catechism, with Luther's annotations in his own handwriting—and the Prayer Book of the Electress Elizabeth, daughter of James I., in her own writing.

From Heidelberg we took the railroad to Carlsruhe. This is the capital of the Grand Duchy of Baden, and contains between twenty and thirty thousand inhabitants. This city is laid out in a very singular manner. The palace is surrounded by a circular court-yard, a handsome row of houses forming a circle about it. All the streets of the city, like the spokes of a wheel, terminate in this centre; so that in a walk round this circle, you can see through all the main streets, and in a few moments obtain a good general view of the town.

There is also a beautiful avenue of Lombardy poplars, two miles long, leading to Durlach; none of these poplars are less than ninety feet and some a hundred and twenty feet in height. After leaving the Rastadt station, a few miles from here is seen an old deserted chateau of the Margraves of Baden, built by Sybilla, wife of Louis of Baden. This lady was very beautiful, and it is said was as vain as she was handsome. There are sixty or seventy portraits of her, taken in different costumes, still hanging in her boudoir. In her old age she became exceedingly bigoted. Her whole time was spent in privation and penance. She wore a hair shirt and a cross of wire net-work with points inside next her skin, and had two circular pieces of the same material to kneel upon. Her bed was a thin rush mat laid upon the floor.

For a number of miles we found wreaths of flowers hung up in every direction, and flags flying from almost every house. On inquiry we found it was the birth-day of the Grand Duke, who was fifty-eight years of age. When we entered Baden, which is a city of great beauty, embosomed among the hills of the Black Forest, and built on the Oos river, we found great preparations making for extensive fireworks in honor of the Grand Duke. This city contains six thousand inhabitants, and has been a celebrated watering place; it is said thirty-two thousand people visited it last year. We went to the old castle where the Margraves of Baden lived six hundred years. The dungeons under the castle are well worth a visit. Following a guide, we were conducted down winding stairs through several narrow dark entries with cells on each side, and came to a passage where, looking up, we discovered the light through a large tunnel leading up to the top of the castle. Here, our guide told us, persons had been let down blindfolded in an arm-chair, never to find their way out. Wander wherever they would, a dark cell would receive them, and a ponderous stone door, at length, by an invisible hand, would shut upon them. These stone doors are composed of one solid slab, a foot and a half thick, and springs concealed in the wall would slowly turn them on a pivot and close them so that no human strength could force them. She showed us also one dungeon in which the instruments of torture were still remaining, and a trap-door beyond which an image of the Virgin stood in a niche. On being told to kiss the Virgin, the prisoner stepping on the trap-door found it fall beneath him, and he was precipitated on a wheel filled with knives and cut to pieces.

At Basle we visited the cathedral in which Erasmus is buried, and the cloisters which were his favorite resort, and went into the room where the famous Council of Basle were accustomed to meet. Here Pope Eugene IV. was dethroned and replaced by Felix V. This room was full of interest to us, as it remains precisely in its original state. In the library of the university we saw, among other curiosities, some manuscripts of Erasmus, who was Professor here.

The country from Basle to Berne is very beautiful. The soil is rich and highly cultivated. But it is a melancholy sight to see the women engaged in the most laborious outdoor duties, and cows yoked together performing the labor of oxen and horses with us, and driven by women. We often met women leading a cow, by a rope round her horns, attached to a load of hay. One of the greatest beauties of the scenery on the continent, is the absence of those ugly fences and rude walls which mar so greatly the aspect of the cultivated parts of our own country. Here, for miles, you see nothing unsightly. The roads are in perfect repair, not a fence even between them and the fields; but one vast beautiful field or garden is spread out to your admiring view. How each land owner, without any visible limit, can understand the boundary of his own possessions, especially after his crop is garnered, is a mystery to me. Or how people can live together in harmony, without quarrels and lawsuits, where no constant visible barrier between mine and thine exists, I cannot comprehend.

Berne is a beautiful city, with twenty or thirty thousand inhabitants. Here we obtained our *first* view (and a most magnificent one it was) of the snowy Alps. The sky was clear, without a cloud, and nearly a dozen peaks of the Bernese Alps rose up in all their beauty and majesty before us, like so many pyramids of snow. You can scarcely imagine our feelings, as we seated ourselves beneath the shade of some old, lofty green tree, on the terrace back of the cathedral, to enjoy the beautiful landscape before us. It was the 30th of August, and every thing about us wore the livery of summer. The river Aar rolled one hundred and eight feet below us, at our feet. The hills about us were clothed with verdure, and yet we were in full sight of the land of eternal snows. There is a great deal to interest and amuse a traveler in Berne. The costumes of the Swiss are a novelty; some of their fashions are very becoming. The town clock, in the centre of the city, is quite a curiosity. A minute before the clock strikes, a wooden cock, by the side of it, crows and flaps its wings; and while a puppet strikes the hour on a bell, a procession of bears issues out and passes in front of a figure upon a throne, who marks the hour by gaping and by lowering his sceptre. They indulge here in a curious partiality for *bears.* Images of this animal are seen everywhere. It is a favorite device, and is the armorial bearing of the canton. Outside one of the gates, two bears are to be found, living at public expense. Quite a large place of solid masonry is built up for their comfort. It would be quite a slight to omit visiting "Barengraben," as it is called. For hundreds of years bears have been kept at public charge. When the French army took possession of Berne, in 1798, the bears were led away captive, and deposited in the "Jardin des Plantes." But when, after a time, matters were settled, the bears were sent for, and provided for as before. Perhaps the Bear is looked upon as the tutelar deity of the city.

At Berne, we found Dr. Hitchcock, President of Amherst College, and his lady, and in company with them we left for Geneva and Mont Blanc.

LETTER NO. VIII

Spending a Sabbath in Berne, we took a Diligence from there to Vevay on Monday. The Diligence is unlike any public conveyance we have in America; it is a great, lumbering vehicle, which, on account of its clumsiness, rolls lazily along. It is divided into several compartments, viz: The "coupee," "l'interieur," "le banquette," "l'imperiale," and "le rotonde." The "coupee" is the most desirable; it will hold three persons, and being exactly behind and below the drivers' seat, with an open front, you have a fine view of the country as you pass along. The seats in this compartment are somewhat higher in price than the others. The "interieur" is the middle division, "le rotonde" is the last, and the "banquette" and "imperiale" are on top. All these divisions will hold sixteen or eighteen persons. They often attach three horses abreast, in front of the wheel horses, and sometimes, in ascending a hill, they put on a pair of oxen ahead of all. These horses have bells about their necks, as with us in sleigh-riding. Beside the driver, there is a conductor, who carries the passengers' passports, attends to the baggage and other matters, and there is often a postillion, who rides one of the front horses. We passed through Freyburg and Bulle—the former of which is noted for its Suspension Bridge, the longest of a single curve in the world—and it has one of the finest organs in Europe, built by the late Aloys Mooser, a native of Freyburg. It has sixty-four stops, and seventy-eight hundred pipes, some of them thirty-two feet long. By paying eleven francs for a party, you may have an opportunity to hear it. The town has eight or ten thousand inhabitants. The country, from Berne to Freyburg, is mostly a grazing country; we saw scarcely any vineyards.

We did not reach Vevay till eight or nine in the evening; but it was moonlight, and so beautiful did our winding way among the hills and vineyards seem, down to the bright and calm Lake of Geneva which lay at our feet, that we talked seriously about turning back the next morning, eight or ten miles, to have another and a day-light view of the same scene. But, as our time was limited, we finally concluded to take a small steamer the next morning from Vevay to Geneva, a distance of fifty-five miles. Vevay is a beautiful little town, located on the east end of Lake Geneva, and the city of Geneva is situated at its western extremity, where the Rhone issues out of it. Vevay is famous for its vineyards and wines. I never saw more delicious grapes.

It was a calm, bright day; the sky was cloudless, and we enjoyed the trip exceedingly. Our view of Mont Blanc, though at a distance of sixty miles, was magnificent. We were told by those on board, who had often traversed the Lake, that we were peculiarly fortunate, as so clear and fine a view was seldom obtained. We could scarcely believe ourselves to be more than ten miles from its base, so distinctly did it stand before us in all its snowy beauty, among the green hills of the Alpine range. On our right, were the towns of Lausanne, Coppet, Ferney, &c. At Lausanne, Gibbon wrote his History of Rome. At Coppet, we saw the chateau of Madame de Stæl. Ferney, about five miles from Geneva, was, for twenty years, the residence of Voltaire; and two of the rooms which he occupied are still preserved as he left them, even to the curtains of his bed, which, it is said, are fast disappearing, from the depredations of visitors. The place where Lord Byron wrote some of his works was pointed out to us also. Geneva is a beautiful place, containing about thirty thousand inhabitants. It is, as every one knows, a famous place for watches, musical boxes, &c. It is said that three thousand people are engaged in watch-making. Here Rousseau was born, and Calvin lived and labored for many years and was buried, and Sir Humphrey Davy died and was buried in the Cemetery of the Plain Palais. No stone marks the grave of Calvin. He forbade the Genevese to erect any monument to his memory, and the site of his grave is not known with any certainty. The Naturalist, Saussure, also, who was the first to ascend Mont Blanc, was born here; and, at the present day, it is the residence of Merle D'Aubigny, author of the History of the Reformation. By the way, he is called *Dr. Merle* here, D'Aubigny being his assumed name as a writer.

We visited John Calvin's house, No. 116 Rue des Chanoines, and we loitered about a long time in St. Peter's

Church, whose walls had so often echoed to his eloquent appeals. Some alterations have taken place in the Church since his day, but much of it remains just as he left it. The old-fashioned sounding board which hung over his head in the pulpit, hangs there still. Families live here in tiers, as they do in Frankfort. We took dinner with a Professor in a Seminary here, who lives in the fifth story. We were obliged to go up one hundred and twenty stairs to the parlor.

The surveillance that is exercised on the Continent, over all the people, we have no conception of in our own country. Even the native inhabitants cannot go from town to town without permission, and their passports are as essential to their well-being, and as rigidly scrutinized, as those of travelers. Foreign residents are more strictly watched still. One gentleman told us, that in getting his passport arranged to leave Geneva for a few weeks only, he happened to see a minute of his most trifling movements recorded by his name in the books of the Bureau, some of which he supposed were known only to himself and family, as they concerned no one else. Our gentlemen, Dr. Hitchcock and Mr. Bullard, called on Rev. Dr. Merle and Rev. Dr. Malan. The latter is quite a patriarch, with white flowing locks; he received them in a very kind and affectionate manner, and on parting, did not even omit the apostolic kiss. Two of his daughters are recently married to American clergymen, one a Rev. Mr. Hall, of Connecticut, and the other, Rev. Mr. Fletcher, Chaplain to the Seamen at Rio Janeiro.

We were shown, at Geneva, some enormous granite boulders, transported from the Alps, two of which, a little distance beyond the port of Geneva, project above the water from the bed of the Lake. They are called "*Pierres de Niton.*" Tradition says they were used as altars to Neptune. They are hollowed out, and instruments of sacrifice have been found near them. After spending two days in

Geneva, we took a "voiture" to Chamouny, a little town lying at the foot of Mont Blanc, a distance of fifty-four miles. We had taken every precaution to have our passports "en regle," as it is called. Had obtained the vise of the Police and of the Sardinian Minister, for the last of which we had to pay four francs. When we reached the boundary of Savoy, we were stopped and the passports demanded and vised again, and in a few rods farther, another police officer stepped up to the carriage and demanded a look at our passports. A gentleman who was behind us, in the Diligence, and had paid his passage to Chamouny, but had come without his passport from Geneva, thinking it unimportant for so short a distance, was not permitted to go on, and was obliged to return and lose the money he had paid for his passage.

Our ride to Chamouny would have been charming, had not our path been beset with beggars. So many assailed our carriage, that we counted fifty-six applicants in fifty-four miles. I never, in any trip anywhere, saw such a system of beggary. The houses were very comfortable, and the gardens and fields about them were thriving and abundant, and the children were neither remarkably ragged or dirty, but the moment a carriage appeared in view, out came the children to beg, whilst the mother, perhaps, stood looking complacently on at the door, to see how the children made out. Almost every woman, and a great majority of the men we met in this journey, were afflicted with the *goitre*, and so horribly were they deformed in many cases by it, that we were compelled to turn away our eyes from the sight. In several, the tumor projecting from their throats was larger than their heads. We were told, moreover, that this disease existed throughout this region—that almost every one was affected more or less by it; and as we progressed on our journey as far as Martigny, to the south of Lake Geneva, and even farther, we found it more and more prevalent, and more frightful in its developments. At Martigny, we were told there was a hospital filled with cases of this disease, under the care of the "Sisters of Charity." Some persons attribute it to the *water* in this region, and some to the great quantity of magnesia in their vegetables, and some to the low living and out-door exposure of the inhabitants; but no satisfactory conclusion seems to have been formed. The water of the Rhone is intensely blue, like indigo, the cause of which Sir Humphrey Davy attributed to the presence of iodine. Now, as iodine is one of the most approved remedies for the goitre, how can its prevalence in the waters of the country produce the disease?

LETTER NO. IX.

At the foot of Mont Blanc,
Chamouny, Sept. 9th, 1850.

We were obliged to leave our "*voiture*" at St. Martin's, some miles from Chamouny, and take a vehicle called a "*char a banc*," a sort of sofa on wheels, in which you ride sideways, with your feet hanging nearly to the ground—a comical looking affair, but the only carriage, they say, in which you can ascend the mountainous region which brings you to the foot of Mont Blanc; but the comfort, convenience or philosophy of its construction I had not the wit to discover. For the first half mile we could only amuse ourselves with our novel and queer mode of conveyance, but we soon found ourselves amid the most wild, romantic and beautiful scenery imaginable. Our eyes could scarcely reach the heights above us, nor could they fathom the depths below. Our path, in some places, was so narrow, that it seemed as if one false step would precipitate us into the ravine; and then again it was wider, bordered with beautiful shrubs and trees, venerable enough to have outlived the storms and snows of ages.

As we descended to Chamouny, Mont Blanc, with its snowy peak, and the glaciers between the needles or peaks around, came full upon our vision. Oh, what a sight! With what anxiety did we wait the developments of the morrow! How earnestly did we wish for a clear and pleasant day, that we might ascend the adjacent mountains and get a nearer view of the Land of Eternal Snows and the Everlasting Sea of Ice!

The day proved all we could have desired; it was cold in the morning, for there was a frost in the night, though only the 6th of September. We started early, taking two guides and four mules, to make the ascent of La Flegere, from which one of the best views of Mont Blanc and the surrounding group of "Aiguilles" is obtained. Our company consisted of eight. We rode up the valley, about two miles, to the hamlet of Les Pres, then turned to the left, and in a few moments arrived at the foot of the mountain. It seemed nearly perpendicular, and I could discern no path whatever. I asked the guide where the road was, and he replied, "we must go straight up." My heart sank within me, and for a moment I recoiled at attempting such an impossibility; but on being assured that the mule could find a way up, with much fear and trembling I commenced the ascent. It was very curious to witness the sagacity and skill of our mules; they would go two or three yards to the right and then turn and go two or three yards to the left, and thus we found ourselves ascending by degrees, when, at the first glance, it seemed too steep to climb at all. After a while we plunged in among the pines and brush, and pursued a winding mule-path around the mountain, sometimes not more than two or three feet wide, and every now and then our mules would hit a loose stone and send it rolling, tumbling, thundering down, down beyond all vision, into the fathomless abyss below; while I often quailed at the idea that a mis-step of the mule might doom me to the same fearful descent. The gentlemen, who walked, were furnished with climbing poles, six or eight feet long, with a sharp iron in the bottom, and holding on the *mules' tails* with the other hand, according to the guides' direction, they were aided and pulled along up. We cut a ridiculous figure on our "winding way," but were amply repaid for our fatigue and apprehension by the enchanting and sublime prospect before us, when we reached the little house for travelers.

Just before we reached the top, we were startled by two or three reports of a cannon below, which our guide assured us was occasioned by the arrival of some traveler at the top of Mont Blanc, when it was always customary, on a given signal, to announce such an event in that way. With a spy-glass, furnished at the house of entertainment on the Flegere, we had a view of the English gentleman and his guides, who had made this difficult ascent; he was fifteen miles distant. He was accompanied by six guides, to whom, we afterwards learned, he paid one hundred francs, or twenty dollars, each; and with mules, provisions, &c., the trip cost him two hundred dollars. He went up one day and returned the next, but was so exhausted with fatigue that he could scarcely speak or move when he reached his hotel. This ascent is not only very expensive, but exceedingly difficult and dangerous, and is sometimes attended with very serious consequences. Some persons have been known to bleed at the nose, eyes and ears before reaching the top; one gentleman sustained an injury to his sight from which he never recovered; many, after making the attempt to ascend, are compelled from exhaustion to return, and those who actually attain its summit do not for a long time recover from the fatigue. After feasting our eyes with a most magnificent view of those mountains of snow, we descended by the same path we came up, which, however, was so painful to me in the descent, that I preferred walking; and on reaching the plain, about one o'clock, we sent back our mules and one guide to Chamouny, and concluded to go up the Montagne Vert, opposite, to enjoy a full view of the Mer de Glace. We crossed the river Arve, which flows from the sea of ice, and has made for itself an archway under the ice, which is a hundred feet thick above it, and commenced climbing the steep ascent by the side of the glacier, where mules never go up and travelers seldom do. Dr. Hitchcock, President of Amherst College, and his lady, were of our party. The sun came down with scorching power, but we scrambled among rocks and bushes for one long hour and then found ourselves only half way to the house erected on the side of the glacier for the refreshment of weary pilgrims. Two avalanches of ice and snow came booming and thundering down, and as they reached the bottom fell into millions of fragments. The noise they made as they first separated from the whole mass was like the distant report of cannon. We were not in a situation to fear any thing from their descent, and, of course, enjoyed the sight extremely.

You can scarcely imagine how beautiful and strange a sight this sea of ice was to us, as we sat down to rest from our fatigue. With the scorching mid-day sun upon us and the exertion of climbing we were in a glow of heat. We were seated on the grass; around us were blooming wild flowers of every variety; strawberries and whortleberries we found growing on the mountain side, and trees and shrubs of all descriptions surrounded us; while at our feet lay this ocean of ice, extending several miles in length and a mile in width: summer and winter meeting together—such a sight as never before had met our eyes. As we afterwards stood upon the ice and threw stones down the crevices through which the deep blue waters yawned, we could hear them thump and rattle down, down to a fearful depth, and at last plunge into the water, showing how the accumulating snows of ages had added to its immensity.

Before us rose the towering peaks of other mountains, one of which, directly opposite us, with its thousand pinnacles almost touching the very heavens, seemed like a grand and beautiful temple of Nature, fit for the Majestic King of these wonderful domains—the King of kings and Lord of lords. The ascent of the mountain grew more and more steep and difficult, and I began to think I must end my days there: it seemed impossible to ascend, and almost as great an impossibility to return. The guide, however, with the help of another, by placing two long poles under my arms, lifted me along over the rocks and bushes; and almost perfectly exhausted, all of us reached the little inn of Montagne Vert at 4 o'clock. Here we rested and took refreshment, and then went out to examine nearer this wonderful Mer de Glace. Quiet and motionless as it seems, this immense mass of ice is said to move a foot a day. A rock of many tons, on which the names of Pococke and Wyndham were engraved in 1741, has in this slow moving process been brought on this mass of ice some miles from the place where the inscriptions were made.

After loitering about awhile we returned to Chamouny, on foot, by the mule path, on the other side, a distance of eight miles. We reached our hotel at 8 o'clock in the evening, much fatigued, but well repaid for the adventure of the day.

LETTER NO. X.

MILAN, September 12, 1850.

In my last, I gave you a brief account of our rambles among the Alps, over "La Flegere and "Montagne Vert," to the "Mer de Glace." Our next expedition was over the "Tete Noire" to Martigny, on our route over the Simplon pass to Italy. The "Col de Balme" has one view which surpasses any in the "Tete Noire," but as the general scenery of the last is superior, we concluded to take the latter course. With our guide and four mules, and the same company in which we made our other excursions, we left Chamouny early in the morning; and after winding about in a zig-zag course over loose and dangerous slopes, through the wildest scenery imaginable, we entered a tunnel, pierced through a rock overhanging a dark and fearful gorge, and in six hours after we left Chamouny found ourselves at a little cabin, where we dined. We then commenced a more difficult and steep ascent, amid dark pine forests and awful precipices, which most of us preferred to climb on foot rather than on mules. We found the descent to Martigny, which occupied perhaps two hours, even more difficult than the ascent; so steep and rocky was it that the mules were often obliged to *jump* from place to place; but the view of the valley of the Rhone from the height, for miles before we reached Martigny, which lies at the mountain's base, was exceedingly beautiful. This little village is very unhealthy and undesirable as a residence, but from its position on the high road of the Simplon, at the termination of the car-road from the St. Bernard, (the famous monastery of which is only ten hours' ride hence,) and the mule path to Chamouny, it is a great and constant resort of travelers. The town is situated at the junction of the Rhone and the Dranse, in a valley hemmed in on all sides by the Alps; and the village has been nearly destroyed twice by an inundation of these rivers, once in 1543, and again in 1818. Almost all the inhabitants are affected by the goitre. They are exceedingly dwarfish, deformed and sickly in their appearance. In no place that we have visited have we seen a costume so unique and curious as here. Their bonnets and head-dresses are wonderful. The monks of St. Bernard have their head-quarters here in a convent, and at intervals they relieve the members stationed at the Hospice of the Great St. Bernard.

The hotels in Martigny, for so small and retired a place, are unusually good. Throughout the continent, you find no regular public breakfast table as in our country. Every one calls for his breakfast when he wishes it, and pays for what he orders, and nothing is set before him *except* what he calls for specially. I could not but smile at one of our "Brother Jonathans," who came in one day and said "he would like his breakfast." "What will you have, sir?" said the waiter, very respectfully. "Oh, any thing," said the Yankee, "it makes no difference — I had no supper last night, and I want a *good* breakfast." The waiter seemed quite confounded. "Will you have coffee, sir — and what else?" "Oh, yes," said he, "coffee and meat and so on; any thing you *happen to have*." The waiter went off. I did not see the end; but I presume the "green" one had quite a bill to pay for his breakfast. There is always *one* public table at 5 or 6 o'clock in the afternoon, the "*table d'hote*," as they call it in French; and they generally ask you when you breakfast, if you will dine at the "*table d'hote*." As these dinners consume two hours or more, and are so late for a Yankee dinner, and moreover so luxurious and expensive, we have not often partaken of them, choosing a more simple repast, consuming less time and at a more seasonable hour. We have, however, dined often enough at the "*table d'hote*" to see the mode of "doing up" a dinner in all the different countries or provinces where we might be.

On the continent you are not charged by the day for three meals, whether you eat them or not, and for your lodging, but so many florins, or francs, or batzens, or lires, or pauls, or carlinis, according to the country you are in, for your *room*, and for as many meals as you take, and according to what you call for at these meals. Then you are charged from ten to thirty cents a day for "services," and so much for candles and fire. They will generally bring up to your room two flaming wax candles and set them down on your table, for which they will charge you twenty cents apiece, even if you do not burn them an hour. One gentleman, who had for some time been paying largely for his candles, found that in a few weeks more, at the rate he had been charged, he should have paid $25 for his candles to light him to bed. The only way is to tell them you prefer ordinary candles, or carry your own with you. It is always best to inquire the price of your room for a day, as soon as shown to it, else you will often have a startling price to pay. The people here seem to think nothing is too good for the English and Americans, and, moreover, that they are made of silver and gold. But I have digressed from the point at which I started. I intended to describe a "*table d'hote*" dinner at the little town of Martigny, as it is a good general specimen of a dinner in Switzerland.

When you seat yourself at the table you see nothing before you of dinner but your plate, on which is a napkin and a piece of bread, a tumbler, wine-glass and decanter of ordinary wine, (which is as free here as water in our country,) and without extra charge, two knives, two forks, and a spoon. There is nothing in the centre of the table but the casters, and every half yard or so up and down the table is a tumbler of wooden toothpicks, or an image of a porcupine in porcelain bristling with the same, with which you are expected to pick your teeth during the intervals between the courses. When all were seated, the order of exercises was as follows: first, soup — then the boiled meat of which the soup was made and mashed potatoes — then fish boiled—fish fried — (each dish passed separately behind us at the table, ready carved, and plates changed every time — the dish of meat then placed on the table till the next course was served) — then came pancakes of some sort mixed with a vegetable — then a dish which none of us could puzzle out satisfactorily, but very common in Switzerland, Piedmont and Italy, made of the brains of something or other, fried in batter (I expect) — then beef, veal, partridges and roast chickens — then stringed beans passed separately — after which were peas, then greens, and finally salad and cheese, changing plates for each. Thus ended the *first* lesson. Then came pudding, afterwards grapes, peaches, plums, maccaroni, nuts, bons-bons, &c. In Germany, they give you soup, fish and several dishes of meat, and then pudding, and afterwards bring on *roast beef*, chickens, &c.

After spending a Sabbath here, we bade farewell to our traveling companions, Dr. and Mrs. Hitchcock, who returned to Geneva, while we proceeded to Milan. We were so fortunate, however, as to find other acquaintances, two English gentleman from Birmingham, with whom we took a private carriage on Monday, (as the Diligence left Sabbath evening,) and traveled as far as Visp, a miserable little village, finely situated at the junction of the Visp with the Rhone. Here our friends left us, striking off to the foot of Monte Rosa by the pass of the Moro, and we took a char-a-banc to Brieg, seven or eight miles further, where we spent the night at the foot of the Simplon pass.

It is amazing to see the shoals of people traveling this season on the continent for pleasure. Although the travel has been increasing for several years, it has far exceeded this summer any previous one. We were repeatedly told that more Americans had visited the continent this year than ever before. It was quite interesting to examine the arrivals at the various hotels; we found the names of many whom we knew by reputation as well as personally, from America, who perhaps had preceded us only a few days. We constantly found amusement as we rode or walked about, in meeting travelers in Switzerland, all equipped in the same style, with traveling-bags or knapsacks slung over their shoulders, a staff in one hand, and an open guide-book in the other, going on a pilgrimage among the Alps, and studying out their course and the curiosities by the way.

The distance from Brieg to Domo d'Ossola is about forty English miles, and it takes ten hours to travel the distance—seven to reach Simplon, and three to go down the mountain to Domo d'Ossola. This day's journey was one of the most delightful and exciting I ever made. The Simplon road, leaving the valley of the Rhone at Brieg, begins to ascend immediately from the post-house, and you wind around and around the mountain till, after six hours' travel, you look down the valley, and there lies the little town of Brieg, like a map, at your feet, just as distinctly seen as when you first began the ascent. This pass is certainly one of the wonders of the age; and your admiration of this gigantic enterprise and of Napoleon's wisdom, skill, inventive genius, and unconquerable will, is increased by the remembrance that such an undertaking was then a novel thing—that nothing of its grandeur or magnitude had preceded it. To have an idea of its immensity, you must not only know that thirty thousand men were at work upon at one time, that it took six years to build it, and that six hundred and eleven bridges, great and small, are constructed for the passage of the road, and that terraces of massive masonry extend for miles, and ten tunnels are pierced through the overhanging rocks, or are built up of stone, and that there are twenty houses of refuge for travelers and workmen who keep it in repair; but you must *see* how smooth and perfect it is in its construction. Its breadth is from twenty-five to thirty feet, and the average slope nowhere exceeds six inches in six and a half feet. You must look down the awful ravines and gorges which it skirts, and up, overhead, at the black and bristling rocks which seem to threaten you, and at the fearful height from which the avalanches come tumbling down, and often carry everything before them. You must see the Gorge of Gondo, which is one of the greatest natural curiosities in the world, and see the road wind through it, and you will think none but Napoleon could ever have conceived the idea of attempting a pass in such a savage place. Our travelers, most of them, walked several miles, not that they were appalled by personal danger in riding, for the road is so wide and safely guarded that nothing is to be apprehended at this season of the year, but to enjoy more perfectly the grandeur and sublimity of the scenery.

Although early in September, we broke off icicles two feet long that had congealed as the water was dripping down from the snow-capped mountains above, while within a rod we picked flowers in full bloom. The Gallery of Gondo, or Tunnel, as we should say, is a cut through solid rock, measuring five hundred and ninety-six feet, and cost immense labor to make it, as the rock is of granite. It is said it required the incessant labor of one hundred workmen, in gangs of eight relieving each other day and night, to pierce a passage in eighteen months. "The progress of the work would have been still more tedious, had the laborers confined themselves to the two ends; but the engineer ordered two side openings to be made, thus working in four places at once. To make these lateral perforations, it was necessary to suspend the miners by ropes over the outside of the rock, till a lodgement was effected; these now serve as windows to light the interior." Near the mouth of this tunnel is a roaring water-fall, carried over a covered bridge of beautiful construction, which is quite a curiosity. We stopped at the famed Hospice on the summit, and were shown about by the Monks, and took a lunch at their table. Father Barras, so long the head of the Great St. Bernard Hospice, is now removed here. While they were taking us to see some of the famous St. Bernard *dogs*, the conductor of the diligence called us and we were obliged to hasten away. As we descended the mountain to Domo d'Ossola, we emerged into a land of greenness and beauty. We found chesnuts and firs, vines and maize, and soon a warmer climate, and began to realize that we were in Italy, the land of beauty and of song. We spent the night at Domo d'Ossola, a small place and not interesting; and next day, following the shore of the beautiful Lago Maggiore, we passed the famous Borromean Islands, of which we had a good view in the diligence. The road to Milan is over a monotonous flat, between avenues of trees, extending for miles; grapevines are festooned between the trees, and grow very luxuriantly. We passed a remarkable *cypress tree*, of great age, said to have been a tree in the time of Julius Cæsar. It is one hundred and twenty-one feet high and twenty-three feet in circumference. Napoleon, in constructing the Simplon, gave orders that the road should diverge from a straight line to save it. Near this tree was fought the first great battle between Scipio and Hannibal, called the battle of Ticinus, in which Scipio was defeated.

We entered Milan through the magnificent *Arch of Peace*, begun by Napoleon and finished in 1838 by the Austrian Government. This is built of pure white marble, and is a splendid specimen of architecture. Milan is a beautiful city, of which you shall hear in my next.

LETTER NO. XI.

VENICE, September 17, 1850.

Milan is a splendid city. As you enter it by the Arch of Peace, erected at the termination of the Simplon road, through a long avenue of trees, it presents a very imposing appearance. A large open space remains in front of this magnificent arch, on which Napoleon intended to have built one of the most beautiful palaces in the world. A design was prepared by Antolini, but only two of the buildings planned have been erected. The space intended for a forum, is now used for exercising the military. There is much in Milan to interest a traveler; but the greatest magnet of attraction is the Cathedral, renowned, world-wide, for its exquisite beauty. It is built entirely of white marble, and exceeds anything I ever saw. I surveyed it from every point of the compass, and wandered over its marble roofs in every direction, and wound myself up the cork-screw stairs of the different turrets, and gazed, till my eyes ached, at the multitude of exquisite statues; but I was so enchanted with the beauty of the exterior, that I have entirely lost all recollection of the interior of the church, and, indeed, cannot remember that I went into it at all. There are seven thousand marble statues about it, no two alike, and five thousand more are necessary to complete the original design. It has one hundred and six turrets, which have fifteen thousand points, and thirty-two are still to be finished. It has already cost five hundred and sixty-three millions of francs, and when completed, will have cost eight hundred and forty-five millions. What seems curious to me is, that scarcely any of these beautiful edifices are *finished*. Palaces, churches and castles are either in ruins, or half done. I might except some that Napoleon finished—for "when *he* spake it was done," and had he carried out his plans here, every thing would have been "done up straight," as we say, like his Simplon road.

The paintings and statuary in Milan are very beautiful. There are many by Titian, Raphael, Guido, Tintoretto, Rembrandt, Correggio, Paul Veronese, Domenichino, Rubens, and others. In the "Santa Maria della Grazie" is to be seen the "Last Supper," by Leonardo da Vinci, which, however, has been exceedingly injured by smoke and dampness. The Amphitheatre at Milan, near the Arch of Peace, built by Napoleon, and capable of containing thirty thousand people, is quite a curiosity.

From Milan, we proceeded by railroad to Treviglio, about twenty-two miles; then took the Diligence and reached Verona at 2 o'clock in the morning. Here we saw an Amphitheatre, built by the Romans, in the greatest preservation of anything of the kind now known. It is supposed to have been built about the time of the Coliseum, at Rome. We visited, also, the new marble Cemetery, covering several acres of ground, and forming a colonnade on three sides of a square. Had we remained in Verona two or three days longer, we should have had an opportunity of seeing the Archduke Charles of Austria review about twenty-thousand of his troops; but, unfortunately, we lost this. At eleven

A. M., we left Verona by railroad, and, passing through Padua, reached Venice at three o'clock, P. M.

I thought I had seen Venice in so many representations, that I knew exactly how it looked; but I have visited no city for which I was so unprepared, and which filled me with such admiration on entrance as this. I fairly cried with delight. The first view, as it burst upon me, *a city in the sea*, was beautiful beyond all description. It seemed to rise out of the water, without any earthly foundation; scarce a tree, and *no* vestige of hill or valley meets the eye. Lofty domes, marble palaces, and glittering spires, stood before us in the water, as the railroad car whirled us with magic speed over a bridge three miles long, from the main land. I could scarcely believe my eyes, and I looked and looked again, to be sure it was no vision of imaginative beauty that deceived me. But, no! there it was—a real city; the far-famed, once glorious, but now expiring city of Venice—a city whose sun is set! As we landed at the railroad station, we were perfectly bewildered with the strangeness and novelty of our situation. No carriages, omnibuses, and noisy drivers, with whip in hand, assailed us—but long, black, funeral-like boats, shaped like a Chinese lady's shoe, pointed and turned up at both ends, lay in long rows in the water-streets of the city, and strange men, speaking in an unknown tongue, insisted upon seating us in this new vehicle. We preferred to *walk*, but looking this way and that, up and down, we saw no way of crossing the water, and no side-walks even, but the pavement about the depot. So, showing the name of the hotel to which we had been recommended, we seated ourselves in a gondola and were rowed silently and noiselessly up the grand street of the city. In the centre of the boat is a little place enclosed, containing seats for four persons, cushioned with black, two behind and one on each side, with a door so low that you stoop on entering. This caboose is covered with black velvet, and is ornamented with black rosettes. So funeral-like is its appearance, that you feel as if you were creeping into a hearse. We rowed in front of many palaces and splendid buildings, turned many corners into narrow canals, and finally landed at a beautiful marble palace whose steps, three of them, were actually in the water. We entered a large and handsome door, and found ourselves in a hollow square, paved with stones, and filled with flowers and birds. Ascending another stairway, we reached a piazza which was lined with paintings of enormous size. Of this hotel, once the "Palais de Grassi," the landlord told us the following story: In the palace opposite, once lived a young lady to whom a gentleman of Venice was deeply attached, and wished to marry. But the father of the lady objected to the match, giving as his ground of objection, that the young man had *no home* for his bride. The father of the young gentleman declared that difficulty should soon be removed, for "he would build a house for his son, *whose windows should be larger than his neighbor's doors*." And so the Palais de Grassi was built in splendid style and quite eclipsed all the rest in the neighborhood, and this lady was married and lived here. But the nobility of Venice, where are they now? Exiled, imprisoned, or dead! and these princely halls and magnificent white marble buildings are now used for store-houses, hotels, wine-shops, &c. One I noticed, was stuffed from top to bottom with *hay*. At the door of another, surrounded with barrels, hogsheads, and baskets of grapes, we saw a man whose trowsers were rolled up to his knees, and whose legs and feet were red with the juice of the grape. We had often heard that the juice of the grape was pressed out by men's feet; we told our gondolier to stop a moment, and he rowed us to the door, and we went in and found it even so. The grapes are thrown into a vat or hogshead, and a man or boy, with naked feet, gets in, and, holding on to the side of the vat with his hands, he jumps up and down in the grapes till the juice is expressed. He hops out whenever he takes a notion, and runs about in the dirt, and then wipes his feet on the grass or a board, and pops in again to finish his work. This process (it is now the time of vintage) we have seen repeatedly. It seems strange to see no carriages and no horses, and to hear no sound of a wheel or a horse's hoof. The quietness is quite annoying. There are few or no gardens, and no back-yards to the houses. The front doors open to the water, and the back doors into the narrow streets between the canals; they are well paved with large, smooth flag-stones, and connect with all parts of the city by little bridges which are formed like stairs, up and down, over the canals, to leave room for the gondolas to run underneath. It is melancholy to see Venice as she is, and remember what she was. Austria designs to humble and ruin this beautiful city, and is doing all in her power to destroy both Milan and Venice. No exertions are wanting to direct trade and commercial enterprise from Venice and build up Trieste on its ruins. Nearly all the noble, rich and influential men have already left here. We have seen many marks of the recent hard-fought battles here, in the roofs and walls of the churches and houses, which are perforated with balls and bombs. We have visited the Church of San Marco, the pride and boast of Venice. Did not admire it, as a whole. It has too much the appearance of a heathen temple, with its many domes. It is adorned with numerous paintings, and is certainly wonderful for the display of beautiful marbles of all sorts, and for its mosaics. It has, in all, five hundred pillars of various marbles. *Here* is a painting of Ceres, and *there* one of the Evangelists—a painting of Proserpine drawn by dragons, in a chariot, and another of the marriage in Cana of Galilee—scripture scenes and heathen mythology all mixed up together. As you enter the great door, you observe in the pavement some pieces of red marble in a circle, which indicate the precise place where Pope Alexander III., and the Emperor Frederick Barbarossa were, on July 23, 1177, reconciled through the intervention of the Venetian Republic. The Pope placed his foot on the head of the prostrate Emperor, repeating the words of the psalm, "Thou shalt tread upon the lion and the adder." The specimens of mosaic, the columns of porphyry, verd antique, serpentine, and other marbles of the richest hue, the bas reliefs, statues, monuments, &c., are of great beauty.

The strange mixture of mythology and Bible history, executed in bas reliefs or in painting, is accounted for from the fact that materials and relics from all countries and climes were brought together to enrich this church. Every vessel that left Venice was obliged to bring back pillars, statuary, marbles, or something for this work. The great Campanile Tower of St. Marc, which contains the bells, stands separate, but near it. This is forty-two feet square at the base and three hundred and twenty-three feet high. This is adorned with several bas reliefs in marble, and with four statues—Pallas, Apollo, Mercury, and Peace—in bronze.

The view from the belfry of the Campanile is very fine. Adjoining St. Marc's is the Doge's Palace, or Palazza Ducale; this we visited. Each side of the front entrance, at the head of the superb staircase which leads to it, you can see an opening in the wall, like those into which we drop letters into our post-offices. These places were formerly covered with a lion's head, mouth open, into which all accusations against any of the distinguished inhabitants of Venice were secretly dropped, and which resulted in the immediate summons and imprisonment, and often secret death, of those calumniated. We were taken down by the guide, with a lighted candle, to see the *pozzi* or dark cells underneath the palace, in which many of the nobles and private citizens, for political crimes or imaginary treason, on secret accusations, were immured; some were there smothered, and others, never again seeing the light of day, were conducted over a covered bridge—the celebrated Bridge of Sighs, or "Ponte de Sopiri," from their dark vaults to the prison, separated from the palace only by a little street canal. They were never heard of afterwards. In this palace, the Librarian has the splendid Greek cameo found in Ephesus in 1793, called the Jupiter Ægiocus, and the celebrated Map of the World, drawn in 1460 by Fra Mauro, showing the surface of the globe as it was then known. There are several halls of paintings, many of which are by Titian, Tintoretto, Paul Veronese, and other great masters.

The Manfrini Palace, so famous for its pictures, we could not see; we did not visit it at the right time.

The churches are, many of them, very beautiful. "Santa Maria Gloriosa de Frari" is full of fine tombs. Here Titian is buried, and a fine monument to his memory is now in process of erection at the sole expense of the Emperor of Austria. It has been building five years, and is still boarded up, so that we could not see it. Opposite his tomb, in the same church, is a monument to Canova, the famous sculptor—the most beautiful piece of sculpture I ever beheld in monumental style. It is a very large pyramid of white marble, into whose open doors Genius, Art, and other beautiful figures, as mourners, are walking in funeral procession. I could have gazed at this exquisite work of art for hours. Canova designed and sculptured it himself for his friend Titian; but it has been used for his own tomb. I have not time even to *name* particularly the numerous paintings, statues and frescos which deserve notice in this elegant church.

The "Academia delle Belle Arte" is full of the rich paintings of the Venitian School. "The Assumption of the Virgin," by Titian; "Adam and Eve taking the forbidden fruit," by Tintoretto; "the Venitian Slave delivered by St. Mark," by the same; "a Portrait of Titian's Mother," by himself; "the Presentation of the Virgin in the Temple," by Titian; and his last unfinished work, "the Deposition from the Cross," with many others, are extremely beautiful. The churches, paintings and statuary alone in Venice, to be viewed as they should be, would occupy several days. We went out in a gondola three or four miles to the Armenian Convent, situated on an island, founded by the Abbot Mechitar, in the beginning of the last century. The Armenian merchants of Calcutta do much for the support of this institution.

In Venice, we were so fortunate as to meet with the Rev. Mr. Langworthy, of Chelsea, and Mr. A. Kingman, of Boston; with them we shall go to Rome. The currency in Venice affords us much amusement. Every thing must be paid for in lires, swanzigers, or centimes, which, added to our ignorance of the Italian language, sometimes quite flusters us. Our chief recreation, when not sight-seeing, is *reckoning up* and *studying out our money*, and "*catching fleas*," which occupies really more time than you can imagine. The Italians do not understand the first principles of neatness, and the country is as full of fleas as Missouri is of musquitoes. Our last business at night, and our first in the morning, is *hunting fleas;* and all the leisure time we can command during the day, we are compelled to appropriate in that way. More anon.

LETTER XII.

FLORENCE, September 23, 1850.

We are sometimes compelled to think that "the chief end of man" in Italy is to *attend to his passport.* Americans, who can travel in their own country from "Dan to Beersheba" without being asked who they are, where they are going, or what they are after, cannot fail to be annoyed and perplexed with this most farcical of all customs, carrying a passport. My companion's ran thus: first, name and age—then height, tall—hair, grey—eyes, blue—chin, sharp—and so on. Fortunately, he had his passport done up in pocket-book fashion, or it certainly would have been nearly worn out by this time. That of one of our gentlemen was quite ragged, it had encountered so many *vises.* We were told in New York, and by the American Minister in London, that when a lady was traveling with her husband, it was unnecessary for her to have a passport, and I often congratulated myself upon being able to travel without one. When we entered a city, our driver would come to a dead halt, and somebody would pop his head into the carriage and say, *passport?* and when we went out of the walls, another would stop us to inquire if it had been looked at in the *other* end of the city; so that the passport must always be at hand for inspection. Sometimes it would be taken and carried away, and we would be at our "wit's end" lest it should never return, knowing that we were undone without it. When we had stopped at a hotel and had taken our rooms, a servant would open the door and ask for the passport—for it is the landlord's immediate duty, on the arrival of a traveler at his house, to *report* him to the Police. Then our passport must be *vised* by the Minister of the next province or kingdom to which we are going, and by the Minister of our own country resident in the city we are in, and finally by the Police. So much must be done before we leave one kingdom or province; and so soon as we reach the boundary of the next one, the passports must be looked at to see that all is right, and the luggage overhauled. We found baggage so troublesome and expensive, that we have long since left all behind but our carpet-bags. In some places you pay for every pound of baggage you have.

We left Venice for Padua by railroad, twenty-three miles. There we concluded to take a *vettura* for Bologna, by way of Ferrara, five of us in company. There is a great deal of highway robbery in Italy, and only two weeks before this, the diligence to Ferrara, containing sixteen passengers, was beset by four men armed, in mid-day. Only a few days since, thirty-five robbers were condemned at Bologna, nine to be imprisoned for life and twenty-six to be shot; but ten, being under age, had their sentence commuted to ten years' hard labor: sixteen were actually shot the 5th of this month.

The distance from Padua to Bologna is about eighty-six English miles. We made a contract with our *vetturino* to start early in the morning, and to halt before dark. We were anxious to reach Ferrara to spend the first night, but it was nearly sunset when we arrived at the river Po, which divides the Austrian from the Papal territory. After crossing the river, our baggage must be examined at the custom house on the other side, and we had then a few miles further to go. Before crossing the river, the passports were called for by the Austrian officer at the landing, and, as usual, I remained in the carriage, while the gentlemen went in to have them examined. To my great surprise and consternation, I was called in and told, I could proceed no further, as *I had no passport.* It was in vain he was told I had experienced no difficulty in any other place, and that it was said to be unnecessary when a family were traveling together. He was inexorable. All that he would say to our entreaties, was in French, with an Italian shrug of his shoulders, "*c'est impossible!*" "What can I do?" exclaimed I, in French. "Oh, you can go back to Rovigo," he replied, "and all the rest can go on." We then made another appeal. We talked a little French and a little Latin and a little more English, and called in another man who could talk German and broken English to help us—adding all the gesticulations, imploring looks and bursts of eloquence which such a dilemma as we were in might be supposed to inspire. Whether all this manœuvre was merely to magnify his office and make a show of authority, I don't know; but after a while it seemed to enter his perecranium that I was the wife of one of the gentlemen, whereupon, after making the other two give him a *written certificate* who I was, that I was myself and nobody else, he let us go, and we "went on our way rejoicing." It was in this neighborhood, that a little more than a year since, (February, 1849,) Marshal Haynau crossed the Po with 10,000 men, and appeared at the gate of Ferrara and demanded, in behalf of the Pope, the delivery of the city gates to the Imperial troops, and the payment of 206,000 scudi, or dollars, in twenty-four hours. This sum was paid through the generosity of an English resident, and the Austrians evacuated the city.

We crossed the Po on a "flying bridge" ferry, being drawn over with ropes, and drove to the custom-house, where our luggage was overhauled, and with these detentions it was quite dark when we arrived at Ferrara. However, we were not beset by robbers. We reached Bologna at one o'clock next day. Bologna is the second capital of the "States of the Church," and is situated at the foot of the Appenines. It has a population of seventy thousand. There is much of interest here in its churches, and there are many excellent paintings. Bologna *has* been celebrated for its University; it enjoyed a greater reputation formerly than it does now. It is the oldest in Italy, and has had one peculiarity—that of learned *female* Professors. In the fourteenth century, Novella d'Andrea used often to occupy her father's chair. It is said she was very beautiful, and, lest the attention of the students should be more absorbed in the *lecturer* than the lecture, a curtain was drawn before her. Moore, in alluding to this, says:

> ——— "drawn before her
> Lest, if her charms were seen, the students
> Should let their young eyes wander o'er her,
> And quite forget their jurisprudence."

Laura Bassi was once Professor of Mathematics and Natural History here. She received the title of L. L. D., and her lectures were attended by ladies of France and Germany, who were members of the institution. *Madonna Manzolini* graduated in Surgery, and was Professor of Anatomy; and in our own times, the Greek chair was filled by *Matilda Tambroni.*

As you leave Bologna, you have a fine view of the magnificent Colonnade, extending three miles from the gate called La Porta di Saragozza, to the church of the Madonna di S. Luca, on a mountain out of the city. We traveled by diligence over the Appenines to Florence. It was a delightful day, and the scenery was truly enchanting. The Appenines separate the Plains of Lombardy from Tuscany. In order to have a full view of the country, we took our seats in the "imperial" of the diligence. The mountains have nothing of the grandeur and boldness of the Alps, but they are picturesque and beautiful. The road, though very good, as *all* the roads are on the continent, is excessively steep in some places. We had three pairs of horses, two postillions, one driver, and a conductor, to navigate us; and you may judge of our astonishment, as we stopped at one house by the road-side, to see a woman come out of the yard, leading by a rope, attached to their yoke, two monstrous white oxen, which she, with perfect self-possession, hitched on ahead of the horses, *going before the whole team herself*, still pulling along her oxen by the rope, while one of the postillions occasionally aided her efforts by applying the butt end of the whip to their sides. When we had reached the summit of the hill, she unhitched her oxen, and receiving her pay for their use from the conductor, she returned home. In this country women are engaged in all kinds of out-door employment. I have seen them ploughing, reaping, mowing, pitching hay, driving hay-carts, &c. Sometimes you will see a woman carrying a pail or jug of water on her head, knitting as she goes along, and driving a flock of goats, all at the same time.

As we descended the Appenines, we obtained our first view of the valley of the Arno. It is one of the most beautiful sights I ever beheld. Florence with its domes and battlements, twenty miles distant, is spread out in all its beauty at your feet. Pistoia also, a walled city, is full in view, besides innumerable villages and hamlets dotted over this immense valley. As we left the mountains for a warmer atmosphere, everything became more luxuriant and beautiful. Whole fields of olives burst upon our view. Figs and pomegranates were growing also in abundance, and vineyards covered the hill-sides. We began to realize that we had reached "a land of oil and wine."

The descent to Florence over a fine road is one of the most enchanting drives in the world. Owing to the steepness of the descent, it was necessary to drag the wheels, which became so hot from the friction, that when half way down we were obliged to stop and have cold water poured on them to prevent the carriage from taking fire. They smoked like a cauldron. I do not wonder that Florence is called "Farenze la bella," or that it has been celebrated in all ages for the beauty of its situation. It contains more than one hundred thousand inhabitants. The buildings on the banks of the Arno, which runs through the city, are grand and imposing; but the Arno is now sluggish and shallow, almost a stream of mud. At other seasons of the year it has doubtless a different appearance. The Cathedral in Florence is as unique, though not as beautiful in its architecture, as that of Milan. It is an immense building, and its exterior is covered with mosaic. It has also a Campanile, or bell-tower, which is equally curious in architecture. The Baptistery near it, was once a temple of Mars. Its bronze doors are splendidly executed. It is said Michael Angelo, when examining them, declared they were worthy of being "the gates of Paradise." The lover of paintings will find enough to study and to admire in Florence. We visited churches and examined paintings till our eyes were dim, and we gazed at statuary till we almost turned into statues ourselves. We visited the studios of our countrymen, Greenough and Powers. The latter has some exquisite pieces of statuary. He was just finishing a bust of Calhoun. He is also at work on a splendid figure, which he calls America. It is superb.

In the church of "Santa Croce" are some very beautiful tombs. One is that of Michael Angelo, and another, which struck me as the finest of any I had seen except Canova's, was that of the Polish Countess Lamoiska, by Bartoline. The stained glass in the churches of Florence is very beautiful.

The church of San Lorenzo contains in the "Capella del Deponti" some few monuments of rare beauty, erected to the Medici family; and the Medicean Chapel, which is back of the choir and yet unfinished, is unlike anything I have yet seen. It contains perhaps a dozen tombs only. The entire walls of the room, which is quite large, are covered with the richest marbles and precious stones—jasper, chalcedony, agate, lapis lazuli, verd antique, and others still more rich and costly.

The richest and most varied collection of paintings in the world is in the "Gallerie Imperiale e Reale." The "Palazza Pitti" has also many that are exquisite. The "Boboli Gardens," connected with this palace, are some of the finest in the world. Our guide told us in imperfect English that the extreme cold, last winter, nearly ruined it. He said the cold was so great, "it died a great many people and nearly half the trees." Connected with the "Palais Pitti," which is the Palace of the Dukes of Tuscany, is a Museum. The Anatomical Museum is the most complete and curious, probably, of any in existence.

In one of the halls of the "Gallerie Imperiale e Reale" is a table of Florentine mosaic so elaborate and beautiful, that it occupied twenty-two workmen twenty-five years! There is also the richest collection of cameos in the world in this palace.

LETTER NO. XIII.

ROME, September 30, 1850.

My last letter was written from Florence, a city of peculiar interest to the traveler. Its local beauty, the healthiness of its climate, its superior attractions to lovers of the fine arts, and the cheapness of living, all combine to make it a favorite resort for people of every clime. Its churches, picture galleries, statuary, and mosaics, claim more than the hasty glance which the sojourn of a few days only allows. Weeks, instead of days, can be profitably spent in Florence, in examining its rare works of art. The Florentine mosaic is there manufactured in every variety. The most exquisite specimens probably in the world are found in the "Gallerie Imperiale e Reale." The manufacture of mosaic is carried on at the public expense. It is said to be very injurious to health, and when the workmen arrive at the age of sixty, they receive a pension from government for the rest of their lives. This style of mosaic is altogether different from the Roman mosaic, the former being made entirely of stones, shaded by the varied tints of their natural color; while the latter is formed of a species of glass, artificially colored. I saw many elaborate specimens of the art, which had cost the labor of a great many years.

There is no place in Italy probably, unless it be Naples, where a person can live cheaper than at Florence. A furnished room and service can be obtained for three or four pauls a day. (A paul is worth ten cents.) The city is full of cafes and restaurants, and they are thronged by ladies as well as gentlemen. An excellent breakfast of coffee, bread, butter and eggs can be obtained at a cafe for thirteen or fifteen cents. Many families hire furnished rooms, and take their breakfasts at cafes, and have their dinners sent in from a "trottoir," or eating-house, and live at a trifling expense, without the trouble of house-keeping. Some pay, perhaps, eight pauls a day for a parlor and bed-room furnished, and two pauls a day for "service," as it is called; which includes not only the attention of a servant, but the use of table-linen, crockery, &c. When they wish breakfast, if they ring a bell, a servant appears and sets the table, bringing also a teakettle of boiling hot water, with which they make tea on the table, English fashion; and they send the servant to buy, or they provide themselves such things as they need. These furnished apartments can be found to let in London, Paris, Frankfort, and in fact in almost all the large cities on the continent. I mention these facts especially for the benefit of families traveling with small means, or of any young "artist" who may wish, at a small expense, to avail himself of the advantages here offered to perfect himself in his profession.

There is a custom here among flower-girls of presenting bouquets to strangers, daily, which is peculiar to Florence, I believe. The very first day we arrived, a flower-girl, with a broad-brimmed leghorn hat, followed us into a cafe, and offered each of us a bouquet. Not understanding that it was intended as a compliment, we refused. She, however, insisted on its acceptance, and finally left on the table a bouquet for three of us. One was offered also to a gentleman, a stranger, who declined it; but she urged it upon him, and finally stuck it in his button-hole. Every day during our stay in Florence she met us at the cafe, or sought us out in the city, and proffered her complimental bouquet. We learned it is a custom, and that no recompense is expected; indeed, it is often refused, if offered; though, if you remain some time, and are supplied daily, a trifling gift will be received on your departure from the city.

My expectations in regard to Italy are disappointed in two or three particulars. I have not yet found the *peculiar* golden sunsets, balmy air, and paradisiacal beauties, which my imagination had pictured from the glowing descriptions of Italian travelers. The north of Italy is so much like Kentucky and Missouri in the rankness and luxuriance of its vegetation, in the majestic beauty of its forests, and in its picturesque scenery, that I could not refrain from exclaiming frequently, how exactly the climate and the general appearance of things is like the south and west of the United States. For the first time, after we crossed the Appenines and descended into Italy, since we left the Ohio river, could I say that I was comfortably and thoroughly *warm*. It was clear and pleasant weather; the sky was cloudless, the sunsets beautiful day after day, but no more so than in Missouri day after day and week after week. I finally came to the conclusion, that although Italy was a beautiful country indeed, it was no more so than our own country in the south and west; and that all the glowing, unearthly descriptions of "sunny Italy" were written by Englishmen, who had lived so eternally in rain, mist or fog, and so seldom in their lives had seen a blazing noon-day sun and seen it *go down* in its glory, that it was the most natural thing in the world that an enthusiastic lover of nature should go off in ecstasies on finding a country with cloudless skies, balmy air and gorgeous sunsets. I listened in vain, moreover, in this "land of song" for those exquisite bursts of melody which have bewitched so many travelers; *but nobody sung while I was there.* The song even of the gondolier in Venice was hushed; but who *could* sing in Venice *now?*

I had expected to find the Italian ladies a peculiar race—brunettes generally, with dark, fascinating eyes, and raven hair; instead of which, I saw as many blondes as brunettes —many very beautiful women indeed, especially in Florence, but with complexions as fair and blooming, and eyes as varied as at home. Women, who are exposed to the sun and engaged in out-door labor here, have the same sickly, sallow hue as those who have suffered from chills and fever and exposure to a southern climate with us.

We found an Episcopal church in Florence, which we attended, but their congregation is small, and they have the curious custom of demanding of every person, as he enters, three pauls, or thirty cents, admittance fee. It is said the same policy is pursued in others of the English churches in Italy.

We hurried away from Florence before we were satisfied with seeing its wonders, in order to arrive at Leghorn in time to take the steamer to Civita Vecchia and Naples. The distance from Florence to Leghorn is sixty-one miles, and a railroad is completed the whole distance. We stopped at Pisa two hours, to visit the celebrated Leaning Tower, the Cathedral, Baptistery, and Campo Santo, which are all in one group, and are well worth a visit. I was satisfied with viewing the Leaning Tower on all sides, without climbing to its summit, thinking, if it should *happen* to topple over while I was there, my situation would be anything but agreeable. It is one hundred and seventy-eight feet high and fifty feet in diameter, and *leans thirteen feet!* It was built in the twelfth century, and it is supposed that the defect arises from a bad foundation. The Cathedral is a beautiful specimen of architecture, and is very rich in ornaments, frescoes, paintings, &c. It is said the silver of one altar cost thirty-six thousand crowns. The Campo Santo, or Cemetery, was founded also in the twelfth century, by Archbishop Ubaldo, and is interesting from the sepulchral monuments within it, as well as from the circumstances of its origin. Fifty-three vessels, *laden with earth from Mount Calvary*, were brought to make it. It is said that in twenty-four hours, dead bodies buried within it *would be reduced to dust!* This sacred dust is enclosed by a massive building, forming a hollow square. The building itself has now so many ancient sepulchral monuments within it, that it is in fact a museum of curiosities.

Leghorn can be reached in twenty-five minutes by railroad from Pisa. We found Leghorn the most busy, bustling place that we had seen on the continent. It contains seventy or eighty thousand inhabitants. It possesses very few objects of art, or curious specimens of antiquity. Its importance as a commercial city is great, and it ranks as the fifth on the Mediterranean, after Marseilles, Genoa, Naples and Smyrna. The monastery of Monte Nero, near the city, on a hill, is visited by most travelers for its pleasing prospect, and also to see a famous picture of the Virgin, which for five hundred years has been the object of great veneration by the Livornese. It is said the picture sailed by *itself*, in 1345, from the island of Negropont to the shore of Ardenya, and that a shepherd, directed by the Virgin, found it and brought it to the monastery.

At Leghorn, we took a steamer for Civita Vecchia, at six o'clock, P. M., and reached there at seven in the morning, a distance of one hundred and sixty-five miles. The steamer was small, dirty and uncomfortable. I was put into an upper berth in the ladies' cabin, without any sheets or pillow; and, not being able to speak Italian, I could not get any. As usual, I became sea-sick and could not sleep. About twelve o'clock in the night, a man came creeping stealthily into our cabin, and through a gap in my curtain I saw him peep slily into the lower berths, as I supposed to ascertain if their inmates were asleep, and then move carefully to the valises and bags, which were heaped together just below where I lay. I suppose he heard a noise, as he turned suddenly and went out. I was alarmed, and placed myself in a situation where I could see every movement. In about half an hour he returned and came to my berth, which was an upper one, and slowly and cautiously drew the curtain aside. I jumped up suddenly and asked him, in French, what he wanted; at which he seemed quite flustered for a moment, and then replied that he "thought he would come and let me now that my little boy was sound asleep." He then went out, but his object, doubtless, was to rob us of our watches, and perhaps search our carpet-bags. I passed a sleepless night.

At Civita Vecchia, the process of landing was tedious enough. The vessels anchor out some distance from the town, and little boats come out for the passengers, and also convey all the freight to the shore. Travelers are not allowed to land till the captain has shown his papers and all the passports have been duly examined. We found a quarantine existed at Naples, which led us to resolve to take a diligence at Civita Vecchia and proceed first to Rome. On leaving town, our luggage was examined twice, first by the police and second by the custom-house officers, each of which expected two pauls; then our passport was vised, for which we paid one dollar, which, with two pauls to the boatman who brought us to shore, and a fee to the porter, made us feel that we were called upon to give to every man we met.

The road to Rome skirts the sea-coast, and for several miles we had a fine view of the Mediterranean. It was with no ordinary feelings we found ourselves drawing near to Rome. Its antiquities, its ruins, its classical associations, all combine to render it the most interesting of all places a traveler can visit, except, perhaps, Jerusalem. Much depends on first impressions, and we had hoped to have entered Rome by sunlight, and prepared our minds, by a glorious entrance within its walls, for a feast of enjoyment in our researches afterwards. Instead of that, the diligence rolled lazily along, and it was half-past ten at night when we arrived at the outer gate of the Eternal City, which was shut, and called for admittance. Safe within the walls and the gate locked, we were next assailed by the police officers with their usual bow-wow-ing, not a word of which we could understand but *passport*, of which the Italians contrive to make four syllables. These were all taken away and carried off, and receipts given for them; and then we were driven to the custom-house, where our baggage was searched again, notwithstanding its recent overhauling at Civita Vecchia, and before we reached our hotel it was past one o'clock in the night.

LETTER NO. XIV.

Rome, October 6, 1850.

In my last, I mentioned that, although we reached the city at ten o'clock at night, we did not get through the examination of our passports and baggage, and find ourselves quietly settled at our hotel, till between one and two o'clock in the morning. We learned, at breakfast, that a great ceremony was to take place on this day, which was Sunday, at which the Pope was to be present; we could not ascertain exactly what it was, but as there was no Protestant service in the city, (for the English and American clergymen had not yet returned, owing to the unhealthiness of Rome as a summer residence,) we hastened away to the Church, that we might

ENGRAVED BY J. SARTAIN.

PIUS IX.

be there in time to obtain seats. We found the streets were lined with people, but we pressed on bravely and reached the gate with difficulty. There we encountered four soldiers with bristling bayonets, who resisted our entrance because we had no written permission. Amid the bustle, however, our friend, Mr. ———, contrived to slip in, and walked on undiscovered. We, however, stood under the arch of the gateway, wedged in by the crowd. To go on was impossible, and to retreat as much so—so we stood still and looked on. The large yard surrounding the Church was filled with soldiers and carriages. The Pope had arrived before us, and the ceremony was in progress. We learned, afterwards, from persons who were so fortunate as to be within, that the Pope first examined a school of young ladies in the convent adjoining, inspecting their embroideries and worsted work, and also the raw material which they used, (wool, &c.,) after which they entered the church. At length, we were startled by the booming of cannon, and on enquiring the cause, we were told the Pope was *canonizing a saint*, Mademoiselle Maria Anna a Jesu de Paredes, of South America. One of the Cardinals, after bowing and kissing the Pope's toe, (or rather his scarlet slipper, embroidered with gold,) presented a petition which the Pope kindly granted, and a printed certificate of the canonization is now posted in every part of the city—the substance of which is, that in consequence of the Pope's earnest prayers and endeavors, and the unceasing petitions of God's people for many years, and in consideration of the extraordinary virtues of the lady, her devoted life and great sufferings, her beatification was now insured, and she might henceforth be reverenced as a saint. After the conclusion of this ceremony, the Pope made his appearance in the balcony "*to bless the people*," which he did by spreading his hands over the crowd below and repeating a few words in an unknown tongue, and then entering his carriage with his Secretary, several other carriages filled with Cardinals following, attended by the Swiss Guards, who are the Pope's body-guard, and the Roman Guards, composed of the young nobility of Rome, he was escorted home with martial music. It is said the Pope has no confidence in his own people, and therefore selects the Swiss soldiery for his body-guard. The stairs and porch of the Church were covered with flowers, olive leaves, and evergreens, for the Pope to walk upon. As he rode through the gate, I had a fair view of His Holiness. He is quite a handsome man, and has, certainly, one of the most benignant countenances I ever looked upon. All agree that he possesses a kind and amiable disposition, and is in favor of yielding to all the reasonable wishes of his people. Although he is the Supreme Head of the Church, nominally, he is said to be *ruled himself* by others. Cardinal Antonelli is the secret moving spring of Church and State affairs. He is Secretary of State, is President of the Council of State, and presides at Cabinet meetings in absence of the Pope. He is a tall, slender Italian, with dark, restless eyes, whose single glance is so stealthy and insinuating as to betray the artful and intriguing character of the owner. Nothing can exceed the splendor of the Pope's equipage, and the pomp and pageant of his retinue. His body-guard look like butterflies. His carriage is covered with gold, and his six horses are enormous fellows, black as jet, with gold trappings; and the Pope's crown is branded on the left flank of each horse; the livery of the postillions and footmen of the whole suit, is exceedingly rich and gay.

Monday, we started on our peregrinations. Very naturally, we first sought the Capitol, from which to take a general survey of the city. At the bottom of the stone steps which lead up on one side to this building, they profess to show you the identical spot where the twin brothers, Romulus and Remus, the founders of this city, were found with their wolf-nurse. From the Capitol, we obtained a fine view of Ancient and Modern Rome, and located in our minds the seven hills on which it was built—the Capitoline, Palatine, Aventine, Cœlian, Esquiline, Quirinal and Viminal—and all the prominent points of interest pointed out to us by our guide. We saw, also, the Bastions to the left of the gate San Pancrazio, on the Janiculum, where the French made the first breach, under Gen. Oudinot, in entering the city last year. We then descended, and began a more minute exploration of the arch of Septimus Severus, of Jupiter Tonans, of the arch of Constantine, and the arch of Titus, erected to commemorate the destruction of Jerusalem; and we wondered at the splendid bas-reliefs, and puzzled over the inscriptions which nobody, yet, has been able fully to read. We went up and down and about where the old Roman Forum stood—where once walked the Cæsars and Pompeys—where Cicero declaimed and Cataline conspired—and where Caligula, and Nero, and Constantine, had plotted and planned, perhaps, and where Virgil, and Horace, and Livy, had stood—where Paul, the Apostle, too, had, doubtless, often trod, during the two years he lived in Rome, "in his own hired house," which spot we also visited. It is near the "Palace Doria," and is now occupied by the church of San Marcia in Via Lata. There is a spring of water underneath this church, which tradition says miraculously sprung up to enable the Apostle to baptize his disciples. We went through the ruins of the palace of the Cæsars. The gardens are now partially covered with vineyards, and the vine-dressers allowed us to pick and eat freely of the grapes; they were the most delicious I ever tasted. This palace, once so beautiful and extensive, is but a mass of ruins—of walls and of arches—of columns and frescoes—heaps upon heaps; the location is exceedingly fine, overlooking the country far and wide, but nothing remains to give you any distinct idea of its former magnificence. From there we went to the Coliseum, the most magnificent ruin I have yet seen. This was commenced by Vespasian in 72, and completed by his son Titus, A. D., 80, ten years after the destruction of Jerusalem. Many thousands of the captive Jews were employed in its construction. The edifice is of an oval form; it is one thousand six hundred and forty-one feet in circumference, and one hundred and fifty-seven feet high. I can never describe the feelings with which I walked about and finally perched myself near the top of this vast ruin, and recalled to memory the scenes of its former days. With what sighs and tears, and heaviness of heart, did the captive Jews build up this monument of their downfall! Of what scenes of gaiety, and splendor, and cruelty, has this been the receptacle! Of what a parade of beauty, of vanity, and of folly as well as suffering, has this been the theatre! In imagination, I peopled those seats with one hundred thousand spectators, said to be present at its dedication, and with them witnessed the games in honor of it, which lasted one hundred days. I saw the sacrifice of two thousand gladiators and five thousand wild beasts, which then took place. I saw Ignatius torn to pieces by wild beasts, and the many Christian martyrs who, in this arena, gave up their lives. Although I visited the Coliseum in the very noon-tide of a bright and beautiful day, it wore such a sombre and dreary aspect to me, from the associations connected with it, that I had no desire to visit it by moonlight, as most travelers do, to add to it the gloominess and silence of midnight, the company of owls and bats, or the awfulness of solitude in such a bloody circus as this has been. Ruin as it is, two or three French soldiers stand at its portals, armed; I cannot imagine for what, for nothing is seen in its enclosures, or disturbs its awful silence, but the lizards that run up and down its walls, and the few strangers that come to look and wonder, and retire, save now and then a devotee who comes in to kiss the cross, erected in the centre of the arena, under a printed pledge given on its transverse piece, in Italian, that whoever shall "kiss the cross once, shall have plenary indulgence two hundred days."

Of St. Peter's Church, one of Rome's greatest attractions, I can find no words to express my admiration. I have now been in Rome several days, and every day I have been in once or twice, to gaze and admire. Its grandeur, its beauty, its elegance and taste—its architecture, paintings, statuary, mosaics, marbles, bas-reliefs, &c., are all unequalled by any thing I have yet seen. To give you some idea of its splendor, it is said that the actual cost of this building has been more than three hundred millions of dollars. The annual expenditure on repairs, superintendence, &c., is three hundred thousand dollars. You will be amazed, but it is even so. I can scarcely imagine how the interior can be more beautiful, but I was disappointed in the exterior; it is neither grand nor imposing. During the siege of Rome, in 1849, considerable damage was done to the roof of the Church; nineteen balls were picked up about the edifice, and it was perforated in eighty different places. Many of the altars are adorned with beautiful mosaics, copied from the paintings of the greatest masters, and you can have some idea of the immense work in them from the fact that some have cost the labor of twelve and twenty years. We visited the manufactory of mosaics in the Vatican, by special permission. It is a great curiosity. Above some of the statues are balconies, which contain relics held in great veneration. Over San Veronica is kept the "sudarium" or handkerchief, bearing the impression of the Saviour's face, which is shown to the people during Holy Week. Over St. Helena is a piece of the true Cross, and over Saint Andrew is the head of that Saint, which was *lost* two years ago, and created a great sensation at the time. I found the following account of it the other day, which I will send you:

"In March, 1848, this relic was stolen from its balcony by some one, who was evidently familiar with the internal arrangements of St. Peter's. The popular belief was, that the Emperor of Austria or the Emperor of Russia had something to do with the affair. The Pope was deeply affected by the sacrilege; religious services were ordered, and a reward of five hundred dollars was offered to any one, not even excepting the culprit, for the recovery. Independent of its sanctity, it had a value of another kind, for it is enclosed in a silver bust, set with jewels, the value of which has been estimated at eighteen thousand scudi or dollars. It was at last found with the jewels detached, but deposited near it, buried in the earth beyond the Porta St. Pancrazio; the secret is said to have been revealed through the confessional; the judicial investigation was, therefore, suspended. Pius IX. wept for joy when it was brought and given into his own hands. The event was announced to the citizens by the Cardinal Vicar. All the bells in Rome rang a joyous peal for half an hour after the *Ave Maria*, the cupola of St. Peter's was illuminated, and, by a spontaneous act on the part of the people, so was the whole city. Te Deum was sung the next day at St. Andrea della Valle and St. Peter's; and on the 5th of April, in the following week, the relic was carried from the former to the latter Church, in a procession equally vast and magnificent with that of the *Corpus Domini.* All the ecclesiastical orders, religious orders, chapters of basilicas, parochial clergy, &c., preceded the gorgeous shrine borne by the canons of the Vatican. The relic was placed in a glass coffer, on a kind of car, and a wide silk canopy supported over it; after which walked His Holiness, followed by the Sacred College, the Senate, the Roman Princes, the members of all the Casini, and (a new feature in such assemblies) a procession of noble ladies, all in black, with lace veils over their faces, and carrying tapers, as did the rest. The noble guard, the municipality, and all the military in Rome, brought up the rear. In St. Peter's,

His Holiness gave the benediction with the relic, and at night another illumination, both of the city and St. Peter's took place, which was still more brilliant than the first."

I was sorry we could not see St. Peter's illuminated; it must be a very imposing spectacle. Just imagine its exterior lighted with rows of lamps from top to bottom. It takes sixty-eight hundred lamps and three hundred and eighty-two men to light them. On the Festival of St. Peter, there are two illuminations the same evening: the first called the *silver*, and the second the *golden* illumination. The former commences at dusk, and is made by lamps enclosed in paper lanterns; the second is made of iron plates filled with blazing tar and turpentine. Precisely at nine o'clock, nine hundred lamps are lighted instantaneously, and, in eight seconds, all the sixty-eight hundred are in full blaze. These illuminations cost six hundred crowns.

On Thursday after our arrival, a great ceremony took place, at which we were so fortunate as to be present, which was no less than the consecration of several Cardinals, among whom was the celebrated Dr. Wiseman, of England. I will give you an account of it in my next.

LETTER NO. XV.

ROME, October 9, 1850.

Soon after our arrival in Rome, we heard that fourteen new Cardinals were to be consecrated during the following week, but notwithstanding all our inquiries, we could not, for two or three days, learn definitely *when* or *where* the ceremony was to take place. Some of the Italians, seeing our interest in the matter, made several attempts to ascertain particulars for us, but in vain. The people here have no means of informing themselves of what is going on in the world, or what is taking place among themselves, except as the developments are made before their eyes. Among a population of one hundred and seventy or one hundred and eighty thousand inhabitants, but two newspapers are published, and these quite small; one is the "Giornale Romano," official, and the "Observatore Romano," semi-official. The people, of course, learn from these nothing, except what their political rulers choose they should know. "All foreign newspapers, expressing any opinions unfavorable to the Papal Court, or to any of the branches of administration, are rigorously excluded. All the Democratic press of England, France and Tuscany, is prohibited, and even journals addressed to resident diplomatists, often meet with the same severity." Not a religious newspaper (Protestant, I mean,) can be found here. One gentleman we met had not seen one for a year, and expressed the greatest sorrow at this deprivation. He knew nothing that was transpiring in the religious world, except such items of information as he occasionally gleaned from travelers.

At length, in a visit to the Vatican, one of the Pope's palaces adjoining St. Peter's, we were shown, among other rooms, the "Sistine Chapel," and the "Sala Ducale," where we found carpenters and upholsterers at work, fitting up the rooms with crimson curtains, golden fringes, &c.; and, on inquiry, were told, in French, that the ceremony was to come off there on Thursday morning, at ten o'clock. We learned that fourteen new Cardinals had been added to the Consistory in the usual private way, but that four, only, would be publicly consecrated at this time, as they were not in Rome. Dr. Wiseman, of England, was one of the four. We were told that ladies, in order to be admitted, must be dressed in black, without bonnets.

Supposing there would be a crowd on the occasion, we went early; and were told we must wait in the "Sala Regia,' or Royal Hall, until after the Pope had arrived. The Swiss Guards and the Roman soldiers, in equal numbers, were arranged in and about the "Sistine Chapel and the "Sala Ducale," in the latter of which the Cardinals, all dressed in scarlet, took their seats in rows on each side. Quite a number of priests and monks, of various orders, were also present.

The sound of music was at length heard, proclaiming the approach of the Pope, and the ladies, perhaps fifty in number, were allowed to pass in, not by the same door as His Holiness, and arrange themselves in a low gallery on the left of his chair; and here we had a fine opportunity to witness all the ceremonies of the occasion. All the ladies had black veils folded over their heads, the ends hanging gracefully on each side.

The Pope, at length, with pomp, was ushered in. He wore his golden mitre and his robe of state. Two Cardinals, one on each side, supported him, and some one followed, bearing his train. The ceremony of seating the Pope in his Chair of State, was quite an operation. With all due deference to the Pope's dignity, I must say I was reminded forcibly of scenes I have witnessed in the chamber of an aged invalid—when the dear old lady was able, to our great joy and delight, to sit up in the easy chair. Two would support her to her seat, and smooth her wrapper and tuck her up carefully; one would stick up her cap in due form and order; another get a soft cricket for her feet and run for a cologne bottle, and others stood by ready for an emergency in case she should faint away or tumble out of her chair. But, seriously, when his holiness was seated, his robe was carefully arranged, his train was disposed of according to rule, and a stool adjusted properly under his feet, while two officials remained standing by his chair. The Cardinals, of whom thirty or forty were present, I should judge, (the Consistory numbers seventy-two,) came forward one by one, and ascending three steps to the Pope's throne, bowed the knee, and kissing first his hand and then each cheek, retired to their seats. A short speech was then made in an unknown tongue—whether an address to man, or a prayer to God, I know not, nor could I learn the purport of it, or ascertain the name of the speaker. After this was ended, the Pope despatched the Cardinals for those who were to be consecrated, and who were, during this time, waiting in the "Sistine Chapel." They came in procession, and, one by one, the four new Cardinals approached His Holiness to be consecrated, separately. Each one knelt and kissed the Pope's "toe," or rather his scarlet slipper embroidered with gold, then his hand and each cheek. It was a wonder that His Holiness survived such an overwhelming manifestation of affection, but he did. The new Cardinal remained kneeling, with his head bowed in the Pope's lap, while His Holiness read a few words to him, sitting, from a book he held in one hand, while with the other he set him apart to his new office. When the four were thus duly consecrated, they were escorted by the old cardinals, the priests and monks also joining in procession and singing with book in hand, through the Sala Regia to the "Sistine Chapel," where we all followed to see the end. The Pope retired through the other door, and we did not see him again. The new cardinals, after prostrating themselves on the steps, covered with scarlet broadcloth in front of the Pope's throne in the Chapel, for a few moments, rose and received the congratulations of their brethren in office by a kiss on the hand and one on each cheek. Cardinal Wiseman is quite a fat, jolly looking personage; he had a smile or a joke for all who greeted him, and seemed to enjoy his honors, kisses and all, amazingly. Finding this was the close of the devotional and religious ceremonies of the occasion, we withdrew, and continued our explorations of the Vatican. I do not suppose there were one hundred persons present besides the cardinals, priests, monks, and other officials. There were very few Italians; the majority were English or Americans. On expressing our surprise at seeing so few persons on so great an occasion, we were told it was a specimen of the present feeling of the people towards their government and their religion; that three or four years ago, twenty thousand spectators would have flocked together on such an occasion.

The Sistine Chapel contains a series of remarkable and beautiful frescoes, executed by the most eminent masters. One side is devoted to representations of passages in the life of Moses, and the other to scenes in the life of Christ. The roof of the chapel is also covered with cartoons delineating other scenes in Scripture history, such as the Creation of Adam, and the Creation of Eve, the Fall and Expulsion from Paradise, the Deluge, the Sacrifice of Noah, &c. Opposite the entrance of the chapel is the great fresco of the Last Judgment, designed by Michael Angelo in his sixtieth year. It cost the labor of eight years. It was commenced at the request of Clement VII. The Pope was anxious to have it painted in oils, but Michael Angelo would execute it only in fresco, saying "oil painting was fit only for *women and people who had time to squander*," and so he had his own way. The fresco is sixty feet high and thirty feet broad, and is as curious as it is magnificent. Solemn and imposing as such a scene must be, there is such a mingling of scriptural and mythological ideas as to render portions of it ridiculous enough. The Saviour and the Virgin occupy a prominent position, and our Saviour is evidently passing sentence on the wicked. On his right is a group of apostles, patriarchs and saints, and on his left a crowd of martyrs. Below is the angel sounding the last trump, and others bearing the books of life and death. On their left is the representation of the Fall of the Condemned, and demons seizing their unwilling victims; while in another place is Charon, ferrying a group over the river Styx, and striking down with his oar some of the rebellious.—Opposite are the blessed rising from their graves, assisted by the angels, &c. Paul IV., who was pope when the picture was finished, objected to the nudity of some of the figures, and ordered another artist to cover the most prominent ones with drapery, which quite offended Michael Angelo. So, in the corner at the right hand of the picture, Michael introduced Biagio, (who was the first to suggest the indelicacy of the figures,) in a correct likeness, standing in hell, as Midas, with ass's ears and a serpent around his body. Biagio complained to the pope, who requested him to alter it; but Michael Angelo sent him word, "that although his holiness could release Biagio from purgatory, he had no power over *hell:*" and Biagio is there still, with his ass's ears, suffering the vengeance of eternal fire.

The Vatican is the palace of palaces. Its buildings and gardens occupy almost as much space as a small city. The palace proper has twenty courts and four thousand four hundred and twenty-two apartments. The museum here requires days instead of hours to see and appreciate its curiosities. It contains a vast number of the best fresco paintings in the world; galleries of statues of exquisite beauty, both ancient and modern; and an endless variety of paintings which have been collecting for ages, halls of tapestry, and sepulchral monuments and inscriptions without end; to say nothing of the variety of curiosities embraced in the hall of animals, hall of busts, hall of the Muses, cabinet of the masks, circular hall, hall of the Greek cross, hall of the Biga, Museo Gregoriano (consisting of eleven chambers), gallery of the candelabra, gallery of maps, &c. &c. And then there are numberless halls, which contain the library, the gardens, and the pontifical armory, all full of wonderful things. The gallery of paintings in the Vatican contains probably some of the best specimens in the world: there are not more than fifty in all, but they are exquisite. "The Transfiguration," the last and greatest work of Raphael; the Communion of St. Jerome," the master-piece of Domenichino; "The Crucifixion of St. Peter," by Guido; "The Entombment of Christ," by Caravaggio, and "The Madonna and Child, surrounded by Angels," by Titian, are perfect gems. I visited this gallery twice, but I wished I had a week to spend in these four rooms alone.

There are seven Basilica in Rome, four within the walls and three without. They are called Basilica, because they have served at different times as the seats of public tribunals or courts of justice. St. Peter's occupies the spot where it is said the Apostle was interred after his crucifixion, and where thousands of the early Christians suffered martyrdom. "St. John Lateran" is the Basilica where the coronation of the popes always takes place.

In a vault underneath the chapel we saw the famous Pieta by Bernini. It is beautiful, and I cannot imagine why it is placed where it is so dark that a candle is necessary, and where it is in a fair way to be ruined by the carelessness of the guide, who has already marred its beauty by smoking it with the candle, as he professes to point out its peculiar excellencies. Connected with this church is the "Scala Santa," of great renown. It contains twenty-eight marble steps, said to have been Pilate's staircase, and to be the identical stairs which Jesus Christ descended when he left the judgment-seat. No one is allowed to go up these steps but penitents on their knees; and so great is the number who visit it, that the edges are protected by boards, which it has been necessary to renew three times. Holes are bored in the wood through which to kiss the steps and save the marble from the touch of polluted lips. One of our company, an American gentleman, was so naughty that he ran up these stairs like a cat, to the great astonishment and dismay of a poor woman who was crawling up on her knees. We, however, went up and came down on the stairs made and provided for the impenitent. I had a great desire to see a painting kept in the chapel here; it is attributed to *St. Luke*, and said to be a *correct likeness of the Saviour when he was twelve years old.* Luke, we are told in holy writ, was the "beloved physician," but nothing is said of him as an artist. Being one of Eve's daughters, I had a great curiosity to see his style of painting, and as much to know how Christ looked when a boy. But we could not gain access. We caught a glimpse of one or two priests at the head of the stairway as we were ascending, but when we had arrived at the top they had disappeared—like snails, they had crept into their shells.

In the cloisters belonging to St. John Lateran, we were shown several remarkable curiosities, among which was the mouth of a well called "the well of the woman of Samaria." It was of stone, round, and three or four feet high. We saw two columns of Pilate's house," and "the column that was split in twain when the wall of the temple was rent!" The slab was shown us on which "the soldiers cast lots for Christ's garments"—it was of porphyry; also a slab supported by four columns, said to be the exact height of our Saviour—six feet! One of our gentlemen stood under it, and the guide remarked that he was just the size of the Saviour! Here we saw also an altar-table of stone, an inch thick, through which, when a priest doubted the real presence, the wafer fell from his hand, and left a hole! But more anon.

LETTER NO. XVI.

Rome, October 12, 1850.

St. Peter's Church is open at all times in the day, and I always found many persons there. Some were praying to the Virgin or one of the saints; others were in devotional attitudes in various parts of the church; while perhaps two or three congregations were, besides, in the midst of their services in some of the chapels. The rich and the poor, the aged and the young, the sorrowful and distressed, here all met together. How delightful was the thought to me, as I passed round among them, that *God knows* the heart; he *knows* who worship him in sincerity and truth; he sees, with unerring eye, all those who *truly seek him with all the heart.* I never appreciated and rejoiced in God's omniscience as here. Walking up the nave or centre of this vast temple, I discovered, in a high chair at my right, an image of a "black saint" as I thought, and wondering much who it could be, I drew near and found it no less a personage than *St. Peter*, in bronze. Quite ashamed of my ignorance and stupidity in making such a mistake in regard to the first Pope of the Church, I paused to obtain a better view of His Holiness. I noticed that every person who passed me, stopped before the statue, and, wiping the right foot, which is extended, with his pocket handkerchief, imprinted a kiss on the *great toe.* The next comer wiped off the last kiss, and gave another. Mothers with babes in their arms, not only kissed the toe themselves, but made their babes do it, and children too small to reach it were lifted up. The toe is partly *kissed off;* the nail has entirely disappeared. It is said this statue of St. Peter was once the statue of Jupiter, now changed into an angel of light. We applied for admittance into the subterranean chapel, where it is said St. Peter and St. Paul are buried. The gentlemen were allowed to go down, but I was told that "*women* were not permitted to see their graves!" So they left me bewailing my misfortune in being born a woman. I however endeavored to console myself by walking around the High Altar, which is covered with a splendid canopy of solid bronze, supported by four pillars, gilded. This canopy cost one hundred thousand dollars. The altar is exactly over St. Peter's grave, and is only used when the Pope officiates in person, which is very seldom, and only on great occasions. The confessional is surrounded by a circular ballustrade, around which a hundred and twelve lamps are continually burning night and day; they are never allowed to go out. A flight of steps leads down to the shrine, and one of Canova's exquisite statues, Pius VI., is kneeling before the door which leads into the Apostle's tomb.

The tribune, which is at the extreme end of the church, and opposite the entrance, is said to contain the *identical* chair in which Peter and some of his successors officiated. This chair is supported by four colossal statues of the Fathers of the Church — St. Augustin and St. Ambrose of the Latin, and St. Chrysostom and St. Athanasius of the Greek Church.

The chapels are all on the side aisles, and the altar in each chapel is decorated with Scripture scenes in mosaic, beautifully executed. These, with the endless variety of mausoleums, statues, bas-reliefs, gilt and stucco ornaments, in each, require days and weeks to examine. The pavement of the church is composed of marbles, arranged in different figures, many of them stars, diamonds, &c., like patchwork quilts. The piers supporting the arches which separate the nave from the side aisles, are faced with thin marbles of various hues, as furniture is *veneered* with mahogany, &c. It is impossible for any one on entering this vast temple to comprehend at once the immense scale of its architecture. It is only by comparing its statues with the human figures which are wandering about it, and measuring its pillars and ascertaining its dimensions, and comparing the size of various objects with others familiar to you, that you can understand its vast proportions. For instance, soon after you enter, your attention is arrested by two *little* cherubs, plump and beautiful, holding marble vases of holy water. You do not admire the angelic beauty of their faces more than the beauty of their proportions. You are therefore surprised, as you take a nearer view, to find these *sweet babes* are six feet high! It seems quite a long walk from the entrance of the church to the high altar, which stands immediately under the dome, the magnificent and stupendous height of whose vault fills you with amazement. The nave of the church, which is the centre between the side aisles, is ninety feet wide, and it is a hundred and fifty-two feet from the pavement to the ceiling in height.

The whole length of the church from the door to the tribune, exclusive of the thickness of the walls, is six hundred and eight feet. From the pavement to the top of the dome is four hundred and five feet, and to the top of the cross is about four hundred and thirty-five feet. The four piers which support this dome are two hundred and thirty-four feet in circumference, the walk around a pier being three feet longer than the length of the Planters' House, St. Louis, which is two hundred and thirty-one feet front. As you look up into this vault from below, your eye is ravished with the beauty of its ornaments, its mosaics, and gilded stuccoes: amid them you discover four medallions representing the four Evangelists. They seem in size like ordinary portraits, and yet when, in ascending the dome, you enter a gallery about midway from the pavement, and look about you, you find that they are of enormous size, and that the *pen* even which St. Mark holds is six feet long; and as you look down upon those who are walking, kneeling or sitting in the chapel, they seem as children in size.

The first time I entered St. Peter's I had walked some distance, when the sound of music, as I thought, fell faintly on my ear. I spoke of it to my companions, but they did not hear it. Soon, however, it became more distinct, and we found as we advanced an organ and full choir in performance. There were also four congregations at worship in different chapels, no one interfering with the other.

St. Peter's is nearly *three* times the length of the Planters' House. Suppose a hall ran through the house ninety feet wide—suppose also, that huge pillars separated the hall from side aisles twenty-one feet wide, and that beyond them, east of the aisles, were chapels or alcoves next to the outer wall forty-seven feet in width, and separated from each other by walls, as the rooms now are, only of greater thickness; an organ might be playing in the south-east room, (if you entered the Planters' on Pine street,) in the centre of the building, and if the ceiling was a hundred and twenty-five feet above the hall floor, you would find it difficult to hear it.

I visited this church many times and at different hours. Of course, I could not attend so many services, witness so many ceremonies as I did, observe such numerous and fanciful costumes among the officials, and such strange manœuvres, without having my mind considerably exercised thereby. The costumes of themselves, I should think, were some of them the study and work of a life-time. There are long dresses and short ones, thick ones and thin, flannel and lace. Some of the priests wore very becoming purple robes: these, I was informed, were the canonicals of St. Peter's; all dressed in this style belonged to the establishment in some shape or other. Sometimes the services were conducted within an enclosure, from which all but priests and monks, and certain others dressed in regimentals, were excluded. Of course, I was inquisitive to know to what order the white flannel priests or monks belonged, and the brown flannel and red flannel, &c.

I wondered much to see so many interesting boys and handsome young men, from ten to twenty-five, all with a little spot on their heads shaved, of the size of a dollar, and was told they belonged to the nobility, and were set apart to the priesthood, and were taking lessons accordingly. I pitied them as they trailed about from pillar to post, with candles taller than themselves, which the little fellows, sometimes, from very weariness, held in any but an upright position;

it certainly seemed like children's play, walking about in procession with blazing lights in mid-day, and reminded me of an incident that occurred in my childhood's days, when I was left in a room to take care of some little shavers younger than myself. In order to make myself agreeable, and afford a pleasant entertainment to my young charge, I collected all the candles about the chambers, and having lighted and ranged them in a circle, we proceeded forthwith to have a regular dance around them. One of us, however, taking fire in the performance, it became necessary to call in the aid of very unwelcome spectators.

Of what possible use could all these candles be in *broad daylight?* For the moment, I was of the opinion of Judas Iscariot, and mentally exclaimed, as I gazed at the walking candles, and the hundreds that were blazing about the painting of some saint or other, "Why were not these candles sold for five hundred pence, and given to the poor?"

These little boys were as fancifully dressed as their elders; on some occasions they wore scarlet wrappers, and on others they had on lace night-gowns. Every thing seemed to have "a season" and "a time," as Solomon says. I concluded there was "a time" for a black dress," and "a time" for a red one—"a time" for a broadcloth, and "a time" for a lace—"a time" to kneel down, and "a time" to get up—"a time" to *put on* a cap, and "a time" to *take it off*—"a time" to turn round one way, and "a time" to turn round the other; but it seemed, as I looked on intently, that it must take a wiser than Solomon *to keep up with the times.* As I could not understand anything said by the priests, or know when they were praying or talking, I knew not when to shut my eyes or when to keep them open; so I kept them open all the time. I knew not either when to stand up or when to sit down, so also in this matter I consulted my convenience. With all the sensitiveness of a woman, I was greatly annoyed at seeing the elegant and costly dresses of some of the officials trailing in the dust up and down the steps and through the aisles, and had a strong desire to run up a tuck in them, or give them a graceful loop; and I was as much amazed as interested at the expertness of some of the young priests in throwing up the censers. On one occasion, I became as intensely engaged and excited as if I had been witnessing the progress of any game of chance, or of cup and ball. With chains two yards long, the cup of incense was thrown up, and came down each time approaching nearer and nearer the heads of the two individuals who were performing the office, till it seemed that the next throw must inevitably hit their unfortunate pates. With breathless anxiety I watched and dreaded the result, when, to my astonishment and delight, at the same instant they both caught the threatening cups with inimitable grace and composure of manner; I then discovered it was an accomplishment, acquired by as much practice as fencing or any other art.

Who could see the elegant lace capes, mantillas and cloaks of the priests, (I do not know that I call them by their right names,) without examining their texture and following out the pattern, and reckoning up the probable cost and utter uselessness of such finery in the representatives of our blessed Master, "the carpenter's Son," and the "fishermen of Galilee!"

Who could see the frequent and dexterous prostrations of the knee before every picture and at every corner, and not smile at the solemn and ungainly and ridiculous manner in which it was performed by some, and indulge in a momentary admiration of the ease and gracefulness exhibited by others? For my part, I practised this bowing of the knee at sundry times from sheer curiosity, and, from my unsuccessful efforts to master the performance, I concluded *this* ceremony was as much a study and required as much practice as dancing or calisthenics.

Who can see the statues of Jupiter, Venus, &c., of pagan, idolatrous times, in different museums and palaces, and not recognize in the statues of the saints and the Virgin *the same gods and goddesses*, under *new* names? Who does not feel as he scours Rome, and gazes at the ruins of its idolatrous temples, their bas-reliefs and inscriptions, and then visits its churches, that Rome is almost as *heathen now* in its worship as it was in the days of yore?

I watched the priests closely to see if they were more devotional than myself, and, in several instances, crowded myself almost up to the altar for a better view. At one time I saw the officiating priest in one of the most solemn services, as I supposed, at mass, turn round and angrily reprimand one of the infant priests, for bringing a candle too near, or setting it down in the wrong place. On another occasion, several very interesting young priests, dressed in long golden robes of exquisite workmanship, had occasion to kneel, one below the other, on different steps; the one behind discovered an unfortunate fold in the dress of the other, which he arranged while praying, and then, observing an unseemly pucker in his own magnificent robe, gave it rather a violent push behind with his foot and straightened it out. But with such frequent changes of posture, and such constant attention to the minor matters of dress, and position and ceremony, what devotional feelings can be expected? What can be done with the *heart* when the hands and feet have so much to do? If the thoughts are wholly absorbed with outward ceremonies, what becomes of meditation?

If the stranger is filled with wonder and admiration as he walks up and down, and sometimes loses his way and his companions also, in the church below, with what surprise and astonishment does he ascend the dome of this magnificent temple! To do this, you must obtain an order from the Director of the Fabbrica of St. Peter, by a written application from the Consul; you have also to pay three or four pauls at the foot of the stairs. The staircase is spiral, and composed of broad, thin stones, of the most easy and gentle ascent imaginable. It is said horses could travel up to the top of the church with ease. When you reach the roof, you are amazed to find yourself in a little village of shops and tenements; for the workmen employed in repairs, live and work up here. A fountain is also flowing, and the roof is paved with broad flat stones, and you can scarcely believe that you are on the top of a building. After you have surveyed this *village*, and wondered long enough how people can possibly live on the "roof-top," you will, of course, ascend the dome itself, which is not as easy a matter as to come up from below.

I ought to say, that, before you commence the ascent of the dome, you must take another look at the statues of Christ and his Twelve Apostles, which stand in a row on the front of the roof of the church. These statues are seventeen feet high, although, as you view them from the ground, they seem of the ordinary size. We traveled up to the base of the ball, which looks from the street no larger than a man's head; it is, however, eight feet in diameter, and will hold sixteen persons. At the bottom of the ball is a balcony, from which a view of surpassing beauty and interest is enjoyed—said to be one of the finest scenes in Europe. Ancient and modern Rome are spread out before you, with the Appenines on one side and the Mediterranean on the other. While enjoying this delightful prospect, most of our party went up into the ball to look out, and we then returned below.

Farewell to St. Peter's! Never again do I expect to behold its like, till I enter the *upper* temple, "made without hands, eternal in the heavens."

LETTER NO. XVII.

ROME, October 14, 1850.

The Church of St. John Lateran is the Basilica, next in importance to St. Peter's. Here the Pope is always crowned. This Church was built by Constantine, and takes its name from the Senator Plautinus Lateranus, whose house once occupied the site. He is said, by Tacitus, to have been put to death by Nero, for having been concerned in the conspiracy of Piso. The place then passed into the hands of the family of Marcus Aurelius, who was born near it. It was afterwards conferred by Constantine on the Bishop of Rome as his episcopal residence, and the Basilica was founded soon after. This Church is interesting to the traveler, from the fact that five general councils have been held here, at one of which, in 1179, the doctrines of the Waldenses and Albigenses were condemned. Another was held in 1215, at which it was said "the Latin Patriarch of Constantinople, the Patriarch of Jerusalem, four hundred Bishops, and the Ambassadors of France, England, Hungary, Arragon, Sicily, Cyprus, &c., were present." The recollection of such events gives deep interest to the place. There are many statues, paintings, columns, &c., here, which are very fine and worthy of examination. As they profess to be in possession of the *very table on which the last supper was eaten by Christ and his Apostles*, we requested to see it. It is kept locked up in a little closet, and stands on its side, covered with a green baize curtain, which the guide lifted, and displayed an old oak table, well worn, about five feet long, I should think, and three or four feet wide.

Santa Maria Maggiore is the third Basilica in rank, and is the most magnificent and largest Roman Church dedicated to the Virgin. The interior of this edifice is said to be one of the finest in existence. One of the chapels contains the "holy cradle," or cradle of the Saviour, which is made the subject of great ceremony and show on Christmas Eve, in which, I believe, the Bambino, or wooden baby, is paraded about.

The Basilica of *Santa Croce in Gerusalemme* is the fourth, and derives its name from a portion of the *true cross*, which is here deposited, and which is shown on one day of Easter week. They have a great many relics here, among which are some of Thomas a Becket's *bones*.

The Basilica of *San Paolo fuori le Mure*, the fifth Basilica, is one mile and a quarter beyond the walls of Rome, on the road to Ostia. Here are to be seen the magnificent pillars of Egyptian alabaster, sent to the Pope by the Pacha of Egypt. We obtained an order from the American Charge d'Affairs, and were admitted to see them. They are not yet in the places designed for them, as St. Paul is rebuilding, having been burnt down some years since. The columns are lying in a work-shop adjoining, covered with great care; they are, probably, the most splendid specimens of alabaster in the world. If I recollect right, they are forty feet long and twelve feet in circumference, and each column is *one solid piece.* One of the four columns has, unfortunately, been broken.

Near St. Paul, the guide professes to show you the block of marble on which *St. Paul was beheaded*, and three fountains which have sprung up *where the Apostle's head bounded three times from the earth.* The Basilica of *San Lorenzo* is a mile from Rome, on the road to Tivoli; it contains a great many holy relics and the catacombs of Santa Cyriaca.

We visited the seventh and last Basilica, that of *San Sebastiano*, which is two miles beyond the gate of that name, on the Appian way, to see the famous catacombs of *San Calisto*, which are entered from the Church. There is nothing else in this Basilica worthy of notice. Greatly to our disappointment, we found the doors barred and sealed with sealing wax. These catacombs are said to extend twenty miles. They run in every direction. It is supposed these immense subterranean chambers were originally excavated to procure clay for the great potteries of the ancient Romans, but ever since the third century, they have been used for burying the dead. Nearly all the monuments and inscriptions in marble, that have been found here, have been removed to the Vatican, and may be seen in the Hall of Monuments. For years, the early Christians resorted to some of these numerous chambers to hold divine worship and to conceal themselves. It has also been a hiding place and receptacle for the many thieves that have infested the Appian way. It is considered quite dangerous to explore the catacombs, the winding passages are so irregular, and so many accidents have occurred. We were told that a teacher once visited them, with thirty of his scholars, and was never heard of afterwards! Whether they lost their way and died of starvation, or became victims to the bad air of some of the chambers, or fell into some concealed pit, no research or investigation has been able to ascertain.

We visited several other churches in Rome, all interesting from events in their history, or from the magnificence and splendor of their ornaments. Among them were *S. Maria del Populo*, built on the spot where Nero's ashes were discovered and scattered to the winds; *Gesu*, the Church of the Jesuits, one of the richest in Rome, containing, among other things, a *silver* statue of St. Ignatius, and the largest mass of lapis lazuli in the known world; *San*

Pietro in Vincoli, a majestic edifice, which contains one of the last works of Michael Angelo, a statue of Moses, whom this queer artist has represented *with horns*, but in spite of the comical effect of his horns, you are awed by the dignity and authority of the law-giver, and filled with admiration at the surprising power of the artist's chisel; *Trinita de Monti*, above the Piazza di Spagna, with a staircase of one hundred and thirty-five steps. This contains the master-piece of Daniele da Volterra, "The Descent from the Cross"—said, by some, to be the third greatest picture in the world—inferior only to "Raphael's Transfiguration," and to the "St. Jerome" of Domenichino.

At the Capuchin church, we saw three very fine paintings —"The Archangel, Michael," by Guido; "The Ecstacy of St. Francis," by Domenichino; and "The Dead Christ," by Andrea Camassei.

Under this Church is the cemetery of the Capuchin Convent, which, although it is not lawful for a woman to see, I had heard so much about it that I found myself, nevertheless, in this city of miracles, *inspired* to attempt an exploration.

The Capuchin Friars are distinguished by their dress, which is a dark brown, loose, woolen garment, worn with a rope about the waist, hanging down with long ends; a cowl or head-piece is attached to the neck of the garment, which is generally worn down, but occasionally drawn up over the head. Their heads are partly shaven; they wear long beards, and no shoes or stockings, but a kind of sandal made of strips of leather, laced over their feet.

They seem to have taken the vow of filthiness as well as poverty. We occasionally rode with them in the Diligence, and met them everywhere in the hotels and streets, greatly to our annoyance, they were so uncleanly. As to their *sanctity*, I can scarcely believe there is such a thing as a *dirty Christian;* a *real* Christian must be clean *inside and out.*

This Cemetery consists of four low, arched chambers, half above ground, the windows opening into a yard attached to the Convent. The earth in which the monks are buried was brought from Jerusalem. We found no difficulty in obtaining an entrance to the yard, and were told by a person who was engaged in repairs, and who probably was not aware of the sinfulness of allowing access to lady-visitors, to walk in. We found the walls, which were whitewashed, covered with human bones, fantastically arranged in diamonds, stars, fans, &c., made with ribs and finger bones. Twenty-four skeletons of monks were standing up, lying down, or sitting in niches around the rooms. These skeletons were dressed up in the brown robes of the order, with the rope around the waist, while the bony fingers of these dead men were seemingly counting their beads or holding a book.

Between the niches were piles of bones six feet high, made of the legs and arms of dead monks, a skull now and then placed among them to keep the pile even, and give it a neat, regular and fanciful appearance. We were told that whenever a Capuchin Friar dies, the bones of the monk longest buried are removed from their coffin to make room for the new occupant, and the old monk is piled up with his brethren, bating the few delicate bones which may be needed to work into the fanciful designs with which they beautify and adorn this strange and revolting charnel-house.

As there are more than three hundred churches in Rome, and most of them rendered interesting by tradition, or valuable productions of art, you can readily perceive the traveler may occupy much time in visiting churches alone.

The time would fail me to tell of all the forums, arches, tombs, fountains, baths, palaces and ruins, of nobody knows what, we visited. I will only name a few.

The Baths of Titus are said to occupy the site formerly covered by the house and gardens of Maecenas, and subsequently by the Golden Palace of Nero. No one can imagine what a rush of thought and feeling takes possession of the traveler as he walks up and down the long corridors, and gazes upon the painted ceilings of which the colors are still fresh, and realizes that he is in the palace of Nero, that monster of humanity, whose plots of iniquity had their birth, perhaps, in these very halls, and whose vaulted chambers had echoed, perhaps, to the avowal of his dark, fiendish plans.

We went down into the tomb of the Scipios, in a vineyard near the Porta San Sebastiano, and the Columbarium of the Pompeys. These Columbaria, of which there are many, are very curious; that of the Pompeys is entire, and the objects found in it remain in their original positions. You go down into the ground by a flight of stairs, and find yourself in a room perhaps twenty feet square. The walls of this room are full of pigeon holes, in which urns or monuments of various size and shape, but small, are placed. I opened one, and took up some of the ashes and fragments of burnt bones in my hand. Who was buried here? thought I; doubtless a dear and cherished friend, but who mourns his loss now? Who can tell whether his death was a gain or a loss to the world? And yet, perhaps unknown, uncared for, unmourned as he is by all earth's inhabitants *now*, his *influence* may still be felt, world-wide, and will live on through all time and eternity. It is a solemn thing to die and be entirely forgotten in *this* world; but with no home or friends, or treasures laid up in another, it is more solemn still.

The tomb of Cecilia Metella is another monument which all must visit, and yet, who was *she*? All that is known of her is, that she must have been *wealthy* and *beloved*, from the magnificent resting-place provided for her.

The tomb of Caius Cestius is built precisely, it is said, in the style of the Egyptian pyramids; it is one hundred and twenty-five feet high, and the breadth at the base is one hundred feet. Although composed of pure white Carrara marble, it is now grey with age.

The Mausoleum of Augustus cannot be visited without feelings of regret and indignation at its present condition. We are told it "was raised to considerable elevation on foundations of white marble, and covered to the summit with evergreen plantations. A bronze statue of Augustus surmounted the whole. Round the inner circumference were sepulchral chambers, containing his remains and those of his family and friends. The grounds around the mausoleum were laid out in groves and public walks." The first person buried in it was the young Marcellus, who died A. D. 22. Here, also, are the remains of Augustus, Octavia, Agrippa, Livia, Drusus, Germanicus, Tiberius and Caligula. Such is the description we have of this mausoleum. How altered now! It is in ruins, grey with age, and wedged in among miserable dwellings, where we had much difficulty to find it. It has been occupied for a fortress, as an amphitheatre for bull-fights, and is now used for fireworks and for exhibitions of rope-dancing.

The Mausoleum of Hadrian is now converted into a fortress, the famous "Castle St. Angelo." Here Antoninus Pius was buried—Marcus Aurelius, Commodus, Septimus Severus, &c. The most important prisoners of State are confined here, and it is said subterranean passages lead from it to the Vatican and St. Peter's. It was in this place Dr. Achilli was imprisoned last year.

The Pantheon is another of Rome's wonders. No one can visit this temple without peculiar emotions. Having been built by Agrippa twenty-six years before Christ, and having been converted from a heathen temple to a Christian church, and still maintaining its original appearance with very little alteration, (except being robbed of its ornaments,) it is certainly calculated from its associations, to be regarded with deep interest. It is probably the best preserved monument of Rome. The bronze doors in front are a great curiosity; they are the original doors of Agrippa. On the outside of the Pantheon, in the frieze of the entablature, is the inscription, "M. Agrippa, L. F. Cos. Tertium, fecit." Raphael's tomb is in one of its chapels.

We looked over the Tarpeian Rock, where so many traitors have been made to leap, and we wandered about the Mamertine Prisons, where Jugurtha was starved to death, and the accomplices of Cataline were strangled by Cicero's order: we were also shown the place where tradition says Peter was confined by command of Nero. They profess to show the pillar to which he was fastened, and a fountain which sprang up miraculously, that he might have water to baptize his jailors, whose names, they say, were Processus and Martinian. Candles were burning and people were praying and worshipping in this dark place.

We paid a visit to Cloaca Maxima; and much did I wish the fathers of our good city of St. Louis, in whom is vested the power to direct our civil engineering, could have taken a peep at this stupendous and useful work, which has already stood, unimpaired, the ravages of twenty-four hundred years! It is a subterranean tunnel, reaching to the Tiber, the common sewer of Ancient Rome. It was built for draining the marshy ground between the Palatine and the Capitoline. Its length is three hundred paces. The blocks of stone are five feet long, many of them, and three feet thick, and are put together without cement, like all Etruscan works. We groped our way over stones laid in the water to the extremity of this remarkable sewer, and looked through its arches. A load of hay could drive through it in some places. Here we found the Acqua Argentina, a clear spring, which some of the Romans think will cure certain diseases. We visited, in a ramble one day among the green fields, the *fountain of Egeria*, famed in classic lore as the favorite retreat of Numa. It was a wild, retired and beautiful place, shaded with lofty, spreading trees. Some of the statues are there still; one, the river-god, is much mutilated. The view of the famous Roman Aqueduct was very fine, as we strolled about it in the campagna. I had, previously, no correct idea of this stupendous and picturesque work of the Romans. A line of arches, six miles in length, is to be seen now, winding about the desolate fields of Ancient Rome. The water ran above ground in a vast tunnel of solid masonry, supported by gigantic arches, twenty feet high, or more. The water, for many miles, was carried under ground till within a few miles of the city, when the aqueduct suddenly makes its appearance like an endless colossal bridge, winding about the city till it reaches and is lost to sight in the surrounding wall.

In my next, we will visit some of the Palaces of Rome, and then, bidding farewell to this most interesting city, take a three days' journey over the famous Pontine marshes to Naples, Mount Vesuvius and Pompeii.

LETTER NO. XVIII.

ROME, October 14, 1850.

In a former letter, I made allusion to the Vatican, the Grand Palace of the Pope, adjoining St. Peters. This is probably the most interesting palace in the world. It has been used for more than a thousand years, and how much longer is not certainly known. Charlemagne, it is said, resided here at the time he was crowned by Leo III., in the eighth century. Its length is eleven hundred and fifty-one English feet—about five times as long as the Planters' House—and its breadth is seven hundred and sixty-seven feet. It has no regularity or outward architectural beauty to recommend it, for it has received so many additions on different plans, and undergone so many changes during the reign of its numerous occupants, each of whom has pulled down or built up according to his own taste, that the most you can say of its exterior is, that it is a huge pile. But its museums of antiquities and of exquisite works of art are unrivalled. The number of paintings, frescoes and mosaics, to say nothing of the relics of past ages that are garnered here, is almost incredible. No labor or expense has been spared to make this the depository of every thing that is beautiful in art or wonderful and interesting in antiquity. It has, as I have mentioned, four thousand four hundred and twenty-two apartments, and one of these, the Hall of the Candelabra, is one thousand feet long. Not only are the walls of the various rooms covered with rich paintings, but the ceiling overhead is adorned with many of the finest frescoes in the world. Every scene, almost, described in the Bible, you will here find represented in tapestry, mosaic, fresco or oils; and the historical events of ages, with the heroes of every age, and the mythological and allegorical figures of classic lore, all are embodied before you. In the *Galleria Lapidaria*, you almost feel that you are walking through a cemetery. Embedded in the wall on the sides of the room are all the marble inscriptions that have been removed from the ruined tombs and columbaria, to the number of three thousand or more. On one side are the Pagan inscriptions, and on the other are those of the early Christians, in Greek or Latin, many of them originally found in the catacombs.

I was greatly interested in the *Hall of Busts*. Here I saw Alexander Severus, Julius Cæsar, Augustus, Marcus Agrippa, Marcus Aurelius, Cato, Septimus Severus, Nero, Hadrian, Julia, the daughter of Titus, &c.

In the *Hall of the Greek Cross* are two sarcophagi of great beauty. They are made of porphyry and are of immense size. One contains the remains of St. Constantia, and the other the Empress Helena.

The Library contains manuscripts, Greek, Latin and Oriental, to the amount of twenty-three thousand five hundred and eighty. There is no other such collection in the world. The number of printed books is only thirty thousand. Among the treasures of the Library is a Virgil of the fourth century, with a portrait of Virgil himself; a large Hebrew Bible, in folio, for which the Jews of Venice once offered its weight in gold; seventeen letters of Henry VIII. to Anne Boleyn, nine in French and eight in English; several manuscripts of Luther, and numberless other literary curiosities.

The Capitol contains many very fine works of Art. Here is the celebrated Dying Gladiator. It is a master-piece of statuary. I noticed also a mosaic, called "Pliny's Doves," one of the finest specimens of ancient mosaic. It represents four doves, drinking; and is composed of natural stones of such extreme minuteness, that seven hundred and sixty are contained in one square inch. Here, among the busts, I saw Titus, Julian the apostate, Antoninus Pius, Plotina, the wife of Trajan, and Julia Sabina, the wife of Hadrian; also, Virgil, Cicero, Socrates, Seneca, Diogenes, Pythagoras, Demosthenes, Homer, Sappho, and many other distinguished characters.

Rome contains more private palaces, probably, than any other city in the world. Some say there are seventy-five. They are, many of them, of enormous size, costly and magnificent, and yet there are many inconsistencies about them to surprise the traveler. For instance, the Palace *Doria* is very beautiful in architectural proportions and ornaments, and yet the lower windows on the street are covered with iron bars, giving the edifice a prison-like appearance, while hay and straw are peeping out of some of the windows, and others are filled with cobwebs, evidently spun many years ago, so rope-like have they become from the accumulation of dust. These lower apartments, I learned, are used for stables, coach-houses, &c. The grand staircase of these palaces is often built of marble, and yet so neglected has it been, or so has the dust of years marred its beauty, that you can scarcely tell the original color of the stone. Many of the spacious rooms, containing perhaps a fortune in paintings, and elegant gilded chairs with crimson, blue or green damask cushions, have no carpets or fireplaces, but dark, dirty brick floors. I often thought, as I wandered about, (and could not help smiling at the idea,) that I *should not be comfortable* in this or that palace. Even the most elegant rooms, adorned with the finest frescoes of the greatest masters above mentioned—and tapestries around the walls—and silk damask curtains so heavy and rich that they would almost stand up of themselves at the windows, without being hung—and floors inlaid with cedar, ebony, satin-wood, &c.,

in the most fanciful and tasteful manner,—imposing as they are upon entrance, are so lofty, and large, and desolate, as to be absolutely destitute of any thing like *comfort.*

A little incident occurred to one of our traveling companions, in a very stylish hotel, that afforded me a great deal of amusement. The lady was rather delicate in health, and very particular about her accommodations. Her husband called for a *good* room, and, having business abroad, left his wife to take possession of it alone. It was dusk when the servant took up their baggage and showed her to her chamber. It was spacious and handsomely furnished, but the floor had evidently been just washed, and the room was decidedly damp. Her first impulse was to call for another apartment, stating her reason; but, remembering she could not make herself understood on account of the language, she concluded to wait for her husband's return. She sat down by the window—he was gone a long, long time—her feet became damp—she grew chilly, and found herself at length quite "stuffed up with a cold"—and feeling she was risking her life by remaining any longer in so damp a room, she returned to the parlor till his return. When he came, she told him he must order another apartment; that she had taken a violent cold and felt very unwell in consequence of remaining there some time, and she dared not sleep in so wet a room. He went up to see it with her, when lo, and behold! the floor was so highly *waxed* it had the appearance of being wet! She joined in the general laugh in spite of her cold, and her chilliness and symptoms of influenza speedily disappeared. The floors are often so highly polished, that you cannot walk across them without risk to life and limb.

The bedsteads throughout Italy are made of *iron*, and usually painted. It is no small consolation to the weary traveler, who knows the lazy and uncleanly habits of the

Italians, to feel that his bed is *unoccupied by any thing* save himself.

In visiting private palaces, as well as any of the ruins in these foreign cities, an entrance fee is always expected by the "custode;" a paul, ten cents, for one person, or two or three pauls for a party. The revenue from these fees is very large.

The *Palace Barberini* is one of the largest in Rome. Some of the walls are entirely covered with pictures, intended for the glorification of the Barberini family. The celebrated portrait of Beatrice Cenci, by Guido, is to be seen here, and the original "Fornarino," by Raphael, besides some other paintings of great merit. In one of the rooms, we saw Cardinal Barberini himself. The *Borghese Palace* is said to contain the richest private collection of paintings in Rome. "The Chase of Diana," by Domenichino — the "Entombment of Christ," by Raphael, painted before he was twenty-four years of age — his own portrait when he was thirteen, and the "Raphael Frescoes," are among the collection.

In the *Doria Palace* are many beautiful paintings. "The Madonna adoring the sleeping Saviour," by Guido — "The Repose in Egypt," by Filippo Lauri — among others, I admired very much.

The Palace of the Inquisition we did not visit. This is used as a prison for delinquent members of the religious societies. It was suppressed by the Roman Assembly in February, 1849, but is now in full blast.

We visited a palace now being fitted up in great style for the Pope, by himself. We went into the Pope's oratory, his sleeping chamber, his private chapel, his reception room, and his *billiard room*, which is elegantly furnished for the recreation of the Pope and his Cardinals, when weary with their religious duties. "The Annunciation," by Guido, the altar-piece in the Pope's chapel, is exquisitely beautiful.

In the *Palazzo Rospigliosi* is a picture of "Adam and Eve after the Fall," by Domenichino, and a portrait of Calvin, by Titian. Here also is "The Aurora" of Guido, a fresco of great beauty.

The Villa Borghese, formerly the great park of Rome, three miles in extent, in which the Romans were accustomed to resort on all great festal days, and said to be very beautifully laid out, was entirely ruined in this last revolution. The entrance is still beautiful and imposing, but not a tree in a thousand has escaped the work of destruction.

There are said to be several thousand *Jews* in Rome. They live by themselves and are walled in, and the gates locked upon them every night at ten o'clock. The Pope has lately withdrawn all his subjects from their employ, and forbidden any Roman to labor in their families. This is said to cause great trouble among the Jews.

The streets of Rome are very narrow, with no side-walks; they are paved with small stones of lava, which is as hard as flint. The Corso, the main street of the city, which is a mile long, has a side-walk, and is wider than most of the others. The Tiber is now very low and muddy. We find the inhabitants of the city do not generally return from their summer haunts until this time, as it is not considered healthy.

The first Sabbath we were here, there was no English service. Last Sabbath, we attended the Church of England; their meetings are held in a room neatly fitted up for public worship just outside of the city gates. The Rev. Mr. Hastings, sent out by the American and Foreign Christian Union, has been here since last December, and will preach here next Sabbath. He has spent the unhealthy season at Albano, fifteen miles distant, and meantime, with the Pope's consent, has fitted up a room in the Via de Pontifici for

Protestant worship in the heart of the city, near the tomb of Augustus.

Dr. Malan, of Geneva, gave us a letter of introduction to Mr. Hastings, which, after some days, was sent to him in the country by Mr. Cass, American Charge d'Affaires. Imagine our surprise and astonishment, the evening after the letter was sent to him, on hearing an earnest tap at our door at the Hotel d'Angleterre, which we hastened to open, to find in this Rev. Mr. Hastings an old friend, whom we had known for years in America, and who, we supposed, was still preaching in Western New York. The interview was as delightful to him as to ourselves, in this foreign land. Immediately on receiving our letter of introduction, finding we were old acquaintances, he hastened to town, and reached the hotel late in the evening, to give us a welcome. He has taken us to see his chapel—"the upper room," as he calls it—which he has fittted up in a neat, simple manner. It is just finished. The arms of the American Ambassador are to be placed over the door. Permission to establish a place of worship for Americans, is owing to the influence of the American Minister in preventing the Propaganda Fidei College from being used as barracks, and the scholars from being turned out, during the revolution. The pupils of the College have presented Mr. Cass with a very handsomely bound book, containing the Lord's Prayer in sixty different languages, written by themselves, as a testimony of their gratitude for his interference in their behalf. All this looks liberal and right. Some incidents have, however, occurred within the last few days which savor a little of the Jesuitism of the Propaganda. Mr. Healey, a brother-in-law of Dr. Achilli, is a member of Mr. Hastings' congregation, and, during Mr. H.'s stay in the country, has made all the necessary arrangements in fitting up the room selected for public worship. Since our arrival, Mr. Healey's house has been visited in the evening by eight or ten officers of the Police, a part standing outside the door, and a part commencing a search of his house, opening all his trunks and drawers, pulling out and opening and retaining such of his letters as they chose, among which are Mr. Hastings' notes from Albano. They carried off with them his Bible, which was the property of his late wife, and particularly valued on that account. They ordered him also to leave Rome within a given time. On being asked by Mr. Healey the cause of this order, they replied that "it was sufficient for him to know that his residence in Rome was not desired." A Jew, also, who has on one or two occasions received articles for Mr. Hastings, consigned to his care, has recently been summoned before the Police, and charged with too great intimacy with Protestants. On denying that he favored the Protestant any more than the Roman Catholic religion, as he was *a Jew*, he was dismissed with a reprimand for this time, and such a significant and authoritative command "to look out for himself hereafter," as made the poor man tremble in his shoes. If Mr. Hastings is to meet with such annoying circumstances—if he is openly to be bid "God speed" in his enterprises, and privately to be assailed with *spiritual fleas* to embarrass and disturb him, the privileges and toleration he has received at the Pope's hands will amount to nothing at all.

There are quite a number of English and American artists in Rome, whose studios are well worth a visit. Mr. Terry, from the neighborhood of Hartford, Conn., has some very fine paintings. We found in the Vatican and many of the palaces, both ladies and gentlemen copying some of the finest paintings. It is a rare privilege to be admitted to copy the works of the greatest masters; but any one, I believe, who goes through a certain routine to obtain permission, can get it. I learned one singular fact, namely, that no one without a regular permission from some one of the artists employed by Government, is allowed to sketch any thing in doors or out, of God's works or man's.

LETTER NO. XIX.

NAPLES, October, 1850.

We found on our arrival at Rome, that a quarantine was in force, and that no person could go, by land or sea, to Naples, under fourteen days after he entered the city. It was soon, however, changed to ten days; but, at the end of that time, the diligences were overflowing, and we could not all obtain seats for the same trip. The diligences, moreover, traveled day and night, exposing us to the malaria of the marshes and to robbers, as well as preventing a view of many deeply interesting objects on the route. Our party, at length, seven in number, hired a "vettura," a comfortable carriage with four horses, having four seats inside, and a "coupee" with two places, which, with one seat with the "vetturino," afforded us excellent accommodations.

But we found it as difficult a matter to get *out* of Rome as it was to get *in*. Nearly a day was occupied in making the necessary arrangements to start. In the first place, a written contract was drawn up, specifying the vehicle, the terms, the time and the service required for performing this journey of one hundred and fifty miles. In Italy, verbal engagements are not binding enough, and it is necessary to be wide awake or you will certainly be overreached or imposed upon in some way. The carriage and horses were *seen* before closing the contract, and at length all was adjusted to the satisfaction of each party to the engagement. Our contract specified that we should reach Naples in three days, stopping every night at dusk. Our "vetturino" was to furnish us two meals a day, at good inns; a breakfast before eleven o'clock, of coffee, eggs, bread and butter; and a dinner at six o'clock, of soup, two kinds of meat, dessert, &c., for ten dollars each. Half the money was paid in advance in Roman "scudi," and the other half at the end of the journey. The contract, written in Italian, was given to one of our party, our captain pro tem., and the duplicate was left at Rome. When all this was duly arranged, our next duty was *to ask leave to depart.* We sent to the Police Office for our passports, which had been there in safe keeping ever since our arrival; we then went to the American Consul to obtain his *vise*, which cost our five gentlemen ten dollars, or two dollars each; from thence they were carried to the Neapolitan Consul and his *vise* procured, for which one dollar was paid; then they were all taken back again to the Police to get their *vise*, for which we paid four pauls more each; and, finally, they were examined again just before we went out of the city gate, to see if all was correct. And thus, having obtained leave of absence from the Eternal City by paying for the privilege, and having notified the principal authorities of our intended departure and place of destination, we shook off the dust from our feet and departed.

The day was delightful. We left the city by the gate of St. John Lateran at the south. Our road lay over the Appian Way, through the rich fields of Ancient Rome, ruins on every side. A long line of aqueducts skirted our path at a distance on one side, while the tombs on the other every few moments claimed our attention. Near *Frattochie* is said to be the place where Claudius was murdered by Milo in a quarrel, which is the subject of one of Cicero's orations, "pro Milone." We passed the mausoleum of Ascanius, the son of Virgil, and stopped to gather some flowers. The Pope's summer palace stood off at our left, and the tomb of Pompey the Great we saw about half a mile from Albano.

As we ascended the hill on which Albano is built, and looked back upon Rome to take our final leave, we were entranced with the beauty of the scene. Here is the place, of all others, to see Rome. All its towers and palaces and obelisks are in distinct view, while the ruins of old Rome stand around in melancholy contrast—a growing, beautiful city, and a ruined city, side by side—a city of life and a city of death together. The Mediterranean lay at our left, as we turned about to gaze at this magnificent and impressive scene.

Albano, a city of five thousand inhabitants, is the fashionable summer resort of the Roman nobility. Its location is high and healthy, and it is supposed to occupy a part of the villas of Pompey and Domitian. Many ruins are still visible. Here we breakfasted at eleven o'clock, at a fine hotel, originally a palace. Between *Albano* and *Cisterna*, where we arrived at five o'clock, to spend the night, we passed the towns of *Genzano* and *Velletri*. The former is a small village situated on *Lake Nemi*, a beautiful sheet of water five miles in circumference, occupying an extinct crater, it is supposed. *Velletri* is the ancient capital of the Volsci, and the birth-place of the Emperor Octavius Augustus. This was once the favorite residence of Tiberius, of Nerva, of Caligula, and of Nero. This city now contains a population of twelve thousand. There is nothing remarkable about its appearance. Its location is on the summit of a hill and it enjoys a commanding prospect, but it is badly built, and its streets are narrow and crooked. We stopped for the night, early, at *Cisterna*, as it is on the confines of the *Pontine Marshes*, which it is not prudent for travelers to enter upon at night. These marshes cover an area of one hundred and forty-four miles, but the road through them, over which we passed to *Terracina*, is only twenty-five miles in length. This spot was interesting to us from the fact, that near here, if not at this very place, stood the "*Three Taverns*" where Paul stopped on his journey to Rome, and where he met a deputation from Rome, and "thanked God, and took courage." Our hotel was very comfortable; we rose early, and without any breakfast started off at four o'clock. For several miles we traveled over the *very road* that Paul traversed eighteen hundred years ago.

At *La Torre del Tre Ponte*, a few miles from *Cisterna*, the Pontine Marshes opened to our view. Curious as I was to see this desert, I did not anticipate much pleasure from traveling over it, except as it would afford an opportunity to see the actual place where the most delightful country houses of Augustus, Pompey, Atticus, and other illustrious Romans, were once situated, and the occasional ruins of ancient walls, aqueducts and fortifications. I was agreeably disappointed to find a level, wide, delightful road, built up some feet from the marsh, running straight as an arrow as far as the eye could reach, each side of which was bordered with magnificent elms, whose shade was refreshing, and whose boughs, interlacing far above our heads, formed the most beautiful arbor imaginable. Through this fine arbor, on a road as smooth as a plank, we rode to *Terracina*. By our side ran the canal called the "*Naviglio Grande*," of which Horace speaks, and upon which he went to *Brindisi*. Not far from *Bocca di Fiume*, west of us, near the Tower of Asturo, was once a little port, where Cicero embarked for his country house the very day that he was assassinated. Here also was the young Corradin arrested who basely betrayed the Lord of Astura, who had afforded him an asylum. A few miles farther, on the sea-shore, at Nettuno, were found those inimitable pieces of statuary, "the Apollo," of the Vatican, and "the Dying Gladiator," of the Capitol. In this neighborhood, also, is St. Felix, a little town, where, according to the poets, the palace of *Circe* stood, and the prisons where the companions of Ulysses were confined. Saw herds of tame buffaloes in this vicinity.

We stopped at *Terracina* to breakfast about noon — but instead of coffee, as our contract specified, we had wine put on the table, and was told there was neither milk nor butter in this town of nine thousand inhabitants, "as the cows had all gone into the country to spend the summer, and would not be home for some time." Here we staid three hours.

Beside the hotel, a bald, scraggy rock reared its head some hundred feet above us, while the deep blue Mediterranean was sweeping by at its base. I had a strong desire to creep up to the top of that marvellous rock and look abroad into the world, and imagined if I could but gain its summit, I should almost see "all the kingdoms of the world in a moment of time;" but our landlord told us a story, that soon cooled my ardor and made me satisfied with a more lowly prospect. An adventurous Englishman, some years since, succeeded by great effort in reaching this vast height, and, having satisfied his curiosity, found to his surprise and horror that he could not get down without aid. No one knew his predicament, nor could he attract attention. Three days and three nights, in the scorching sun and the blighting dew, did he wander about on this mountain-rock, half starved and half dead with fearful apprehensions, before he was discovered and assisted in his efforts to come down. So I turned my thoughts to the sea-shore, and amused myself with gathering some beautiful little shells washed up on the beach. *Terracina* was once quite a port, but nothing remains now to show it save the rings to which the vessels were fastened. A handsome palace was built here about seventy-five years ago by Pius VI.

La Torre del Confini, beyond *Terracina*, is the last town of the Ecclesiastical States. Here our baggage was overhauled, and by the payment of a fee it was sealed and a certificate given, which, it was said, would prevent our being delayed at the next place, *Portello*, the first settlement in the Neapolitan kingdom. It, however, was only a ruse to obtain money, and we went through all the formalities of search notwithstanding our certificates.

Fondi, the next city, is a walled town of four thousand seven hundred inhabitants, celebrated in history as the place where the famous Corsair Barberousse disembarked in the night, and attempted to carry off the beautiful Julie Gonzague, widow of Vespasian Colonna, in which he was defeated; and in his wrath he pillaged the town, and carried off many of the inhabitants into slavery.

The lower part of the walls of this city is said to be older than Rome itself. We had not time to stop here, not even to see the study of Thomas Aquinas, which is shown to strangers. *Itri* is a small and exceedingly ancient town, containing five hundred souls. It was formerly the Latin city *Mamurra*, mentioned by Horace. The remains of the Cyclopean walls and of an old temple are still visible, and here, as we passed through the town, we saw at a distance the tomb of Cicero.

During this day's travel we saw more poverty, nakedness, filth and savage wildness than ever before. Few people live on the marshes, but those that do seem to be the dregs of creation. From *Terracina* to *Mola di Gaeta* we had an opportunity to witness the glory of the vintage. Hundreds of the peasantry were returning from the vineyards, loaded with grapes. The women and young girls carried baskets on their heads, filled with clusters of such marvellous size and beauty as to call forth our repeated expressions of admiration and astonishment. They equalled the clusters of Canaan, *in my old primer*, brought as specimens by Caleb and Joshua—the sight of whose wonderful bunches, in my young days, always destroyed my comfort for the time being. Donkeys and men were bowed down with leathern bottles, filled almost to bursting with wine, and with casks of the skins from which the juice had been expressed. As it drew towards night, the road became filled with men, women, children and donkeys. Oh, the poor donkeys! If they did not groan under their loads, I did. Some of them were so laden that nothing could be seen of the animals but their ears and their tails. They looked like moving masses of old bags and tubs. Beside the cabins, mostly built of straw, we saw many treading out the wine with their feet, hopping up and down in hogsheads cut in two, as we saw them at Venice.

The dress of the people was quite novel to us, and afforded us much amusement. It is said "rags" form one of the exports of Italy. I should certainly think, judging from appearances in this part of the country, that they had rather *im*ported the article from all other nations. It seemed as if the *rag-bag* must constitute their only wardrobe.

The grapes here are trained up on upright bamboo sticks, with bamboos running herizontally between, to sustain the enormous and abundant clusters. Orchards of olives, oranges, figs and pomegranates abounded. Century plants, cacti, cyclamens and flowers in great variety bordered the way-side. The scenery of the country grew more and more beautiful. Sometimes we rode, and sometimes we walked and gathered flowers for our "herbariums," and ate the grapes the peasants gave us, expressing our thankfulness by our greediness. We were all half crazy with delight the whole day. No part of our journey through Italy had afforded us more beautiful specimens of country scenery, more interesting localities, more original and picturesque, more laughable or deplorable specimens of humanity. The old towns of *Fondi* and *Itri* looked as if they were thousands of years old, and as if the idea of "*change*" had never traveled either into the dictionaries or the sconces of the people. The fields of olives, containing trees thousands of years old, were a perfect curiosity.* I felt I had never seen *old* trees and *old* orchards before, nor had I any true conception of the hoary and venerable appearance to which trees could attain. Here these old orchards had remained centuries unchanged; and these aged sentinels, what had they not endured, from age to age, in pitiless blasts and never-ending dews! They had outlived the armed millions that had poured over their hill-sides. Temples, monuments and fortifications, destined to last through all time and immortalize the memory of the great, had arisen around them and crumbled before them, and nobody, now living, could find their *certain* history. If these *old trees* could be made to *speak*, what would they not say! Oh, that they had tongues! I almost wished to shake their huge, old, gnarled limbs and *make* them speak out and gratify our curiosity, which was well nigh desperate. But no! there they stood, regardless of us and our longings, silent as the dead slumberers beneath the sod, with the secrets of ages locked up in their old hearts, to torture, for ages hence, others of Eve's curious progeny. There they stood, *ever* silent, save when the passing blast drew forth from their sweeping branches an involuntary requiem to ages gone by.

* Naturalists say that the Olive attains the age of three or four thousand years. We are told, it does not begin to bear till it is fifty years old.

Mola di Gaeta, where we spent our second night, contains two thousand inhabitants, and is in sight of the *Gulf of Gaeta* and the city of *Gaeta*, where Pope Pius IX. found a refuge in the late revolution. From the terrace of our hotel, which was situated on an elevated point but a few rods from the sea, we had a splendid view of the promontory on which the beautiful city of Gaeta is built. As we stood facing the sea, the sun just dipping into the water, Gaeta, with its magnificent peak, Corvo, rose on our right. At its summit stands *La Tour de Roland*, which is the ancient tomb of Lucius Manutius Plancus, and another tower, supposed to be a temple of Mercury. At our left, had it been perfectly clear, we should have had our first glimpse of Vesuvius, to complete the scene.

At a little distance from Mola is *Castelleone*, once *Formio*, in whose environs Cicero was assassinated.

LETTER NO. XX.

NAPLES, October, 1850.

We found excellent accommodations at the *Mola*, and left at four o'clock in the morning, traveling as far as *Capua* before we breakfasted. We passed *Sessa*, a town most beautifully located, and famous in the time of Horace for its wines. *Capua* stands at the foot of *Mt. St. Nicolas*, a part of the chain of the *Tiphates* mountains, and in the neighborhood of the rivers *Clanio* and *Volturno*. *Capua* was interesting to us from the fact, that here Hannibal dwelt among its beautiful hills, and he and his army were ruined by its delicious wines. The old town of *Capua* was about a mile from the present site. The country from this place to Naples is beautiful beyond description. The grapes hung in festoons from lofty elms. Passed the ruins of an old aqueduct, and crossed over a most magnificent iron bridge, the finest but one in all Italy. Saw the plough of primitive times; it was quite amusing to see the awkward and laborious mode of ploughing, compared with our own. Here we began to notice a striking peculiarity in the harness of the horses. The *hames* were built up in the form of a pyramid, and adorned with a profusion of brass ornaments, and rows of little brass bells; even the country horses were caparisoned in the most royal-like manner. The land in the neighborhood of Naples is exceedingly rich and level, like prairie land, a garden of Eden in beauty. Fields of vegetables were as fresh and green as with us in June.

Naples is the most beautiful city I have seen. As we entered its vast gate and drove through the superb street of Toledo, two hundred feet or more wide, with most elegant houses of four or five stories, built of yellow stucco, I was captivated with the splendor and magnificence of all I saw. I had forgotten that, next to London and Paris, it was the most populous city in Europe; it contains three hundred and sixty thousand inhabitants. After passing the formalities of the custom house, we drove to a large, imposing edifice, and halted. The military were drilling before us, and formed quite an interesting spectacle. Priests, monks, and lazzaroni were parading about, and people of all nations, with their varied and novel costumes, attracted our attention. The city was *alive*, in every sense of the word. We had not seen so much bustle, earnestness and activity since we left England. Here we staid a full hour. The gentlemen became quite impatient. I was in a state of enchantment, and was quite satisfied to sit and look about at the wonderful things which met my eye everywhere. But what could have become of our driver? We imagined first one thing and then another, till finally it began to grow dark, and we became not only impatient, but alarmed. At length, a gentleman came to the carriage and informed us that our "vetturino" had been arrested! The carriage and horses also were to be detained, and could go no further. Nobody could tell us *why* this had happened; not even the driver himself could imagine the cause. We knew not but *we* should be arrested, ourselves, next. I began to think Naples was not so fine a place after all, and wished I was out of this land of mystery and miracles. Quite a mob soon collected about the carriage, as the fact was noised about — men, women, children, soldiers and priests. At last, four small vehicles were procured by our "vetturino's" order, and we changed our baggage to them, and after an hour or two of anxiety and apprehension of all sorts of evil, we found ourselves very merry and joyful at the "Hotel du Commerce," with excellent accommodations. We never learned the cause of our driver's arrest. It was supposed to be some informality in that everlasting torment, the passport.

The next morning, early, (Saturday,) we prepared for an excursion to Mount Vesuvius. We rode nearly two miles over the broad and beautiful street on the shore of the gulf, with the shipping and a distant view of the islands at our right, while on our left were elegant edifices, villas and gardens, more imposing in appearance than in any other city I had seen, till we reached the station, where we took the cars to *Portici*, four miles farther, still in full view of the sea. From here we walked to the little village of *Resina*, where we engaged a guide and horses for four of the company, the rest preferring to walk. The sky was cloudy and we feared rain, but eager to feast our eyes with a sight of one of the world's wonders, we were not disposed to defer our visit till another time. *Portici* has about five thousand inhabitants, and contains the Palais Royal with beautiful gardens just at the foot of Vesuvius. Many of the rich Neapolitans have superb country seats here. From *Resina*, we commenced the ascent of the mountain. We wound about through the narrow lanes of the outskirts of the village, till we reached a new, wide road, not yet finished, extending five or six miles, in a gradual ascent up the mountain, our companions on foot striking off on a shorter route, but impassable for horses, where we soon lost sight of them. As we ascended the slope, we rode slow, every now and then turning square about, to enjoy the magnificent view which our position afforded of the city and bay of Naples, of the sea and its islands on one side, and of the chateaux, villas, palaces and vineyards in our immediate neighborhood, and the villages that dotted the plain in the distant view. Green fields and luxuriant vineyards, loaded with Italy's most luscious grapes, bordered our way, while the tall, dark peak of the volcano loomed up before us. No words can paint the beauty of the enchanting scene that filled our vision. We could only gaze and admire and loiter along, worrying each other with expressions of delight, and exhausting our vocabulary of adjectives in all their degrees, positive, comparative and superlative, and then finish by declaring that all we had ever heard and read fell *infinitely* below the reality, and all the sketches and colorings of the best artists did not *begin to compare with nature's own work.* And till we have a sort of "*Transcendental*" dictionary, a little above and beyond the comprehension of mortals in our present state, no representation, save that which the *eye* itself can portray before the mind, will ever give any *true* idea of the magnificent and captivating scenery of this region to the lover of nature. Independent of the volcano and the stirring recollections awakened by its sight, it seems as if all the varied beauties of nature, of science, and of art, had congregated in this spot to form one of earth's most bewitching landscapes. Our road lay amid patches of scoria and vineyards, redeemed from the ruined fields of ages gone by, which, remarkable as it may seem, now produce the most delicious grapes and the richest wines of Italy. The ashes and scoria of the volcano, mingled with the natural soil, together with the favorable exposure of the hill-sides to the sun, the air and the dew, seem to contribute in a wonderful manner to the culture of superior fruit. The grapes almost melted in our mouths. From the vineyards on these mountain sides, is made the famous wine called "*Lachrymæ Christi.*"

At length we reached a plateau, covered with masses of lava as hard as flint, mingled with loose pieces of scoria, with now and then a stray shrub or flower, struggling for life amid the ashes and rubbish of this desolate waste. Here we found a little hermitage, inhabited by a poor "solitaire." To him the words of Goldsmith could be most truthfully applied —

"Man wants but little here below,
Nor wants that little long."

For, living here on the heaving bosom of this uncertain volcano, he certainly could not expect to want *anything long* in *this* world. Here and there upon the mountain side, on the very edge of the black deposits of this fearful burning mountain, we saw some few handsome dwellings, leading us to wonder at the thoughtlessness and recklessness and temerity of those who, ever living in this "region and shadow of death," seem to have become insensible to fear, and utterly regardless of consequences. Before reaching the *house of rest*, a little below the cone of the mountain, there came up a tremendous blow of wind and rain, which added not a little to the variety and romance of our expedition, if not to our comfort and hilarity. Here we met our companions, who had "climbed up some other way," and, all in company, but still on our horses, we traveled on over the melted rocks and spongy excrescences, and black, brittle scoria that filled our path. As to a defined road, we had none. We gave the reins to our horses, and leaving them to pick their way over the stony, sterile ascent, at length reached a temporary shelter at the foot of the "Cone de Gautrey," where we left our horses in the care of a guide. This peak is so called from a Frenchman of that name, who, some years since, in an unaccountable state of excitement, threw himself into the crater, from which his body was thrown out by an eruption two days after. Here we paused to take another view of the landscape below. The rain had ceased, and the sun shone fitfully upon the hill-tops and turrets before us. Naples in its length and breadth lay at our feet. The Gulf of Naples, with its shipping, and the Tyrrhean Sea, with its islands, stretched far away in the distance, till sea and sky were lost in one vast expanse. *Pozzuoli* was in full view. *Posilippo*, with its beautiful coast, and *Cape Miseno*, lay before us.

The island of *Capri* and the promontory of *Sorrento*, with the islands of *Procida* and *Ischia*, with their green hills and dots of villages, stood off at our left, while under and around us were towns and cities upon whom the sleep of ages had settled. Far away down the slope, on all sides were the accumulated eruptions of centuries, blackened and hardened by time, from beneath whose dark, deep, flinty crust it seemed difficult to realize that the terrific mandate of the *resurrection* even could ever call up to life its thousands of slumbering dead. But we had a hard day's work before us, and it would not do to loiter. I took a long and earnest look up to the top of the rough, sombre, almost perpendicular peak to which we aspired. It looked like a vast pyramid of burnt coal and ashes. There were three ways to reach the summit. The most common way for ladies to make the ascent, is to be carried up in an arm-chair, by four men, with poles run under the seat, carried by two men in front, wheelbarrow fashion, and resting on the shoulders of the two behind. But if, by any mischance, thought I, these men should happen *to let me fall*, I should roll down into one of these villages, perhaps, as much to the dismay of the inhabitants as to my own! This mode I declined promptly. The guide then put a leather strap about his waist, and, giving me the long end, said he would pull me up after him. I tried this awhile, but concluded, finally, I would do as the rest did, *crawl up*. So I betook myself to my hands and feet, and, feeling that I had undertaken a serious job, I summoned all the resolution and fortitude I could command, and scrambled along finely for awhile; but, at length, the scoria being rough and loose, to one step forward, I found myself sliding down two behind. Patiently and perseveringly, however, I clambered along. Sometimes I would make quite an advance, and then, by an unlucky footing, set in motion a pile of stones, that would go thumping and clattering down to the bottom. Sometimes, tired with effort, I would reach a safe place, and turn about and sit down to take breath, and "to consider upon my ways," and, obtaining a fresh view of the scenes before me, be stimulated to renewed exertion, and then travel on. Every now and then I received the kindly aid of a climbing-pole, extended to me by the gentlemen, who would pull me along. At length, with falls and bruises by some, with torn shoes and garments and aching limbs by others, and the loss of a bottle of wine by another, who fell and lost the precious contents in the fall, after an hour's severe effort, we reached the crater quite exhausted, and sat down to rest us and eat the dinner we had brought, before we proceeded to *look in* and inspect more minutely this awful phenomenon of nature. Fissures in the ground were about us in every direction, from which smoke was constantly issuing, and so hot was the air emitted, that we could not hold our hands in them a moment. Sulphur was lying about crystalized and in powder. We walked partly around the rim of the crater. I was surprised to find it half a mile or more in circumference. It is constantly changing its appearance. The last eruption, two years since, has given it a new aspect. A part of the distance, the width of the rim was not more than three feet, composed of rolling sand or ashes—the smoking, boiling abyss on one side, and an old extinct crater on the other.

I think I never experienced a more appalling sense of fear than when walking on this narrow space, and occasionally peeping cautiously over into the smoking cauldron, from which the wind would now and then lift up the smoke for a moment and give us a glimpse of the yawning abyss, I found the ashes giving way beneath my feet and I sliding down into the old crater of '34. I screamed for help. The guide caught me, but his feet sliding too, Dr. M., a young English physician of our party, came to our rescue, and drew us to a safe place, breaking, in his effort to save us, some *eggs* which he had just cooked in one of the crevices of the mountain, by the heated air which was constantly issuing out of it. We rambled about, picking up pieces of sulphur and specimens of scoria; sometimes reaching over into the crater to gather the powdered sulphur, which was actually so hot we could not hold it long in our hands. When it grew towards night, the guide mustered our party, and one of the gentlemen was missing. We feared he had fallen into the crater, and for ten or fifteen minutes were greatly alarmed. He was at length found, and we prepared to go down. We encountered another party, among whom were two ladies, who had come up in the *arm-chair*. They were pale and terrified by their dangerous ascent, and looked, as children sometimes say, "as if they had *seen sights*." I supposed it would be as difficult, nearly, to go down as to come up, and dreaded it. We were told by our guide, that we must go down in the ashes, and not upon the scoria. Our astonishment was equalled only by our uproarious mirth, when we found that the moment we put our feet in the ashes we all began to *slide* down to the bottom of the mountain. The sand was bottomless. Our heads and arms were visible, while the ashes was flying in every direction; but, like "Korah's troop," we were nearly "swallowed up," nor could we stop ourselves in our descent. Go we must, and go we did, till we found ourselves at the bottom. What it took us more than an hour's severe labor to accomplish in ascending, required less than five minutes in the descent. We laughed heartily at the performance itself, and the figure we cut; and quite in good humor, we mounted our horses and wound our way down the mountain, the guide pointing out the places of the different eruptions. The last, two years or more since, burst out at the side instead of the top of the mountain. As we cast our eyes far and wide, and beheld the extent of the ruins on every side, caused by the eruptions of former years, and the apparent insecurity of the inhabitants at its base, our wonder at the strange and astounding catastrophes which have occurred was fully equalled by our surprise at the fool-hardiness of the thousands, who seem to court destruction by planting themselves exactly at death's door. Our view of the country and the sea was more beautiful even, in our descent to Naples, than when we were ascending the mountain. Difficult as was the expedition, and weary as we were when we found ourselves at our hotel, on Saturday night, we felt well repaid for our toil.

LETTER NO. XXI.

NAPLES, October, 1850.

Monday morning we left Naples early, to explore the famous entombed city of Pompeii. Both Herculaneum and Pompeii can be visited in one day, as they are only a few miles apart; but we were told there was not much to be seen now at the former, so we concluded to scour only Pompeii, for our time was short. The traveler who has leisure to see both, stops at Resina, on the way to Pompeii, and goes down to the sea-shore to find Herculaneum, where we took a guide and horses to go up Vesuvius. Our route to Pompeii was by the railroad, through Portici, Resina, Torre del Greco, containing thirteen thousand inhabitants, and Torre del Annunziata, with a population of nine thousand souls. Its distance is about twelve miles from Naples. No one can pass the site of the ancient city of Herculaneum without feelings of deep melancholy. The almost entire oblivion in which it was buried for more than sixteen centuries, with only a tradition that such a city *was*, but nobody knew *where*—the little that we know of it now, with the much that the researches future years will doubtless disclose, shroud it with an antiquity and a mystery that cannot fail most sadly to interest the stranger. If we may believe some writers, it was a bustling city at the time of the siege of Troy, one thousand three hundred and forty-two years before the Christian era. How little did Hercules, its founder, dream of its destiny! And how passing strange is it, that, in its very neighborhood, with the muttering thunders of Vesuvius, like a prophet's voice, echoing in their ears from year to year, the cities of Portici and Resina should dare to plant their walls in the ashes that cover the ruins of their predecessor! But thus it is. Man is so infatuated he *will* rush on to destruction, in spite of warnings, threatenings, and the most terrific and mournful examples, even in the face of death itself.

Not a trace of the river Sarno, which once ran through this buried city, is now visible within several miles. It seems to have been choked and filled up by the shower of ashes which destroyed the city, and its course is now below Pompeii. In the excavations which have been made, the old bed of the river has been found. It was at the depth of eighty feet below the surface, that the richest part of the ancient city was discovered. Think what a deluge of burning cinders must have astonished the bewildered inhabitants who fled from their homes! And what a sea of fire must have enveloped with its burning waves those who were too sick and helpless to flee! Yet nobody here fears a similar catastrophe, although so lately as the eruption of 1834, one hundred houses were buried up.

At the railroad station, near Pompeii, we found a man who said he could talk English well, and, engaging him as our *cicerone*, we walked up to the ruined city; but we soon began to think it would be necessary to get another to *interpret his English*. Many of the guides that are found throughout Italy, and that impose themselves upon the traveler, and *must be* engaged for want of better, are miserably qualified for their profession. They profess to talk German, French, English and Italian generally, and I suppose they serve their various patrons with a like gibberish. We entered Pompeii near the Cathedral and Forum, ascending quite an eminence, from which we had an extensive view. Its location must have been charming originally.

Quite a portion of the city has been uncovered, yet perhaps not one half; and there it stands before you—a mournful spectacle! Many workmen are constantly employed in making excavations, and in restoring the original appearance of the public buildings and dilapidated walls. Every fragment is replaced, and every broken column mended, and all the rubbish that had accumulated for ages has been removed. The streets, more than twenty of which have been cleared and swept, are long, straight and narrow, and look, I suppose, precisely as they did the last days its fated inhabitants walked them. The side-walks are about two or three feet wide, made of lava. The streets are paved with the same material, and are, perhaps, fifteen feet wide between the side-walks. *Ruts* are worn into the stone, in some places, two inches deep, showing not only that the streets had been long traveled, but that the carriages used were very narrow. The carriages or chariots could not have been more than two feet and a half wide, and could not have accommodated more than one person on a seat. With what mingled emotions did I walk up and down these streets! How many thousands in all the vigor of life, and the buoyancy of hope, and chronicled by fame, perhaps world-wide once, had trod where I trod, and been hustled along in the busy crowd of loungers and gapers, beggars and princes, mechanics and merchants, whose names tradition has forgotten to hand down, and history to record—whose deeds have faded from the pillars, perhaps, which were to stand as monuments forever! Naught but the *influence of their lives* for weal or woe to man *now* lives to travel on to eternity. What a solemn thought, that our influence never dies! Whether we will or not, it marches on from generation to generation, till, like a poison or a cure, it spreads into the arteries of society, working death or life, and affects countless multitudes to the end of time. Only in *this* way do any of the master spirits, that moved Pompeii once, live in the world's history now, and its pages will never be read till the universe is assembled to hear.

The houses seem to have been built mostly of bricks, about an inch thick, of a lighter color, harder, and less porous than the bricks of our own times. They were two stories high, with terraced roofs. The roofs, of course, have all disappeared, and everything made of wood in the houses was so charred by the red hot cinders as to have given way, and has been removed with other rubbish. Most things of value have also been taken to the museums of Naples, Portici, Rome, Versailles, &c. But a decree has been passed, of late years, by the king of Naples, prohibiting the removal of any article that may be found hereafter. The walls of the houses remain as they were, but the door-cases and window-frames have disappeared. The names and occupation of some of the business men can be deciphered, and the devices in front of the shops and stores still remain. I walked into a bake shop and looked around. There was the stone-slab counter with the indentures of years upon it, where bread had been delivered to many a hungry soul, and the marble on which many a cracker or pie-crust had been moulded; and, in another place, the oven itself in which they were baked. I put my head into the oven, and rumaged about with my hands, hoping to find a small bit of bread or cake "of olden time." What would I not have given for a *piece of bread* eighteen hundred years old, or a *pie* baked in the time of Titus! But there was nothing in the oven save ashes, showing that the baker had not *swept* his oven as clean as we do in modern times. We went into an oil shop, and a soap factory, and a great washing establishment. In this last place everything had been done on a grand scale. I should judge, from its capacity and arrangements within, that it might have served for a *city* washhouse. We visited the house of Sallust, and picked somewild roses that grew in the court.

The rooms in most of the buildings were quite small, and the walls in many of them were painted in a very handsome style of fresco, the colors still fresh. Baskets of fruit and flowers, cupids, gods and goddesses, without number, and representations of battles, heroes, and events, which, of course, were nameless to us, arrested our attention, as well as the paved and magnificent floors of some of the public buildings. Some of these floors were elegant specimens of mosaic, and the person who showed them to us would rub a space with a wet cloth to give us an idea of their beauty when fresh and unexposed to the dew and air. The *restaurants* were evidently places of great splendor in their day, equal to the present cafes of France and Italy.

We were shown one building, which had been excavated within the last six months. It was probably a musical academy. We judged so from the style of fresco paintings on the walls, where the muses and many musical instruments were represented, and probably included a refreshment room, for Ceres and Pomona and other fabulous divinities, with their rich golden treasures, were also depicted in glowing colors. There was also a beautiful fountain in the centre of a small court, near which a marble statue of Apollo stood, and several animals of pure white marble, left by the king's order, stood around the fountain, some of them maimed, but as fresh looking as when they came from the sculptor's chisel. A little dog, a duck, and a rabbit, I would very willingly have brought away with me, but no one is permitted to carry off any relics. The floors in this establishment were also in mosaic, each piece about one-eighth of an inch square, and laid in very fanciful patterns, like the rich and varied colors and regular figures of a kaleidescope. Quite a number of soldiers are scattered about Pompeii, to guard the most interesting of its antiquities from the depredations of visiters, and to make money out of travelers who explore these ruins. You cannot enter some of these houses without feeing the keeper with a *carlin* or two. A carlin is worth about eight cents. We visited the temple of Isis, and while one of the company took the place of the goddess, I slipped into a private door, up a pair of stairs behind the niche once occupied by the priestess, and delivered *an oracle*, after the manner of the ancients, to auditors as willing to listen as those of yore, but more faithless in the *divine inspiration.* Formerly, a hollow image used to stand here, into which a priest crept and spoke, having access by the private staircase I found, while the poor, ignorant devotees believed the goddess herself was endowed with speech.

We went into a cell in one of the prisons, where two men were found dead, sitting "in the stocks." These skeletons are exhibited in some museum, I forget where.

It is said that in one building, twenty-seven females were found near a door, evidently in the attempt to escape from impending ruin. In another place, near a door, were found the skeletons of two men, one holding a key in one hand and a bag of cameos in the other. We went into a public bathing establishment, which was evidently fitted up originally in great style, and were shown one marble bathing-tub, in which our guide told us Pius IX. had bathed his "infallible" humanity, and which, in his eyes, was now evidently a sacred relic.

We were shown the house of Marcus Arrius Diomede. But little remains except the walls and the wine cellar. The latter is a great curiosity. It is about eight feet wide, and extends around the house, forming a square, fifty feet on the side. It is in a perfect state of preservation. We saw six earthen wine jars, two feet or more high, which would contain several gallons each. Two of them seemed to be whole, and, for aught I know, were filled with wine nearly two thousand years old, but, as all four of our company were teetotalers, we did not examine into the matter, but left them untouched for the benefit of the wine-bibbers who should come after us. The walls of the city are eighteen feet high, and twelve feet thick, and are uncovered for two miles. Six gates have been discovered. But nothing interested me more than the *Cemetery* of Pompeii. The tombs are some of them beautiful in design, costly in material, and exquisite in finish. The inscriptions were in Latin; I regretted that I had not time to copy some of them. One I noticed was built A. D. 12, from the inscription. I would have been glad to have spent hours in wandering about the monuments and decyphering the names upon them, but time would not allow. We walked out of the city in a different direction from the place we entered it, and sauntered through a vineyard and a large cotton field, whose luxuriance and beauty were amazing. But what a multitude of thoughts rushed upon us! We were walking, perhaps, above the buried treasures of a ruined city, which future time may perhaps uncover. Among the most precious articles yet discovered in these cities, are 1696 papyrus rolls, some of which are so charred as to be illegible, and others will at a future time be deciphered, and unravel some of the mystery which now envelops *Herculaneum and Pompeii.*

LETTER NO. XXII.

STEAMER LOMBARDY, Mediterranean,
October, 1850.

There are many objects of interest in Naples, but nothing *more* enchanting than the incomparable beauty of its location. The bay itself, it is said, exceeds all others in the known world, except that of Constantinople, and its beautiful panorama of islands, clustered around it, dotted with their many villages, and the tall, black, smoking volcano, which looms up below it, cannot but extort from the traveler the acknowledgement, that Naples is the *queen* of cities. It is not walled around, like other large cities of the Continent, but is defended by several chateaux, the most remarkable of which is the Chateau St. Elme, the Chateu Neuf, and the Chateau de l'Oeuf. The former is built in a regular hexagonal form, overlooking the entire city and gulf, including Vesuvius, and its foundations are laid on solid rock. Le Chateau Neuf is said to have been built from the design of the old Bastile of Paris; it stands on the shore of the sea and behind the King's Palace. The Chateau the l'Oeuf is so called from its shape, which is like an egg. This stands on the top of a rock, which forms an island, and is connected with the city by a canal one hundred and twenty feet long. This chateau divides the gulf into two parts and overlooks the whole. It is now used for prisoners of State. Many of the princes and noble inhabitants are now prisoners for political offences, among whom are several *ladies*.

Ferdinand II., the present King, is very unpopular. The army is recruited from the best young men, and often great-

8*

ly against their will. We were told of one family, who were entirely dependent on the two sons, who were at the head of a great manufacturing establishment. Both were indispensable to carry on the business. One of the sons was drafted for the army. He could not leave without breaking up the establishment, and was obliged to buy himself off by the payment of $1,000.

The Palais de la Residence Royal is one of the finest in Naples, and the Hotel Royal des Pauvres, a house of refuge for the poor, is magnificent. It encloses four courts, and a church in the centre. Here they admit orphans, who are apprenticed to different trades at a suitable age, or are initiated into the various arts and sciences for which they develop a taste.

There are about three hundred churches in Naples, many of which contain fine paintings, statues, &c., but they are not equal to those in Rome. On the Sabbath, we attended the English service in the chapel of the English Ambassador. It is neatly fitted up for worship, but is difficult to find, and such a constant firing of cannon was kept up exactly under the windows, that it was impossible to hear anything.

There was nothing in the external appearance of the inhabitants to remind us of the Sabbath. The streets were filled with a bustling throng of soldiers, priests, lazzaroni and others, who were crowding their way hither and thither, and the stores displayed, if anything, a greater and richer variety than usual.

The Bourbon Museum, which we visited too late on Monday to gain access, is said to contain more rare, precious and curious objects of antiquity and art than the Vatican. The various rooms are filled with the exhumed treasures of Herculaneum, Pompeii and Stabia. One room alone contains sixteen thousand articles of various kinds, kitchen utensils, musical instruments, keys, &c.

Naples contains colleges, academies, and benevolent institutions of various kinds, also a Conservatoire de Musique, which is in high repute, and which has produced many celebrated compositors of music, among whom are Zingarelli and Bellini. Zingarelli was the composer of the sublime Miserere, which is chanted in the Holy Week at St. Peters with such thrilling effect, as we are told.

Silks, velvets, laces, stockings, gloves, maccaroni, &c., are important articles of commerce. Both ladies' and gentlemen's gloves we found for two carlins or sixteen cents a pair. A carriage and driver could be hired for an hour for one carlin. A person can live here cheaper, probably, than in any other city of Europe. The currency was a source of great annoyance to us. We had just become familiar with the bajocchi and scudi of Rome; and at Naples we found tornesi, grana, carlini, and Neapolitan scudi, which differs somewhat from the Roman scudi.

Many delightful excursions can be made from Naples to localities famed by the fables of the ancients and the pens of historians, among which are Posylippo, the tomb of Virgil, Grotto du Chien, Pozzuoli, Lake Avernus, Grotto of the Sybil, Baiae, Cape Mysene, &c. Posylippo is a celebrated mountain, through which a grotto is cut at its base, 960 feet long, 20 feet wide, and 50 feet high. The grotto is lighted day and night. It is not now known by whom this gigantic work was executed, nor at what period, but it was probably done to shorten the route from Naples to Pozzuoli, and to avoid the ascent of the mountain. Beyond this grotto is Virgil's tomb. The road to Pozzuoli is beautiful, but the country about, including Baiae, once renowned as the seat of splendor and luxury, presents to the eye a desolate waste. Here was once the seat of superstition and the centre of earthly enjoyment. Here Caligula lived in splendor, power, luxury and crime. Everything that wealth and art, and science and pleasure could gather into one place, was concentrated in this beautiful region—this Campagna Felice of the Romans. I could *imagine* how beautiful it was. The scenery by land and at sea was exquisite. The climate delightful. It was a land of oil, and wine and honey. With a soil incomparably rich, everything that nature could crave might grow almost spontaneously. The waters were full of fish. Country and city, with their verdant beauties and architectural gems, land and water, mountain and valley, all conspired to form a bewitching landscape. Horace thought there was no place on earth like Baiae; and Virgil, and Cicero, and Seneca, and hosts of other renowned characters, once gazed on this very spot with emotions of delight. But these cities, and their pomp and array, and swarming, bustling, gay, pleasure-loving crowds, have long since passed away. There was a traveler who stopped at Pozzuoli more than eighteen hundred years ago. What were his emotions as he looked abroad over this garden of the world! He was a poor, despised, persecuted man—but a man whose memory lives to bless the world, while the memory of Caligula rots. I mean the Apostle Paul, when having tarried three months at Malta, he came up a prisoner to Rome, in chains, and we are told, "the ship fetched a compass and came to Rhegium, and the next day they reached Puteoli"—now called Pozzuoli. Paul and Caligula, what a contrast then! what a contrast forever!

The dog-grotto is about nine feet long, four wide and ten deep. A light vapor constantly issues from it, which is fatal to animal life. It is a singular fact, that this vapor rises only to the height of a few inches from the ground. A dog, placed in the vicinity of this deadly air, after inhaling it a few seconds, is thrown into convulsions, and unless speedily removed into a purer atmosphere, dies. Man, from his stature, may stand there with impunity, whereas, if he should lie down upon the ground and inhale the air, he would be similarly effected. Lake Avernus is of an oval shape, and a mile and a half in circumference. It is surrounded by mountains, which, it is said, were formerly covered with dense forests, whose dark, thick shadows eternally brooded over the waters, from which such a fatal miasma arose as to render its vicinity dangerous. It is not so now, however. The banks of the lake are charming, it is full of excellent fish, and the air is healthy. The depth is 400 feet. The entrance to the famous grotto of the Sybil is opposite this lake, and further on is the famous river Styx, and for aught I know, the grim old ferryman, Charon, was waiting for some passengers—we did not go in to see.

Without seeing half the curiosities worthy of notice in Naples, we were obliged to leave, and taking the steamboat Lombardy at 5 o'clock, P. M., we reached Civita Vecchia, 185 miles, early in the morning. There was only one lady beside myself in the lady's cabin, and we were startled in the night by a noise near us, and looking out of our berths, we found a man rummaging the pockets of our dresses, which were hung up, probably in the expectation of finding money. It seems as if the Italians could not live without begging or stealing. As soon as it was light in the morning, we were told that the health officers were on board and would soon be in the cabin to see what condition we were in. My companion jumped up and hastily dressed herself, but I contented myself with putting my head out from the curtains, and telling the officer that I *was alive.* We were soon, however, summoned up on deck, to be counted and numbered, and go through a comical ceremony, which lasted an hour. Every one was compelled to come forward as his name was called and be numbered, and then march in single file the length of the vessel like a row of State's prisoners, and be counted like a flock of sheep. When it was found that we all answered to our names and number, that nobody was sick, dead or missing, we were told we might go on shore. Had any one of our passengers been ill, we should probably have been obliged to remain in quarantine several days.

Before we could land, we found the Captain was obliged to go to the police office and exhibit his papers and our passports, and report the health of the vessel, &c.—all of which occupied him till nearly noon. Then we found we must pay two pauls each to be rowed from the boat to the land, and pay the police for *liberty* to land, so we concluded, as we had once gone through a series of like ceremonies in this same renowned city, we would remain on board till 5 o'-clock, when the vessel would leave for Leghorn.

Civita Vecchia contains six or seven thousand inhabitants, and is a very important place, as the vessels from Malta, Naples, Leghorn, Genoa and Marseilles are constantly arriving. It is said there are no less than thirty arrivals each month from these ports. Civita Vecchia stands where the Roman settlement of Centumcellae formerly stood. The prisons of Civita Vecchia will contain 1200 prisoners, and are the largest in the Papal States. The brigand, Gasperonia, has been confined here, and twenty of his banditi, for more than eighteen years. He was the celebrated leader of the band who committed so many depredations on travelers passing the Pontine Marshes, through Fondi and St. Agatha. He admits that he has murdered thirty persons, though rumor accuses him of having killed hundreds. He holds a levee between 11 and 12 o'clock, and can be seen by permission of the Consul, by any one who has the curiosity to call on the monster. It is said people not only visit him, but make him *presents* of money. The Pope, some years since, allowed him two pauls a day for his tobacco and brandy. Whether the present Pope regards him with so much interest and attention, I am not able to say. I presume he regards himself as quite a favored and distinguished character. He does not hesitate to say that "the greatest prize he ever took was $4,000." After the death of *Cucumello*, the old leader of the banditti from Rome to Naples, he was chosen successor, and for several years was the terror of all travelers through that region.

And here I must touch a little upon the morality of Italy. Robbery, beggary, murder, stealing, lying and imposition of all kinds is practiced in this country with an effrontery and deliberation, and frequency, that makes you feel every moment you need more than one pair of eyes to make your way. In Rome, one of our company had two silk pocket handkerchiefs stolen in two successive days from his pocket while in market buying grapes. In Naples, after engaging a carriage for two carlins an hour, on paying the driver, he declared that a two carlin piece was only one carlin, and therefore, in consequence of not understanding the currency, he was paid, and took without compunction, *four* carlins. In Verona, one of our company on retiring, requested an extra blanket on his bed. Instead of which, the servant understood that he wished his sheets changed, and walked off with the gentleman's *watch*, which had been placed under his pillow. Our friend soon gave the alarm, as well as he was able in broken language, and the servant was made to give up his prize. In buying maps of Rome, the bookseller charged twelve francs each, but finally took six francs. We found that no one who understood the custom of the country, pretended to give the price asked for a thing, and merchants almost invariably ask more for an article than they expect to receive.

I mention these cases as samples of business transactions. In regard to beggary, as Italy is celebrated for its charitable institutions, you are astonished at the crowds of mendicants that assail you every where. From the priesthood and officers employed by government, down to the wretched and squalid outcasts of society, you find yourself constantly surrounded with supplicants for charity. Some of the priests and monks are *masked*, and will shake a box of coins in your ear, and call to you from the corner of the street to give to something or other.

With a population of 175,000, Rome expends an immense sum in charity. Relief is distributed to the poor at their own houses, by a committee, to the amount of $172,000 annually. The Pope gives $40,000 a year in charity. The annual revenues of their charitable institutions, which are, most of them, magnificently endowed, is said to be not less than $840,000, and all this is independent of the large sums distributed by the different orders and fraternities; and yet Rome is *full* of beggars—wherever you go, they are at your heels.

And then—"tell it not in Gath, publish it not in the streets of Askelon"—the number of *Foundling* institutions in Italy is positively frightful. In Rome even, the city of the Pope, the representative of God himself, with the immaculate example of infallibility ever before the community, and six thousand specimens of spotless humanity embodied in priests, monks and nuns, *three thousand* children "without fathers, without mothers, without descent," are laid at the doors of foundling institutions in Rome every year! In *one* hospital, eight hundred foundlings are received annually. Nobody knows or wonders where these children come from; they come up of a night, probably, like toadstools. It is a blessed fact, however, that most of the children die in infancy, and that He, who has said: "When thy father and thy mother forsake thee, then the Lord will take thee up," remembers his promise, especially in regard to these deserted infants, and that, by estimation, it is supposed that seventy two per cent. of them are withdrawn from this life in infancy annually, to be trained in God's nursery for heavenly service. There most be some radical defect in a religious community, where such startling facts are developed. In a land of *Bibles*, such inhumanity in the gross was never heard of.

LETTER NO. XXIII.

TURIN, October, 1850.

Leaving Civita Vecchia at 5 P. M., we reached Leghorn the next morning, and lay by at that port till 5 P. M., and then left for Genoa, where we arrived Friday morning early. The trip from Naples to Genoa could be accomplished in two days and nights, instead of three days and a half, were it not for the delays at Civita Vecchia and Leghorn to take in freight and passengers. The appearance of Genoa from the sea, as you enter the harbor from Leghorn, is very imposing and beautiful. The city lies before you on the slope of a mountain, in the form of a crescent. The lofty hills in the back-ground are covered with low oaks and olives, and interspersed with palaces, and villas and gardens blooming in luxuriance and gaiety. It would seem to be a city of *kings*, from the number of its palaces. A few of the streets are quite handsome; Balbi, Nuova and Nuovissima are among the finest. In the Strada Nuova are six palaces on the north side, and seven on the south, and the glimpses you get, as you pass, of the courts and statues, and columns and arches, and orange trees and rare flowers, give you an idea of their splendor and magnificence within. The majority of the streets, however, are excessively narrow, while the houses are handsome, and perhaps five or six stories high, and look as if they nearly met at the top. It is impossible for a carriage to pass through many of these streets, and as the houses rise in massive blocks up the hills, you wonder how the people can ever climb up those steep, dark, narrow lanes to their homes, and much more how they supply themselves with furniture and provision, and wood, &c. So we enquired, and found their burdens were carried chiefly on the shoulders of men, and on the backs of mules and donkeys. My heart ached for poor, abused humanity, as I saw *hogsheads* of *molasses* born up the landing from the boats on the shoulders of six men. We were told, that the merchants who live up these narrow streets, take mules at the bottom of the street, while a servant follows on foot, holding on to the mule's tail to help him up, and when the gentleman alights at his own door, the servant rides back again on the mule. One cannot fail to remark in all the Italian cities and harbors the immense labor required to conduct their ordinary business, and the utter want of all the labor-saving machines and contrivances, which are so prevalent every where in America. It seems as if everything is done in the hardest possible manner, and every body goes the most round-about way to work. And, considering what a lazy people the Italians are, we could not but laugh oftentimes, at their awkward and ridiculous, and fatiguing efforts to accomplish what the ingenuity of an Englishman or an American would do with the utmost ease to himself. Genoa is strongly fortified. An inner and an outer wall surround the city; the inner one contains the city proper, and the outer one extends over the sides of the hills and mountains, a length of eighteen miles.

There are said to be 144,000 inhabitants here, besides the garrison. Silks, damasks, velvets and artificial flowers, with embroideries of cambrics and muslin, afford employment to a great number of the people. And the gold and silver fillagre work, peculiar to this city, gives the shops the most brilliant appearance. The fig tree wood is made here into dressing boxes, caskets, &c., of great beauty. The women do not wear bonnets generally, but have a strip of Swiss muslin two yards in length, thrown over their heads, not concealing their faces, but held together under the chin by one hand, while the other is folded across the breast. It is one of the most becoming fashions imaginable. Even the common people and market women surprise you by the clean, fresh look of their white muslin veils, as they pass by. We stopped at the Hotel Feder, formerly the Palace of the Admiralty, a very excellent hotel, from which we had a delightful view of the bay and sea, and of a new portico along the quay of the port, which extends some distance. Upon the terrace is a beautiful promenade with a marble floor, where, in a pleasant moonlight evening, you have a magnificent prospect of the land and sea. Galley slaves are employed on the public works in various parts of the city. They are dressed in red; those who have been guilty of *murder* wear caps of red and black, while the caps of *thieves* are red and yellow. There are many very beautiful paintings in Genoa, both in the palaces and the churches. The works of Guido, Rubens, Vandycke, Tinttoreto, Paul Veronese, Garafolo, Titian, Raphael, &c., afford a feast to the lover of painting. The Palazzo Rosso contains the best private collection. A hundred thousand dollars, we were told, had been expended in ornamenting *one* hall in one of the palaces. The paved marble floors, frescoed ceilings and gilded walls exhibit the greatest splendor. We visited only two churches. The Cathedral, a Gothic edifice, striped with black and white marble, is quite odd and curious, but like many other splendid works of Italy, not half finished. Under one of its altars, it is said, repose the ashes of John the Baptist! L'Annunziata is a very rich and gorgeous church, so covered with gilding inside, that it seems, almost as if built with sunbeams. Genoa is peculiarly interesting to the American traveler as the birthplace of Christopher Columbus. We regretted that we could not remain two or three weeks in Genoa; we could have passed the time delightfully. We left for Turin by way of Novi, Alessandria and Marengo, in the diligence. The scenery was delightful as we climbed the ridge of the Appenines, which skirts Genoa. Vineyards covered the hill sides, and groves of chesnuts of enormous size met our eye every where.

We found Novi a pleasant town of 10,000 inhabitants; it was near here the brave Gen. Joubert lost his life in 1799. We wandered about the place two or three hours, and then took the railroad to Turin. We were all on tip-toe to see the famous battle-field of Marengo. We passed straight through it, and were so fortunate as to find a gentleman in the cars who was familiar with the whole ground, and who, with much enthusiasm, pointed out the locations and explained the manœuvres of the two armies, and the three places where the Austrian force crossed the river Bormida into the plain of Marengo, and advanced upon Napoleon in three separate columns. The Austrian numbered forty thousands; Napoleon had but twenty thousand at command, (for Dessaix and the reserve, were absent) only two thousand five hundred of whom were cavalry.

Our companion showed us where Victor stood, and Lannes and St. Cyr were posted with their divisions, behind which were the Consular Guard and Napoleon himself. He showed us where Dessaix with the reserve, appeared in the outskirts of the field, whose timely presence encouraged Napoleon's army and won the day. The brave Dessaix was the first that fell. We saw where the routed Austrians crossed the Bormida, and where both horses and riders, by hundreds, were drowned, and the river, it is said, flowed with blood. Alessandria, in the neighborhood of Marengo, is a large and flourishing city; and Asti, the next city of note, contains 24,000 inhabitants. Near this last place, are "two wells which, before the earthquake of Lisbon, contained pure water; after this they became sulphuretted and unfit for use till the earthquake in Pignerol, in 1807, when the waters became sweet again." Turin is a magnificent city, containing, it is said, 117,000 inhabitants, exclusive of the soldiery, of which there is a large number. There are few monuments here, as in most cities of Italy, of great antiquity, as it has been repeatedly destroyed and rebuilt. The streets are straight and wide, with sidewalks, and intersect each other at right angles; the houses are handsome and regular, and built of yellow brick, which imparts to the city a very lively appearance; they are very high, some of them of many stories; the doors and windows ornamented, and a cornice around the top. I wondered where *the poor* lived, for surely they could not inhabit such fine dwellings, and was told it was *against the law* to put up an indifferent looking house in Turin. They are generally built much alike —all handsome—and the poor look, *outwardly*, comfortable as the rich. I was delighted with the appearance of the inhabitants. They seemed to be, and we were told they were an industrious, honest, kind-hearted people. We saw few beggars and little apparent poverty. Turin is most beautifully located in the valleys of the Dora and the Po, just above their confluence; the streets have stone slabs laid for carriage-wheels to run upon, in some of them two lines, and it is delightful to run over them, there is so little and so easy a motion. This peculiarity in the streets we found in Milan and some others of the Italian cities.

The women, by hundreds in companies, are to be seen, in a pleasant day, washing by the river side or from the sides of low vessels near the banks. Here, as in Rome and many other places, *family* washings do not enter into the code of domestic economy, but the washings are done cheaper and better, it is said, by women trained in the practice of washing in the rivers. I amused myself half an hour one day, as I sat down on the stone abutment of the bridge, in gazing at these merry washer women. They sang and swashed about the clothes in the river and then piled them up on the stones, and laughed and told stories and enjoyed themselves in fine style, while it seems as if the garments, without hot water, and for aught I know, without soap, must come from their hands anything but clean. In Rome, however, our clothes were washed in this way, and were well done. It costs there two bajocchi, or two cents, to wash and iron a shirt.

We were very desirous to see Vittorie Emanuele, the new King of Sardinia, or as he *prefers* to be styled, the king of *Piedmont*, (not relishing the idea that the little island of Sardinia should give the name to his kingdom.) We visited his palace, and were more delighted, on the whole, with his royal residence than any other we have seen. The rooms we visited, while they contain many of the splendid productions of ancient art, and display many peculiarities of antique style, have so many modern adornments and comforts, as to render them charming. Nothing can exceed the beauty of the mosaic floors. The royal family were not at home, and we were taken into some of the private apartments, which were fitted up in a style of luxury and ease truly magnificent; yet they were not carpeted. I could have spent hours delightfully in wandering through the suite of rooms occupied by the ex-Queen, mother of the present King, Maria Teresa of Tuscany, Archduchess of Austria, and examining all the curious and fanciful things she had gathered together; everything to please the eye and the taste. Her bedquilt and curtains are of the most exquisite crimson silk damask, lined with white silk, and her writing table, and her work room, adjoining, contained almost a museum of curiosities and conveniences. For the first time in my life, I wished I was a queen, and had such useful, convenient and beautiful things. She has a little boudoir, fitted up with a sofa on each side, in which, at the sound of the dinner bell, the family seat themselves, and by means of pulleys, they go down, down, down into the dining room, dumb-waiter fashion, and find themselves at dinner before they know it. This plan was contrived to save their royal personages the trouble of going up and down stairs. One of her rooms was covered with mirrors overhead, so arranged that you are compelled to behold hundreds of fac-similes of your own precious self, and it has such a ludicrous effect to see yourself suddenly multiplied into a *vast assembly*, that you cannot avoid a fit of laughter. Indeed, I was so annoyed by the hundreds of my own eyes gazing at me, and the presence of hundreds of myself about me, that I was glad to escape *from* myself and be *alone.* Rooms of paintings, statues and ancient curiosities belong to her suite of apartments.

In one chamber, every thing remains as Carlo Alberto, the late king, left it. The bed on which he died away from home, has lately been brought and placed here. In this room, the ex-Queen spends many hours. He died, it is said, of a broken heart.

Charles Albert was, perhaps, the leading spirit in the attempt made soon after the French revolution, to combine all

Italy—the Kingdom of Naples, Roman States, Tuscany, Lombardy and Piedmont, in one great Italian nation, leaving at the same time, each existing kingdom an independent sovereignty, like the separate States in our own glorious confederacy. Lombardy had rebelled against Austria, Tuscany and Rome had participated in the struggle, and the King of Naples had yielded to the popular cry and sent 40,000 men to their aid. They had marched as far as Alessandria, within a few miles of Turin, when, as is generally supposed, under the influence of Austria and Russian gold, and a groundless fear that Charles Albert sought to acquire the ascendancy over all Italy, and put the crown on his own head, they withdrew all their forces suddenly, and left Charles Albert and Lombardy, to encounter the whole Austrian army alone. He could not endure the thought of having his people crushed and subjugated as Lombardy had been, and prematurely brought on a decisive battle, which he lost, and in which he fought like a madman, desiring to die on the field. His friends bore him forcibly from certain death, and he abdicated in favor of his son, the present king, in sight of the victorious enemy, and fled from his kingdom and died broken hearted.

LETTER NO. XXIV.

LYONS, October, 1850.

Adjoining the State apartment in the Palace of the King of Piedmont, at Turin, is the Armeria Royal, containing a curious collection of the armory of the middle ages. It is far more extensive and interesting than the Hall of Knights at the White Tower, London. Here we saw the Duke Emanuele Filiberte in his full suite of armor, just as he appeared at the battle of St. Quentin, and the cuirass of Prince Eugene, worn at the battle of Turin, and that worn by king Carlo Emanuele III., at the battle of Guastalla, 1734. We saw, among other curiosities, three small triangular bladed stilettos, such as Italian ladies wear, or *did* wear in days of yore, to rid themselves of their husbands, &c. The Royal Gallery of Pictures and the Royal Academy, contain many treasures of art. Turin at the present time, is rather under the Pope's displeasure, and it would not be strange if he should shortly thunder from the Vatican a bull of excommunication.

A law was some time since promulgated, that the *priesthood* should be subject to the same civil laws, and tried in the civil courts for an offence like other subjects. Formerly they were tried, and punished or acquitted by an ecclesiastical court alone. Pietro di Santa Rosa, Prime Minister, was supposed to be the instigator of this offensive provision in the constitution. He died on the 5th of August last, and was refused extreme unction by his priest, unless he denounced the law and recalled his approbation of it. But he positively and perseveringly refused, and died unshrived. Santa Rosa was an amiable and extremely popular man, and moreover, a good and firm Catholic, and this refusal of his confessor to grant him the usual rite of the church in his last extremity, so exasperated both King and the people, that what might have been a doubtful experiment before, will now become an unalterable law. *

We heard in Genoa that Vittorio Emanuele was a mere boy; that he cared little for his people, and spent his time mostly in hunting and pleasure. In Turin, however, we heard another statement altogether. He is said to have received the crown from his father very reluctantly; he is unambitious of power, and having been trained in the army, feels that his education entirely unfits him for the throne and for a court life. He is greatly beloved by the people generally, and idolized by the army. He is thirty-one years of age. The queen is an uncommonly lovely and interesting lady, and they have five children. He has selected the very best men in his kingdom to compose his Cabinet, and seems anxious for the best good of the people. We met a very beautiful and interesting lady in Turin, from New Jersey, America. She was consumptive, and had been recommended to try the balmy air of Italy. She had been at Marseilles and other places in the South of France and Italy, and had now located herself for the winter in Turin. But change of climate had not benefited her; and the fatigues and discomforts and annoyances of traveling, and the want of many of those accustomed, nameless comforts, found only at home, and in one's native land, led her to declaim most earnestly and feelingly, against the folly and cruelty of sending away invalids to foreign climes for their health. "Do undeceive people," she said, "about this mat-

* The Pope has since, actually excommunicated the King of Piedmont and his whole Government from the Roman Church.

ter, when you return. Tell them it is altogether a mistaken notion to send their friends to Italy for its balmy air and its sunny skies. The changes here are as sudden and inimical to the consumptive patient, as in America; the contrary opinion is all moonshine." We learned, when it was too late for our plans, that a ride of twenty-five miles only would have enabled us to have spent a Sabbath with the *Waldenses*, in their own valley. We, however, consoled ourselves for the disappointment, by attending the *church* of the Waldenses, lately established in Turin. There are several thousands of these far-famed people living in this city. At the present time, there are also many refugees here, from Austria, Lombardy, Tuscany and Rome; the number is estimated at 8,000 families, or 40,000 souls.

The sidewalks of the principal streets are very wide and many of them arched and roofed over, as at Berne, in Switzerland. All kinds of goods are displayed for sale on the sidewalks, and the people, as in other cities of Italy, seem to live and labor out doors. The hotels are excellent and well managed. We found one peculiarity at the table, which at first was quite a puzzle. By the side of every plate lay six or eight sticks, half a yard long, of the size of one's little finger and of a light brown color. "What are we to do with these things," thought I, as I quietly eyed the little wands, and ventured at length to turn them over and up to see what they were. But as I could not divine their quality or their use, I kept my eye on my neighbors to see what *they* did with them. What was my surprise to find they were made to *eat*, and to see a gentleman take one, and begining at one end, soon craunch it down like a piece of celery. As he seemed to be neither strangled or choked in the performance, I ventured upon the same experiment, and soon found it was the famous Piedmontees *bread*, called "Pane grissino," a kind of unbolted bread, which is very excellent and which I soon learned to like so well, that I was sorry to leave it. It is peculiar to Turin. After spending a few days in this pleasant city, we engaged our seats in one of the diligences of Bonafous & Brothers, the best, it is said, in Italy, by way of Mt. Cenis, Chamberry and Lyons to Paris. These diligences are so aristocratic in their customs, that they never pass around to pick up their passengers like our stages, but you most present yourself, bag and baggage, with your ticket paid for and your seat numbered, at the Posthouse to claim your place; nor must you seat yourself till your name and number is called.

We were to leave at 5 o'clock, P. M., and ride all night. Arriving early, we had a fine opportunity to observe the process of stowing away the baggage, which was a sight well worth seeing. Throughout Europe a carefulness and a faithfulness and an attention to all the minor matters of traveling is shown in all the great thoroughfares, which an American, I am sorry to say, does not always see at home. How often do we see a trunk pitched from a stage, regardless which end is up, or whether it splits open, even, in the fall! Here everything is handled with care. Our baggage was all rolled up in straw, every article separate, and so enveloped that it could not chafe, and so carefully packed that it could not get loose. Had we been starting for the North Pole, it need not have been more securely stowed away.

The country about Turin is very beautiful. We rode through an avenue of elms, six miles long, to Rivoli, a town of five thousand inhabitants. Our road to Susa, at the foot of Mt. Cenis, lay through the valley of the Doire and the great plain of Lombardy, sometimes called the Golden Valley, walled in by the Alps, dotted here and there with villages, showing up in the distance an occasional villa, or church or old palace, to render enchantment to the scene. The great beauty of the cattle in this region, and in fact, through all

Italy, cannot fail to arrest the traveler's attention. The cows and oxen are mostly of a cream color or rich auburn, and are noble looking creatures. At our left stood the monastery of San Michele on the Monte Pirichiano, one of the most remarkable monuments of Piedmont. Formerly, three hundred monks lived here, but it is now deserted and a ruin. One of the arches, it is said, still contains the dried corpses of many of these monks. Till within a short time, two rows of these mummies adorned the staircase to the gallery, and you must pass between these skeleton sentinels to go in. Nobody knows why they were thus placed, but they were venerated by the peasants, who occasionally dressed them up, placing fresh bouquets in their bony fingers.

Not far from this is the Monte de Roccia Melone, 11,000 feet high. On its summit is perched a chapel, dedicated to Notre Dame des Neiges, to which the inhabitants of Susa formerly made a pilgrimage every August. It is almost inaccessible, and the pathway was so dangerous, and the rarity of the air so great, and so many accidents happened, that the Virgin has now come down out of the clouds and holds her levee at Susa. The Rector of Mt. Cenis told a traveler that "many persons who fell from the awful precipices over the crags to the rocks below, were so dashed to atoms that the largest piece of their bodies to be found was the *ear.*"

Susa, although containing only 3,000 inhabitants, is a place of much interest, and is the seat of an Archbishop. It contains the celebrated arch of Augustus, built by Cottius eight years before Christ, the oldest monument of antiquity in this part of Italy; and also the Fort of La Brunette, once an important fortress and the key of the valley. In the days of its greatest power, it is said, if a traveler stopped to *look* at it deliberately, he was told 'to pass on,' so jealously was it guarded. From a gentle mist, when we left Turin, it began to rain, and finally to sleet before we commenced the ascent of the mountains, and we were quite startled at seeing a cart coming down with two inches of *snow* on the top. The idea of a snow storm on Mt. Cenis was anything but agreeable, and as we prepared to ascend the mountains, and eight mules were brought to be added to the six horses with which we left Turin, we began to realize the difficulty and danger of the ascent. It was now, moreover, night, and the snow flakes began to fall thick and fast. The moon was at the full, so that it was not dark; and as we had secured the coupee, which is in front, with glass windows before us and at the sides, we could dimly see enough to terrify the imagination as we wound about the edges of awful cliffs, and had an indistinct view of the deep dark gorges below.

Our road was thirty feet wide, smooth and gently ascending, and a thousand times did I bless the memory of Napoleon Bonaparte, for his indomitable genius, enterprise and perseverance in forcing such a path through this wild and rugged country. But the frowning, bristling crags above, and the yawning chasms below, and the trackless waste before us, and the increasing, drifting snow, waked up fearful memories of ancient tales. Avalanches, snow drifts, buried travelers, compassionate monks and sagacious dogs, all passed in sad review before my excited fancy, and I longed for *day break* as some alleviation of our difficulties. It was some comfort to know that twenty-five houses of refuge were stationed up and down the mountain, from Susa on one side to Lanslebourg on the other. Persons are stationed here to keep the road in repair, and to afford assistance to travelers; and in the most dangerous places, especially near the summit, these houses are not many rods apart. The snow increased; we had not yet reached the summit, and daylight only revealed the growing drifts and the almost utter impossibility of distinguishing the road in some places at a distance, except by the poles twelve feet high, stationed every few rods on the edge of the precipices, as a guard and a guide to the bewildered traveler. I could comprehend the terror that must seize hold of the solitary wanderer, benumbed and benighted, and overtaken with one of the wild and raging *tourmentes*, or tempests, so common to this region, and felt if I could once safely emerge into the beauty and warmth of sunlight, I would never desire any further experience of an Alpine storm. Near Refuge No. 22, avalanches often fall, but the dangerous spot is passed in three or four minutes, and I breathed more freely after it was over. No. 20 is called La Ramasse; and here sledges are constantly kept in readiness in the winter, with guides for any travelers who may prefer to take a *slide* down to Lanslebourg in ten *minutes*, instead of going by the road, which takes an *hour and a half.* I could not but laugh at the idea of such a stupendous slide being preferred by some travelers to the longer route: the perpendicular descent is 2000 feet. We were in sight of the Grand Croix, the culminating point, which is 6,780 feet above the level of the sea. The cantonniers perform this sledge-trip with the utmost dexterity and safety, they think. We were told that an Englishman spent eight days here some years since, for the sole purpose of risking his neck by sliding down three times a day! What would our school boys think of such a slide as that!

At length we reached the plain and lake of Cenis on the top of the mountain, and a beautiful place, I doubt not, it is during the brief stay of summer among them, which lasts but a few weeks. The lake itself is frozen over six months in the year, and the mountain peaks, which wall in this dell of beauty, are covered with snow the whole season. The lake is full of delicious trout, and we found quite a little village, containing a hospice and barracks capable of containing one thousand soldiers, &c. At Grand Croix the descent begins, and we were astonished to see, instead of fourteen horses and mules which had brought us up, that only *two horses* were attached to the diligence to take us down.

As we began to descend the mountain, and the snow storm abated, and the air grew clearer and warmer, and finally the snow melted into rain and the rain into mist, I could fully sympathize with *Noah*, when he looked out of the window of the ark and saw the waters abate, and the tops of the hills peep out, and finally the trees, and valleys, and grass appear, and once more stepped out on terra firma, into sunshine with gladness of heart. Thus did we, in less than two hours, emerge from winter's awful snows and all the accumulation of dangers and horrors that shroud these Alpine passes, into a valley of verdure, and beauty, and life, and warmth, when we found ourselves at the little village of Lanslebourg, inhabited by the rude cantonniers. Such a sudden transition from winter to summer, from danger and terror to safety and delight, produces the most curious effect on the mind imaginable.

LETTER NO. XXV.

PARIS, October, 1850.

Our journey from the foot of Mt. Cenis to Paris was accomplished in three days and nights, passing one night at Lyons. Our road lay through Chamberry, a town which contains about ten thousand inhabitants, and is the capital of Savoy. Before the French revolution there were twenty convents here; now however, there are only seven. We found Lyons and its environs very beautiful; the rivers Saone and Rhone, run through the city. It contains two hundred thousand inhabitants, and is the second city in France. At Lyons we met with a little incident, which, as it shows how travelers are often imposed upon, I will relate. Contrary to our usual custom, we had neglected to select our hotel from those names in our guide book before we stopped, and consequently we found ourselves at a loss to know where to go. A runner who could talk English imperfectly, seeing us undetermined where to put up, recommended a place, but not finding its appearance such as we liked, he promised to take us to the Hotel de Europe. Arriving at a hotel of inferior appearance, he said this was the one, and commenced taking our baggage. Confident that he was deceiving us, we told him so, and then pointed to the sign over the door, on which Hotel d'Orient blazed in large letters. He assured us, however, it was the Hotel de Europe, and to convince us called the landlord. When the landlord appeared, he gave him a wink, and inquired if this was not the Hotel de Europe. The landlord replied promptly, with a smile, that it certainly was; of course we had nothing more to say, and took our rooms. We found out, notwithstanding, that we were deceived by the runner, who wished his fee from the landlord, and by the landlord who would not scruple to use any means to fill his house. It was the Hotel d'Orient. These runners obtain a compensation from the inn-keepers for every traveler they bring, and the landlords themselves stand in fear of the runner's displeasure, lest they give a bad name to their hotels and lose custom in consequence. The only safe way is to turn a deaf ear to all agents and runners, and depend entirely upon the traveler's *Guide Book*, with which every one should be supplied. Our sail up the Rhone from Lyons to Dijon was quite pleasant, not only on account of the number of villages we passed, but as giving an opportunity of a day's travel with many of the French people. The steamers on the Rhone are quite small, but handsomely finished and furnished. They have no regular meals on board, but have a coffee room, where each passenger can call for what he chooses at any hour. There is nothing peculiarly interesting in the scenery of the Rhone; it does not compare in any respect with the Rhine. From Dijon we proceeded to Chalons in the diligence, which was there put on the cars, and we entered Paris by the railroad.

Paris is indeed a beautiful city, yet I must say I do not admire its public gardens and parks as I do those of London. There is a lack of cultivation and neatness and finish about them, which detracts greatly from their beauty. The Tuileries abound with wide and delightful walks, but the trees form too much of a shade and render it too forest-like for my taste. They shut out the sun, and of course very little grass grows beneath the foliage, and a ramble among the trees must be made amid dust and gravel, which is anything but agreeable. In England, the trees and parks are cultivated to a state of perfection, of which I had scarce a conception before. Every tree is perfect in shape, whether little or big, and not a dead limb or an ungraceful branch is to be seen. Thes ward underneath is like green velvet; it looks, as Colman says, "as if it was combed with a fine tooth comb" daily, and the walks are constantly swept. I never saw anything so perfectly beautiful in nature, as some of the lawns and parks in England, which in a future letter, I shall describe. We domiciled ourselves at once at Meurice's Hotel, the far-famed resort of all English and American travelers. This overlooks the garden of the Tuileries on the Rue de Rivoli, one of the finest streets in the city. Our lodging room is nearer the 'upper world' than any apartment it was ever before my privilege to occupy, being a journey of one hundred and twenty-one stairs from the street. These stairs, moreover, are waxed every morning and brushed till they shine like mirrors, and I never felt more deeply impressed with the importance and absolute necessity of 'taking, heed to my steps,' as the biole directs, than in my daily walks up and down at this hotel.

One of our first rambles was, of course, through the Tuileries. Here is to be found an assembled world almost every day, from 3 to 6, P. M. Thousands of chairs are spread about under the trees, and fathers, mothers, children servants, loafers, fashionables, and strangers of all tribes and tongues, are walking to and fro, or are seated in the shade in the most home-like manner imaginable. Ladies with and without bonnets, and in caps, are seated, sewing or knitting, in perfect ease and apparent enjoyment, occasionally raising their eyes to witness their childrens' gambols, and to chatter and laugh about some passing novelty. Children in lawns and laces crawl about in the dirt, utterly regardless of their finery — boys dressed in the height of fashion, lay down their canes and turn somersets in their best hats, or roll their hoops amid the crowd, to the consternation of jabbering fashionables who are promenading—girls are jumping the rope, or like fairies, dancing, or sailing about in the circles, singing; and babies innumerable, beautiful as angels and dressed in the most costly and elegant manner, are paraded about to gratify their mother's and nurses' pride, and to awaken the notice and admiration of all spectators. Never before did I see such an exhibition of domestic life outdoors, or such a display of home-scenery and enjoyment in a public promenade. And this is an every day scene, in pleasant weather. The French, like the Italians, live in the street.

The great charm of the Tuileries is, that it is in the *very heart of the city*, and that you can step, in one moment, from the bustling crowd in the business streets, into this paradise of trees and flowers, of walks and statues, and fountains, which from its boundless extent as you look about, and the entire abandonment of its thousands of visitors to gaiety and pleasure, almost bewilders the stranger. Seventy acres are enclosed in this garden. The Palace of the Tuileries is at the eastern boundary of the garden, and if you stand at one end of the wide avenue that runs from the centre of the Palace, you can look beyond the limits of the garden through the Place de la Concorde and the Champs Elysees, terminating with L'Arc de l'Etoile, erected to commemorate Napoleon's victories, a distance of two miles. It is a magnificent view.

Soon after our arrival here, we went with the multitude, that poured into St. Roch, the richest church in Paris, to witness the ceremonies of All Saints' day. It was with difficulty that we obtained a seat. Every one who was seated paid two sous for his chair. The singing on this occasion was very fine; the greatest opera singer in Paris was there. The next day was All Souls' day, and we hastened with the crowd to Pere la Chaise. It was an unpleasant day, nevertheless, thousands upon thousands visited this cemetery to adorn with fresh wreaths and flowers the tombs of their friends. This famous burial place is on the northeast side of Paris, and contains one hundred acres, entirely walled in. It is unlike any other cemetery I ever visited; no more beautiful, however, in point of location and varied scenery than some in our own country, nor is it kept in as perfect order and arranged in as good taste as some in America. The number and costliness, and variety and beauty of its monuments, however, cannot fail to awaken admiration. Chapels, temples, pyramids, mausoleums, obelisks, and every variety of column, altar and urn elegantly ornamented, each, in their turn, attract attention and interest. One of the most beautiful monuments here is that of Abelard and Eloise, who died in the twelfth century. We visited the tombs of Generals St. Cyr and McDonald, of Marshal Suchet, Abbe Siccaud, Marshal Massena, General Gobert, the Russian Countess Demidoff, the Marchioness de Beauharnais, La Fontaine, La Place, Madame Genlis, and a host of others. From their graves I plucked a leaf or flower, which the frost would soon have nipped, but was told afterwards, if I had been observed by any of the keepers, no friends or amount of money would have saved me from imprisonment, so strict are their rules and so sacredly held is every thing within this enclosure. We paused where the remains of Marshal Ney repose. No monument or inscription marks it, but it is surrounded with a railing and laid out like a garden. The concourse of people that thronged Pere la Chaise on this great day was immense. All bore some offerings of affectionate remembrance, which were deposited in the little sepulchral chapels or laid on the tombs of the departed. Some were covered with a dozen or more wreaths, made of white or yellow flowers, which grow in the south of France, similar to our *life-everlasting*.

These wreaths had inscribed on them, with the same flowers, colored black, " A ma mere," " A ma fille," &c. Candles were lighted and burning in all the temples and chapels, and chairs covered with black velvet, stood in the recesses of many tombs, at which we saw many mourners kneeling. Images of the Virgin and various Saints stood about the graves. There is certainly something very touching in this yearly visit to the sanctuary of the dead. We wandered about till nearly dark, and then returned to our hotel. Blocks of houses in Paris are many of them built in a manner entirely different from those of our own country, and so are the hotels. They are built in the form of a hollow square, with only one entrance from the street, through an arch wide enough for the passage of two carriages abreast. The huge door or gate of this arch is closed at dark, and there is no admittance except by ringing a bell which is answered by the porter. Five families, too, occupy a house five stories high, each family appropriating one story to themselves, parlors, kitchens and chambers, all being in the same range of apartments. We dined with a friend living in one of these blocks. It was dark when we arrived at the great entrance, and we rang for admittance. No sooner had we touched the bell than the massive gate flew open, noiselessly and magically to us, for no living creature could be seen. " Did you open that gate ? " said I to my companion almost terrified at the mysterious manner in which it opened for us to enter. The reply was in the negative ; and when we reached the porter's lodge, we found that, by means of a pulley in his own room, he had opened the gate without troubling himself to move from his chair.

We found about thirty houses arranged around the sides of this hollow square, each five stories high, and occupied by one hundred and fifty families, their rent varying from three to five hundred dollars each. Mr. A. lived in the first tier of apartments, Mr. B. in the second, and so on, each family with its own door plate and bell in the entry of the story to which they belonged. One porter only is employed by all the families in the square. He shows every comer to the family for whom he inquires. There are five reservoirs of water in Paris, but it is not conveyed by pipes to the houses. Families have no hydrants as with us, but are supplied with all the water they use by water-carriers, who go around daily with casks, and leave it in such quantities as families wish, they paying for it as we do for milk. It is estimated that 4,000,000 francs, or somewhere about $800,000 of our money, is yearly paid by the inhabitants of Paris, to the water-carriers. "And how do you manage for water for family washings?" inquired I of one lady. "No family does its own washing," she replied, "our clothes, even our servants', are sent into the country to be washed every week. It is done better and cheaper out of the house." Female servants receive from $4 to $6 per month, besides their *wine* daily, or its equivalent in money. Dressmakers very seldom go out into families; they do their work at their own rooms. A seamstress to do plain sewing can be hired for thirty cents a day, if she finds her own 'nourrice,' as she calls it, and for twenty-five cents if she has her board.

In my next I will give you some account of the Louvre, the Palace of Versailles, of the Sevres Porcelain Factory, &c.

LETTER NO. XXVI.

PARIS, November, 1850.

The Tuileries, as its name implies, was a tile-field five hundred years ago; but on becoming the property of Catherine de Medicis, she built here an edifice in 1564, since which time it has been the residence, at various periods, of Henry IV., Louis XIII., Louis XIV., the Duke of Orleans during the minority of Louis XV., of Napoleon, and finally of Louis Philippe. Its historical associations and recollections render it a place of deep interest to the traveler. Since Louis Philippe's flight in February, 1848, it has been used for various purposes, and during the revolution was so injured and pillaged, that its glory has departed. The Place du Carrousel forms its inner court, and the Palace of the Louvre encloses two sides of it. In this court, Napoleon used to review his troops, and in it stands a splendid triumphal arch erected by Bonaparte in 1806.

The national museum in the Louvre contains the most exquisite productions of taste and skill, innumerable objects of antiquity and art, and such a variety of models of every thing, that is supposed to be " in heaven above, or that is in the earth beneath, or that is in the water under the earth," that days, instead of hours, are necessary to walk through the *miles* of rooms it contains, and to view with any minuteness the treasures amassed within its walls.

It was a rich treat to examine the earliest paintings of the middle ages, and to see the best productions of the French, Flemish, German and Italian schools. The Grand Salon, which is said to be the largest and best lighted room for exhibition in the world, is filled with nearly three thousand pictures of the greatest deceased masters. This salon is one thousand three hundred and twenty-two feet in length and forty-two feet in width, and the pictures are — some of them — of immense size. I was bewildered and enchanted with all I saw. I cannot give you any conception of the vast wilderness of specimens of art that met our eyes. Jewels, vases, cups, porcelain, mirrors, cameos and precious stones, of every variety and of immense value, fill many rooms. A few articles, once belonging to the toilet of Marie de Medicis, are valued at thousands and thousands of pounds. The carvings in ivory by the Chinese are marvelous specimens of skill. It seemed as if we saw all the birds, fishes and animals that had been created since the flood, stuffed and paraded before us; and all the ships, boats and water crafts that the ingenuity of human invention had ever contrived, and models of every machine that could be adapted to human purposes, and all the sphynxes and winged bulls and busts, and statues that Pompeii and Nineveh and other buried cities have ever yielded up to mortal sight.

What a wonderful creature is man, after all! I often exclaimed involuntarily, and of what boundless ingenuity and almost infinite skill is he possessed! One day at the Louvre was all the time we could afford.

We visited Sevres, four miles west of Paris, where the famous porcelain manufactory is located.

I suppose there is no similar establishment equal to it in the world. Indeed I had no idea that any thing so exquisitely beautiful in the shape of porcelain ware, could be wrought by human hands, as some of the specimens which were shown us. We wandered through its museum, containing nearly ten thousand articles collected from China, Japan and India, Piedmont, Tuscany, Prussia, Venice and other cities in Italy, from England, Netherlands, Spain, Portugal, Saxony, Austria, Bavaria, and so on. We saw models of all the ornamental vases, services, statues and figures that have been made here since its establishment, more than a hundred years ago. After looking at all the specimens of pottery, earthen ware, delf-ware, stone-ware, &c., gathered from all quarters of the globe, I asked the attendants to show me something from our own country, the United States. I could not help laughing, though I was vexed, when he showed me an old fashioned *slate inkstand* that would weigh a quarter of a pound, full of pen holes, such as many years ago I had seen in the old-fashioned school houses of New Hampshire. This manufactury is sustained by government. The painters employed are of the highest order, and the number of workmen exceeds one hundred and eighty. This porcelain is formed of kaolin, from Limoges, sand, alkali, saltpetre and clay. The enamel is obtained from feldspath. After passing through the hands of the greatest painters of landscapes, portraits, &c., the colors are *baked* in by a peculiar process. The show rooms are magnificent. I gazed at one splendid picture, not large, in a beautifully gilded frame, till I was half crazy to own it. It was a representation of a young and lovely girl, beautiful in death, and robed for the grave; her attendants stood in such apparent anguish that my *own* heart was melted—and above was traced in delicate letters, "like a flower I have perished and passed away." The design, execution and finish of this picture were exquisite. I know not how long I had stood before this painting, lost in admiration, and considering how I could carry it home, and trying to persuade myself, not only that I wanted it so much I *must have it*, but that I could *afford* it, as I had not yet purchased *one* among the thousands I had coveted. In imagination I transplanted it to my own home, and felt that I should be satisfied if I had this *one gem* of art, if I could never afford another. So I called the attendant, full of hope and strong purpose to call it mine, and inquired its price; I was struck dumb with astonishment when he replied, "The price, Madame, is 30,000 francs," $6,000. I concluded at once *not to buy it*, and giving it one despairing, farewell glance, I turned about to gaze at others with a subdued imagination.

Versailles is about eight miles southwest of Paris. Its Palace and gardens are beautiful; and its collection of historical pictures, statues and busts, portraits of royal families, views of royal residences, marine gallery, &c., deserve several visits to be appreciated.

I was told there were about twelve miles of rooms in the several stories of this palace, and determined to set my eyes on all. I was obliged, for want of time, to go through some of the departments almost on the *full run*. Here you may see and be introduced *by catalogue* to all the Kings and Queens of France, from Pharamond to Charles X. I paid my respects to the court beauties of several centuries. I admired some and laughed at others. I experienced the various emotions of dislike, contempt, scorn, &c., or of complacency, admiration and reverence, as I remembered the history or read the hearts of many heroes of olden time in the faces that looked down upon me. I was wonderfully amused at the costumes of different periods, and the curious appearance of many of the little sprigs of nobility that had stood up so prim on these walls for years. I felt quite at home in this vast and quaint assembly of lords and ladies, and should have been delighted to have spent a week at least, in their society. Still a feeling of melancholy crept over me, as I remembered what they were once, full of life and gaiety, and that they were now unmourned and forgotten by all earth's present millions. The historical paintings introduced us to the warriors of other times, and we were hurried into scenes of battle, naval and military, till we grew warlike from sympathy. The views of royal residences were representations of the past, rather than of the present—of edifices and localities as they once excisted, and of costumes of other centuries. Here we saw Napoleon in his youth and in his prime — in war and in peace — at the head of armies and at the head of his family. We saw him in his boyhood with his mother, at his nuptials, in the days of his greatest power, and with his son. We followed him through all his battles but his *last;* his victories are all perpetuated, but his defeat and downfall are not remembered *here.* The chapel is a magnificent spectacle. It is said that Louis XIV. concentrated all the grandeur and taste of the age in the embellishment of this one place. Besides the interest it possesses as giving a just idea of the style and magnificence of those times, it must be remembered that many remarkable religious ceremonies took place here, among the rest, in front of this altar were celebrated the nuptials of Louis XVI. and Marie Antoinette, in 1769. The paintings, marbles, mosaics, statues, &c., are superb. The organ is called the finest in France. Every Sunday a service is held here. We were shown in the palace the bed-chamber of Louis XIV. Everything is magnificent and in perfect order, and remains just as it was when he was carried from it to his grave. We saw the bed on which he died, with the same coverlet and hangings. Nobody has slept in the room since his death. The clock points to the hour and the moment when his decease occurred. To see the private apartments of Marie Antoinette, a special permit is necessary. In the Grande Salle des Gardes is to be seen David's great picture of Napoleon's Coronation, for which the painter received 100,000 francs. The Hall of 1792, as it is called, introduces you to all the military characters of the revolution of 1789; and in the Hall of 1830, you find all the principal events of that revolution, pictured before you. I cannot even allude to the numerous rooms at which we glanced, but suffice it to say, that I felt, when I left the palace of Versailles, that I had had a magnificent *dream*, in which I had seen the faces of the dead and living of all ages, had been a looker-on in scenes of public gaiety and of private court life, of sorrow, revolution and bloodshed; had moved in the circles of royalty and splendor till I was satisfied; in short, that I had passed through the scenes of a lifetime in a day.

The gardens and park here form a little paradise. Jets d'eau of every conceivable variety are playing. You are surrounded by nymphs and cherubs, gods and heroes, saints and sinners, and may wander amid green houses of surpassing beauty, and feel that while the interior of the palace is the perfection of art, its gardens are the perfection of nature. One of the orange-trees here was produced from the seed in 1421; after flourishing under eighteen reigns and blooming in beauty 430 years, it is still likely to live to a good old age, a sort of Methusâleh among the trees. Its branches are encirled by iron rings to support their weight. The fountains are distinguished by the names of the Grandes Eaux and the Petites Eaux. The former never play except on great occasions, and are always announced in the public prints. Every time they play, it costs about 10,000 francs. One of the fountains in these gardens is said to have cost 1,500,000 francs. Le Grand Trianon, and le Petit Trianon the traveler must be sure to visit. The former is a villa at the extremity of the park, built by Louis XIV. for Madame Maintenon. I shall not describe it, but its decorations are elegant, and the grounds about it are laid out into labyrinths, and with its fountains and statues, to a lover of the beautiful, is a bewitching place. The servants who show these apartments have many interesting stories to tell.

Le Petit Trianon was built by Louis XV. for Madame du Barri. These mansions can be seen only by showing a passport. I will here add the fact, that in the museums of Paris, (the Louvre and Versailles,) there are annually sold 200,000 catalogues at one franc, and 100,000 at two francs; 100,000 francs more are taken for depositing canes, umbrellas and parasols. The net revenue from these sources is upwards of 300,000 francs a year, or about $60,000 of our money. As we returned to the city we had a passing view of St. Cloud, but had not time to visit it, which we much regretted. By the side of the railroad, the country was covered for miles with sheets, shirts and clothing, by acres, on lines, to dry, the washings of the city being performed in this region.

LETTER NO. XXVII.

PARIS, November, 1850.

I find there is no end to sight-seeing in this magnificent city. The markets, bridges, aqueducts, fountains, monuments, parks and gardens, churches, palaces, charitable institutions, cemeteries, &c., are either so beautiful in themselves, so interesting from association, or so useful and commendable in design, that the traveler who has leisure, is amply repaid if he visits them all. I do not, however, intend to exhaust your patience, or that of your readers, by descriptions of a *tithe* even, of the wonders and beauties that filled us with admiration, but will only speak of a few of the many. One of the first places to which we naturally resorted, was *the burial place of Lafayette*, the man whom Americans have delighted to honor, and whose memory is enshrined in a million of temples "not built with hands," imperishable — the temples of grateful American hearts. I had seen him in my young days, when the homage of a nation was laid at his feet, and he was overwhelmed with blessings and praises; flowers were strewed in his path, and smiles illuminated his steps, and I would feign see the last resting place accorded to him by his nation. We drove to Rue de Picpus, No. 15, once a Convent of the order of St. Augustin, and now occupied by the Ladies of the Sacred Heart. Within the walls of this establishment is a small private cemetery, a forlorn, uncultivated enclosure, containing, perhaps, fifty graves, in which repose a few noble French families. And here, in this man-forsaken, uncared for spot, was Lafayette's grave, marked by a plain, simple white marble slab, raised a few inches only from the ground; his wife's remains lie besides him and those of Geo. Washington Lafayette, his son. Not a shrub or flower, or testimony of respect, admiration or regard, or any mark of special culture gave token, that here a *great man* was buried. No memento of the spot could I gather but a vile weed, that I dug out of the ground at the head of the grave. I was ashamed of France, that one of her greatest and purest of nature's noblemen, should sleep so unhonored, so forgotten, so neglected. Had he fallen in America, he would not have been buried in a corner, nor would the traveler be compelled to stoop to the earth to read the inscription on his tombstone.

We turned our steps towards the Pantheon, which is beautifully located and has a most stately appearance. Here stood, formerly, the church of Ste. Genevieve, the patron Sainte of Paris. Ste. Genevieve was buried here in 512.

When the old church became dilapidated, Louis XV. erected the present one in its site, on the greatest scale of magnificence. It is not yet one hundred years old. The cost of it was defrayed by a lottery. Eleven steps, the whole length of the front of the building, give access to the portico, which is supported by six Corinthian columns sixty feet high, above which is a triangular pediment, with a very beautiful composition in relief, designed by David.

It represents France, in a figure fifteen feet in height, distributing honors to several of her great men, among whom are Fenelon, Malesherbes, Mirabeau, Voltaire, Rousseau, Lafayette, David, &c., on her right hand, and on her left are figures representing soldiers, with Napoleon in front. History and Liberty are represented as sitting at the feet of France, inscribing the names of great men, and weaving chaplets to adorn them. The interior is beautifully finished with bas-reliefs, allegorical paintings, statues, &c. The dome was painted by Gros: he received one hundred thousand francs for it, and so delighted was Charles X. on visiting the church, that he created the painter a baron. The series of vaults under the church are well worth a visit. We were amazed at the massive structure of the walls and vaulted roof. Some of the stones are fifty feet long, and are constructed without any kind of cement. Here, in temporary sarcophagi, are the remains of Voltaire and Rousseau. Marshal Lannes, Marat and Mirabeau, were buried here. The two last have been removed, by order of the National Government, and Marat was thrown into a common sewer, a fitting grave for so bad a man. We ascended the dome and were repaid with a splendid view of Paris, the finest, it is said, to be had, as this is the most elevated building in the city.

We visited the Hotel des Invalides. Of this institution France may well be proud. Its design is grand. The edifice covers sixteen acres, and encloses fifteen courts. The Hotel will hold five thousand invalids; it has now only three thousand. The number of officers is said to be one hundred and seventy. At the head of the establishment is Marshal Jerome Bonaparte, ex-King of Westphalia. There are twenty-six Sisters of Charity here, and two hundred and sixty servants, of all kinds. I cannot describe the feelings with which I viewed the inmates. None are admitted, except such as are disabled by wounds, or have served thirty years. Such a variety of deformities I never before saw. Scarcely a perfect man is to be found. Some are without arms, some with one leg, or with a wooden one, or with no legs at all. The maimed, the halt, the lame and the blind, can here condole together. One old soldier, a Pole, named Kolombeski, 120 years of age, has just been admitted. He has been in service seventy-five years, and seen ten forms of government in France. We conversed with several of the old soldiers, who knew Napoleon, and it was exceedingly interesting to see how their faces brightened up at Bonaparte's name. The accommodations for the invalids are excellent. They all dress in uniform, but their only duty is to mount guard in their turn. Every soldier receives pay by the month, to the end of his life, besides his board, clothing and wine. If any soldier does not consume his allowance, he can receive an equivalent in money; if he has no legs, he can have money instead of shoes. Every one seems contented and happy. This is his home for life; he has every comfort and convenience, and it is no small matter to live in such a beautiful place, and look out daily on such beautiful things as are in view. The Library, founded by Napoleon, contains 17,000 volumes, and consists of works of all kinds. In the council chamber and adjoining hall, are many drawings and paintings and portraits of illustrious men.

Fifteen hundred pounds of meat are boiled here every day, besides what is used in soups, and sixty bushels of vegetables are a daily allowance. On one spit, is cooked a nice little roast of *four hundred pounds* at a time.

The church, connected with this institution, possesses much interest, because here is *Napoleon's tomb.* It is not yet finished, and the work is concealed from view, as you enter the church, by an immense painting, nearly covering one end of the church. We used all the most refined and approved arts of Yankeedom to gain a peep at the work in progress, but in vain. Even the potent argument, that we had used in other countries with such success, and that had served as a talisman, so magical as to break down all rules and regulations in other places, namely, that we were *Americans*, was " no go " here. So we turned away in disappointment, and amused ourselves with examining the flags taken in war, which are thickly ranged on all sides of the church. Most of them are African trophies, among which are the parasol of command and other colors taken from Morocco in 1844. In Napoleon's time, it is said, 3,000 flags filled the nave of this church, but on the evening before the allied armies entered Paris, in March 1814, they were burnt by order of Joseph Bonaparte. Thrice was the command given before it was obeyed.

We paid a visit also, to the manufactory of the Gobelin Tapestry. This has been a royal establishment since 1604. We passed through three rooms filled with specimens of the tapestry of the seventeenth and eighteenth centuries, most of which were executed here. I could not have believed any process, short of painting, could render objects so lifelike and beautiful. There are six rooms in which are twenty-five looms at work. None of these carpets are ever sold. They have been made solely and expressly for royalty to walk upon, and who will tread over the future carpets of this factory is a problem in the present state of things in France. The colors and shading of these carpets are perfectly beautiful. The designs are the productions of some of the most exquisite painters of the age. Some of these carpets it takes ten years to weave, and they cost 150,000 francs. Now, Messrs. Editors, you will certainly think I am becoming more moderate in my desires, and making a *feeble* effort at least, to be reconciled and conformed to my condition in life, when I tell you that I did not even *wish* for one of these $30,000 carpets to put in my parlor with that beautiful picture that I *thought so strongly of buying* at Sevres. It is said the largest carpet ever made here, was for the gallery of the Louvre, containing seventy-two pieces thirteen hundred feet long.

There are one hundred and twenty workmen in this establishment, and when disabled by age or infirmity, they receive a pension of six hundred or one thousand francs from Government. There are rooms devoted to the processes of preparing and dyeing the wool; also a school of design; and in the winters, a course of lectures on chemistry, applicable to the art of dyeing, is delivered here.

In our wanderings about this great city, we are often compelled by weariness and want of refreshment, to stop at the restaurants and cafes, to rest and refresh ourselves. It is astonishing to see how numerous these establishments are, and how much they are frequented by ladies and gentlemen. Some of them are most elegantly furnished, and everything that can gratify the palate, can be had at a few moments' warning. For nearly a hundred years, these places of refreshment have been in vogue. It is said that they were commenced in the following way: A certain person prepared a room for refreshments and put on his sign this parody of a passage from the Bible: "Venite ad me omnes qui *stomacho* laboratis, et ego *restaurabo* vos." He was successful in his attempt, and from that day to this, establishments of every kind have been increasing. At many of the best of these houses, a good dinner can be had for two francs. In many, a dinner of soup, two dishes of meat, a dessert and wine can be had for twenty-two sous. A person can live in Paris in a very comfortable and respectable manner, for much less than in the cities of our own country. Apartments, ready furnished, are always to let, and there are persons called "traiteurs," whose business it is to send dinners, ready dressed to order. Unfurnished apartments can also be obtained, and furniture hired from the upholsterers. This, where persons remain three months or more, is said to be the most independent and economical plan. In visiting many of the curiosities of the place, it is desirable to hire a valet de place, who can talk both French and English, who can point out and explain many things, which you would not see or learn alone. Their charge is five or six francs a day. There are some antiquities in Paris, which it is well worth the while to see. It was discovered in the last century, that some portions of Paris were *sinking*, and it was ascertained that 200 acres or more had, in ancient times, been used as quarries, and that many roads, churches, palaces, and buildings of various kinds, which had been erected over those cavities underground, were in danger of being engulphed. Engineers were employed to examine and prop up the buildings so endangered, and the thought occurred that these quarries could be converted into catacombs; accordingly in 1786 they were consecrated for that purpose, and many cemeteries were emptied of their contents, and the bones of the dead of ages gone by, were removed to this place. It is supposed the remains of at least 3,000,000 of human beings are here deposited. They are not *buried*, but piled up fancifully and systematically as in the catacombs of Rome, and there are rooms in which all manner of tasteful devices, formed of skulls and bones of different sizes may be seen. There is said to be some danger in visiting this horrible charnel-house, lest the roof may cave in. It is supposed by many that these excavations run under one-sixth part of the city, as variations of surface and extraordinary fissures in the earth, are constantly taking place.

LETTER NO. XXVIII.

PARIS, November, 1850.

Paris far surpasses London in the architectural beauty and taste of its palaces and public edifices. The external appearance of the Louvre is magnificent. I have seen none superior this side of the Alps. The Palace of the Luxembourg is a beautiful edifice, and contains many fine paintings. We visited the Palais Bourbon, now used by the National Assembly. What hosts of recollections pressed upon us as we found ourselves within its walls! What revolutionary scenes have been enacted here! To what wordy contests have these walls echoed! What tumult, and uproar, and confusion, and clamor have raged here, filling many hearts with the most distressing apprehensions and agonizing fears. The old Chamber of Deputies, no longer used, but shown to visitors, is a beautiful apartment of semicircular form, containing five hundred seats, rising in gradation and encircling the tribune. It is all fitted up in crimson velvet and gold. I took the seat once occupied by Napoleon, and lately by Louis Philippe, and felt sufficiently inspired to have delivered a *speech* most feelingly if not eloquently, on the vanity of all human affairs.

The hall which is now used is temporary and exceedingly plain in all its arrangements. Over the President's chair are these words: Liberte, Egalite, Fraternite. And these words greet you throughout Paris, at every corner and on almost every object.

As to Churches, the Madeleine is the most beautiful I have seen here. St. Roch, St. Eustache and Notre Dame de Loretto, are greatly famed for their music. In the former, on All Saints day, I witnessed the greatest pageantry I have ever seen any where. The music was exquisite. The greatest opera singer in Paris was there, among others, to entertain us. Nothing could exceed the splendor and elegance of the lace and golden robes worn on this occasion, or the solemn nonsense of the ceremonies that passed in review. Candles, and show-bread, and staves were marched around and about, to the great delight of the children in the crowd, at least, and certainly to the wonder and astonishment of all such novices as myself, who could neither understand the use or propriety of such puerile exhibitions, except as giving us an opportunity to examine more minutely the magnificence of the priests' robes, and to allow us a passing glance at the handsome priests themselves, which of course, was very gratifying to all of Eve's daughters who chanced to be there. Nothing interested me more, however, than the multifarious manœuvres of the Marshal of the day. I never *fully* comprehended the idea of "magnifying one's office before." I finally concluded this man must have been expressly created for the position he held. He was one of the most magnificent specimens of mankind I ever met, and was dressed in gorgeous regimentals, which were very becoming; and as he marched about in a manner more stately than can be described, before his look and his crook, every individual, man, woman and child retreated as far into nothingness as their materiality would permit. I could not find out who he was. But it is a blessed thing to see a man, anywhere, who has found out his vocation, and who fills it to perfection.

There are said to be 42,000 Catholic clergymen in France besides 8,000 or 9,000 Theological students intended for the priesthood. The salary of the Archbishop of Paris is forty thousand francs—a salary not to be compared to that of the Archbishop of the established church in England. There are 3,000 Convents in France, and 24,000 nuns. Of the clergy of other persuations, there are 411 Calvinists, and 230 Lutherans, and 8 Jewish Rabbins. The Church of England has 40 ministers in France, and there are 86 ministers of other denominations. There are many Americans in Paris, and a church for American Presbyterians is greatly needed and desired. We attended the Wesleyan Church, where service was held in English. The room was small and poor. There are all sorts of charitable institutions here, and it is said they are admirably conducted. Among them, is an institution in the Rue de Reuilly, called the "Maison des Diaconnesses." They are Protestant Sisters of Charity, whose office is to attend the sick-beds of Protestants in the various hospitals of Paris. Another is called "L'Etablissement des Filatures." This gives work to three thousand and eight hundred poor women, who receive hemp to spin and are paid a certain sum. They have also one hundred and sixty weavers, whose looms and tools are gratuitously supplied.

Another, of unspeakable benefit to poor women with young children, bears the name of "Creches," or Nurseries. The mothers deposit their babies there at half past five in the morning, returning to them occasionally during the day, and taking them home at eight o'clock at night, paying twenty centimes (about four cents,) a day to have them taken care of. Each baby has a basket to itself. They receive about seventy children daily. A matron superintends, with six assistants. The Foundling hospital in Rue d'Enfer, No. 74, receives an immense number of children annually. There is a box, called a "tour," in the wall near the gate, in which the baby to be deserted was formerly dropped, and after ringing a bell, the heartless mother absconded; no one was seen, and no questions were asked. The box was turned round on a pivot and the child was taken in. Of late years, this plan of reception has been abolished, but infanticide has so increased since this clandestine mode of leaving the children has been dispensed with, that public opinion is now strongly in favor of the old plan. I found a discussion and report on this subject, in one of the Parisian papers, from which I had intended to make some extracts, but have mislaid it. The healthy children are alone retained in the hospital, and the number generally is about one hundred and seventy; but the youngest and feeblest ones are placed in the country to nurse, and the number generally out at nurse is *thirteen thousand!** The expenditures of this institution amounted in 1848 to two hundred and seventy-five thousand six hundred and forty-two dollars, or more than a million of francs. There is one room, called the reception room, in which all the new comers are placed. After the visit of the physicians, they are assigned to one of four infirmaries—for medical cases, surgical cases, measles, or ophthalmic cases. Cradles are

* In all my statements of figures, I do not speak at random or from hearsay, but am indebted to printed statistical tables, which I have found in the countries I have visited.

placed around the room, and several nurses are in attendance. One child in four dies.

It is as good as a feast to go "shopping" in Paris, or rather, to go about *looking in the windows*, which is the safest and most economical way, if you have not a long purse. The French certainly bear the palm in ingenuity of invention: they can make *anything* out of *nothing*, and of many *nothings* they can make the most beautiful thing in the world to look at, and yet, when you come to examine it, it is *nothing* after all — the simplest things in the world which any body could have made, and you are almost tempted to think you are a fool, never to have tried the experiment. Some of the shops cover immense squares, with innumerable doors on each side. I popped into several of these doors to enquire for articles, and finding myself always in the same place, till quite annoyed by the ubiquity of the concern, I passed into another street, and after trying several doors with the same result there, I concluded the firm was an omnipresent one, and I would shop in another part of the city. Some of the stores always looked tolerably well filled with customers — ladies standing about elegantly dressed. I laughed heartily one day, after waiting very patiently and politely for a lady next to me at the counter to finish her business, and becoming quite provoked at her quiet, stiff and stately manner, I turned towards her ladyship to *look* her into more dispatch, and found her only a *stuffed* lady, created for the purpose of showing off an elegant mantilla. The clerk all the while was wondering, I suppose, at my leisurely way of making known my wants. Young women are found behind the counters in almost all departments of business. They are even employed as bookkeepers, and receivers of the money in the cafes.

The ladies have one custom here, which for house-keepers and mothers, struck me as admirable. It is in regard to receiving calls. A lady selects the day or evening which, on the whole, is most convenient or agreeable for her to see her friends, and issues her card accordingly: "Mrs. ——— will be happy to see her friends on Thursday," or to this effect. She is therefore, devoted to calls that day, from twelve or one o'clock till ten or eleven in the evening. Every other day in the week she is mistress of her own time, and can make her calculations to suit her own convenience. I was assured by an American lady, who had adopted the custom, that it was far more pleasant to receive calls in this way, than to be in hourly expectation of visitors from sunrise to sunset and after. People extend their calls to a later hour in the evening than with us. A gentleman made us a very fashionable call after eleven o'clock at night. We were so unaccustomed to the manners of polite society, that we had actually been a-bed and asleep a whole hour, when he left his card.

The "Jardin des Plantes," founded by Louis XIII. in 1635, is one of the places in Paris that every stranger must visit. The celebrated naturalist, Buffon, for many years superintended this beautiful garden, and devoted himself to its interests. The Cabinet of Comparative Anatomy here, is said to be the richest in the world, and is greatly indebted to Baron Cuvier for its arrangement, &c. Every thing, rare among plants, shrubs and trees from all quarters of the globe is to be found within this enclosure. More than twelve thousand species of plants are cultivated in the botanical department.

The menagerie contains also every variety of animals, in enclosures, huts or sheds, suitable to their habits. Beautiful shady walks lead to their different habitations. Ten thousand specimens of birds are found in one gallery. There is also a hot-house inhabited by snakes and reptiles, almost too odious to look at, living quite at home in their glass-cages. Several days would scarcely suffice to examine all the rare and curious things in this place.

We paid a visit to the chapel of St. Ferdinand, erected on the spot where the Duke of Orleans expired in 1842. He was thrown from his carriage and died immediately after. There is a beautiful marble group in one of the rooms representing the prince on his death-bed, and an angel supporting him, also in another department, a painting of all the members of the royal family as they are standing about the dying Prince; Louis Philippe, the Queen, and Princess Clementine, the Dukes of Aumale and Montpensier, Marshals Soult and Gerard and the Cure of Mery. It is a very touching as well as truthful scene. The Duke of Orleans was a universal favorite and most deeply mourned. Had he lived, how different probably, would now be the situation and prospects of France!

We leave immediately by the railway for Boulogne and Folkstone, for London. You will hear from me next, at the great English Metropolis.

LETTER NO. XXIX.

LONDON, November, 1850.

Leaving Paris by railway, we reached Boulogne in six hours. We could not but laugh at a notice in the cars, in printed letters, which some wag had altered by erasing the word "not," to read thus, "Gentlemen are respectfully requested to *smoke* in the cars, and to put their feet on the cushions." This is a good sample of French drollery. The time occupied in crossing the English channel is not more than two hours, but it was sufficient to give me the most deeply experimental knowledge of sea-sickness which I ever wish to attain. From some cause or other, it is said sea-sickness is more general and more severe in this channel, than any where else. I was more dead than alive when I seated myself in the cars at Foulkstone for London. We were delighted to find ourselves once more where our native tongue was spoken, after having been so long a time strangers in strange lands. England seemed nearer and dearer than ever before.

We are actually *keeping house* in London. We are in Northumberland Court on the Strand, just opposite Trafalgar Square, in the Court End of the great metropolis. Northumberland Court is a narrow but clean and quiet place, containing not more than twenty houses, mostly owned by widows, who have apartments to let. We had no sooner installed ourselves in our new situation, than we received a call from the Rev. Mr. J. and family, of Brooklyn, New York, who occupy apartments in the same house, and intend to spend a year, traveling in Europe.

For the amusement of your lady-readers, let me enter a little more minutely into my house-keeping arrangements. Our room is neatly furnished, with Brussels carpet, hair sofa and chairs, and centre table, having in it also a large mahogany wardrobe, apparently, but in reality, enclosing a bedstead, which turns down; our room, therefore, serves as a parlor by day, and a sleeping room at night. Our landlady charges us two shillings, or fifty cents a day for our room, six-pence or twelve cents a day for service, and six-pence a week for the washing of bed and table linen. She furnishes also our crockery. By ringing a bell, I can summon a fine-looking English damsel to set my table, go to market, &c. She then brings a teakettle of boiling water, with which I make tea on the table, English fashion. We take our breakfast and tea in our room, and our dinner in whatever part of London chance finds us; for, as our business is *seeing the world*, we live mostly in the street. We find this quiet way of disposing of ourselves during our stay in the city, more pleasant, as well as more economical than paying ten dollars a day at Morley's Hotel, with a suite of rooms, and style and etiquette to match. We have milk sent to us, twice a day, from the Duke of Northumberland's dairy, and more beautiful rolls than I ever found in America. The butter here as well as throughout the Continent, has not a particle of salt in it. Every body spreads the butter on the bread, and then sprinkles salt over it. The muffins we get hot from the bakeries, and the mutton and gooseberries we find here, are delicious, and surpass any thing of the kind I ever saw at home. The gooseberries are twice as large as they grow with us.

We have dined out three times; and as an English dinner is somewhat different from an American one, I must tell you about it. The *services*, in one instance, commenced precisely at six o'clock, P. M., and we did not finish the various courses of fish, fowl, meats, pastry and fruits for nearly three hours. Every thing was then removed, but we remained. The table was then again covered, and tea, cakes, &c., were brought on. We sipped our tea and nibbled away at our cakes, and chatted a long time, and then left the table. As we had an engagement at an early hour the next day, we prepared to leave about ten o'clock, quite to the surprise and disappointment of our friends, who begged us to stay till after *supper, which was just ready!* We had been eating nearly four hours *then.*

At another dinner party of twenty-five persons, we had the pleasure of being served on Sevres porcelain, every plate of which cost twenty five dollars or more. Everything was handed on silver waiters, and we eat our dessert with golden teaspoons. Here we had an opportunity to taste the famous fish, sole, and another small fish, of which I have forgotten the name; both are delicious.

Our most stylish dinner was with Mr. ———, member of Parliament, who lives in an elegant place, quite removed from the bustle and noise of the city. We were received at the door by a handsome young gentleman, so elegantly whiskered and dressed in black, with white cravat, gold shirt buttons, silk stockings, pumps and silver buckles, and so gracefully bowed over to the care of a genteel personage in black silk, with a neat blonde cap, that I was in somewhat of a puzzle, till after I was ushered into the drawing room, I surmised that the elegant gentleman was no other than the butler, and the genteel lady was the house-keeper. Other company was expected, and dinner delayed till their arrival, and our host took a walk with us about the premises, showing us his park, hot-house, garden, and finally his *stable*, which he insisted upon our entering. And truly it was a fine sight. The stable was paved with small, round white stones, and as clean and well swept as a house floor.

The stalls were full of noble horses. The carriage was magnificent, in a fine room, well finished off with a fire-place in it to warm it while the carriage was being cleaned. The ostler's room was carpeted and well furnished, and at his master's command, he threw open his closet doors, and displayed with evident pride and satisfaction, all the trimmings, harness, &c., which shone like gold and silver, and were hung up in the most perfect order, everything in its place. The dinner was served in great style. The butler with his white gloves on, and another waiter, but a whit behind him in gentility, served us. The latter handed everything he brought into the room with a bow to the butler, and the butler flourished everything on to the table. English servants have a quiet, graceful, dumb way of waiting, that almost compels you to believe they are machines, and not living realities. After every luxury in the way of soups, fish, meats, puddings and pies had been discussed, the elegant waxed table, which shone like a mirror, was loaded with cut glass and silver, fruits and wines of various kinds, ale, porter, strong beer, &c. Mr. ——'s astonishment and distress at our declinature of all his choice old wines and rare liquors, were only equalled by our amazement at seeing him and his sons drink first a little Sherry, and then a little Madeira and a good deal of Champagne, and then a glass of ale and a little porter, and so on, which I must confess they stood bravely. After spending several hours at the table, we retired to the drawing room, and before we had time to take breath, *tea* was brought in.

We were unable to see Windsor Castle, as it is undergoing repairs; but through the influence of a friend, we were permitted to pay a visit to St. James' Palace, when we were here in August, although it was just closed for the season. Here the Queen holds all her levees, as her predecessors for many years have done. The rooms are more commodious and better arranged for large assemblies, than in any other place. We were shown the Council Chamber, the Reception and Ante-room and Banqueting Hall. The carpets have been down five years. They are Wilton; crimson is the prevailing color, and crimson velvet paper covers the walls. The ceiling is beautifully gilded. The chandeliers, mirrors and tables are superb. The upholsterer was there, preparing the rooms to be shut up for the season. The top, sides and floor, as well as all the furniture were to be covered with brown linen, of which he said it would take seven thousand yards.

The carpets were not to be taken up, only covered. The Queen's chair in the Council Chamber cost two thousand and five hundred dollars. It was a very comfortable chair to sit upon! In the Reception room is a throne and canopy over it, which is encircled by a gilt railing, enclosing perhaps twelve feet square. When individuals are presented to the Queen, she does not receive them sitting on her throne, but she stands outside this enclosure. The young Duke of Cambridge rode up while we were there. He is quite a handsome man. The Queen, I am told, always opens the ball with this favorite cousin. The late Queen Adelaide's apartments are on the opposite side of the Court.

We spent an evening in Madame Tussaud's Wax Gallery, in King street. This exceeds any wax exhibition I have ever seen. The hall was so finely lighted by gas as to outdo old Sol's day-light altogether. The music was excellent, and the crowd gaily dressed. Throughout the hall are groups of wax figures, all distinguished characters, standing or sitting, so elegantly and neatly dressed, and so perfectly life-like in their attitudes and general appearance, as to create many amusing mistakes. None of them are inclosed in glass cases. A fine looking gentleman was sitting on a sofa, gazing at the passing crowd, while two or three ladies sat by him in quite a merry mode. One hand held his hat and cane, and the other rested carelessly upon his knee. After looking at him some time inquisitively, one of my companions said, "Is that man *alive* or not?" "Why," replied I, laughing, "he is alive of course; don't you see how he turns his head around?" This satisfied my friend for a moment, and then his doubts returned; so we concluded to go and sit down near his lordship, and touch him if necessary, to solve the problem, or speak to him and see if he was alive. I moved by him very carefully, lest I should tread on his toes, while he turned his head very deliberately to look at us. After some whispering among ourselves, and as many sly glances as we dared bestow upon him, we found out he was only a *wax* gentleman after all, and his head turned every few minutes by some kind of machinery But the illusion was complete. Some around us, I presume, never discovered that he was not a *bona fide* man. Many of the figures were scattered about purposely, either standing by themselves, or sitting on the sofas and lounges to deceive visitors. Near the entrance of the room we found the Queen, Prince Albert, and four of the little sprigs of royalty. The young prince and princesses were standing by their parents, the baby was asleep in its cradle, looking like life itself, only a *little more so*, with its elegant embroideries, laces and coverings of surpassing beauty and richness. These are all said to have been perfect resemblances to the originals, when taken some few years since. Almost every man, highly distinguished for the last hundred years in France or England, is to be seen here, true to life, in the costume of his time. Two large groups were especially interesting: one was the crowning of Queen Victoria, and the other the Court of Queen Elizabeth. In the former, the Duke of Wellington, Queen Adelaide, the Duchess of Kent, the Duke of Devonshire, &c., were prominent figures.

Queen Elizabeth and the Earl of Leicester, and sundry lords and ladies dressed in all the splendor and quaintness of the olden time, were a truly interesting spectacle. Here stood a flirting couple of ancient times, and there sat a regular courting couple. Here were gentlemen in powdered wigs and knee buckles, and there ladies in laughably short waists and long trains. Here stood Napoleon, talking over matters very earnestly with some of the leading men of his time, and in another place were John Adams, John Randolph, and others of our countrymen. But noblest among them all, and peering above all others, stood our own illustrious George Washington, dressed in simple black—the most dignified and benevolent looking person there. While comparing him with other great men who stood around, in the pride and enthusiasm of the moment, I could scarcely restrain myself from shaking hands with him, in spite of his dignity, and telling him that, to my thinking, he was by far the finest looking and best man in the assembly, and I was as proud of him as I was of the country I belonged to, although the Queen of England was near enough to hear me. As it was, a few Americans of us (for we had found a number of our ship companions, and had gone together to the exhibition,) so loudly praised and admired our own countrymen, and congratulated ourselves so warmly in finding them in such an unexpected place, that we attracted as much attention before we finished our eulogium, as the great Washington himself. In an adjoining room, we were shown several curiosities, among which were the identical carriage in which Napoleon rode for years, and the writing desk he used to the end of his life, which I searched faithfully, hoping to find a scrap of his writing or an expression of some great thought. I got up into the carriage and shut the door, and almost imagined that Bonaparte was there too.

The great charm and peculiarity of Madame Tussaud's Wax Gallery, over all other exhibitions of the kind I have ever seen, is, not only the perfect elegance and finish, and life-like appearance of her figures, but the richness and beauty and costliness, and purity of their dress. In our own country, even in the museum of the matchless Barnum, the neglected, soiled appearance of the few wax figures there, leads you to turn away from them almost with disgust. I could not but think, as I saw the pure white dresses and laces, the unsoiled white gloves and shirt bosoms, the fine glossy broadcloth without a particle of dust upon it, the polished boots, and the elegantly dressed heads, which looked as if they had just escaped from the hair dresser's hands, what an endless business to keep every thing in such trim; every figure looked as if dressed for an evening party.

In my next I will tell you about some of the Churches in London.

LETTER NO. XXX.

London, November, 1850.

The two finest specimens of church architecture in Protestant Europe are said to be St. Paul's Cathedral and Westminster Abbey. The former covers more than two acres of ground, and is the largest Protestant Church in the world. In order to see all parts of St. Paul, you are obliged to pay no less then seven different fees, amounting in all to 75 cents; clock 2d., whispering gallery 2d., ball 1s. 6d., and so on. By mounting six hundred and sixteen steps, you may reach the top of the Church, from which there is a magnificent view of this superb city, which is truly wonderful from its vastness, being thirty miles in circumference. The interior of the great cupola contains several paintings, illustrative of scenes in St. Paul's life; and the baldness of the interior is somewhat relieved by statues and monuments. Among these statues are Dr. Johnson, Howard, the Philantropist, Lord Nelson &c. The pavement up to the altar is beautiful, composed of alternate slabs of black and white marble. The carvings of the stalls in the choir are beautifully executed, but there is a dingy, gloomy look about the chapel, which spoils every thing. We attended church here once, and were surprised to find a small congregation on a pleasant day; probably not over five hundred. The services were not peculiarly interesting, but the singing surpassed any church music I ever heard. Twelve little boys, from ten to fourteen, clothed in white surplices, performed certain parts exquisitely. I almost felt, as I gazed on their beautiful faces, and listened to their sweet voices, that I was listening to the harmony of angels. Three times every day in the year is service performed in this church. The great bell weighs more than eleven thousand pounds, and is ten feet in diameter. It is never tolled but on the death of the King, Queen, or some member of the royal family; or for the bishop of London, or the Dean of St. Paul's.

I am ashamed to own that I was disappointed in Westminster Abbey. I had heard much of this celebrated antiquity, and had anticipated my visit to the graves of the illustrious dead in the Poet's Corner with the greatest enthusiasm. But the beautiful fabric which my fancy had erected, toppled over before I passed the threshold. I entered and gazed around with little more emotion than if I had been a statue. I account for my disappointment in this way: We entered the church from the Poet's corner through a mean and dirty entrance, instead of the great and beautiful gate on the northern side, and the effect on my mind was precisely, I suppose, as it would be to enter a superb and elegant dwelling by the back door, and go through the kitchen into the parlor. First impressions are of great account in matters of taste. If good, they affect us like throwing open a window-shutter and pouring sun-light upon an object. I knew that here were monuments to the memory of Spencer, Milton, Shakspeare, Thomson, Gay, Goldsmith, Addison, Johnson, Handel, Garrick, Dr. Watts, Isaac Newton and hosts of others, and did *not consider*, till I stood upon the spot, that many of them were *simply* beautiful monuments, erected in honor of their memory, but not in the place where their ashes repose; and half the sentiment that would have been awakened by feeling that these splendid monuments actually covered their dust, was dispelled by a knowledge that their remains, in reality, slumbered beneath other sods. Much of the reverence and enthusiasm I should have felt, had I stood at their actual graves, was changed into simple admiration of monumental beauty, such as I should have felt in any *marble-yard*, filled with specimens of elaborate and tasteful sculpture. Had I first passed *around* the Abbey and formed an accurate idea of its height its immensity, and marked its towers and its pinacles, and its antique stained windows, especially the great rose window in front, ninety feet in circumference, and walked up the nave of the church, viewing at my leisure the diverse and picturesque and tasteful, as well as monstrous and antique monumental effigies, which abound within, I might have been as enchanted and enthusiastic, as most are who visit this place. In the Chapels, of which there are eleven, containing tombs, I must say, my expectations were more than realized. Here repose the kings and queens of England; and every variety of sepulcral design, which centuries have elaborated, are displayed to view. On many tombs is a full length marble effigy of the sleeper within. There is something truly touching in this representation of the shrouded dead. Upon some are the images of both parents, while perhaps several children, with hands clasped and eyes raised to Heaven, are kneeling about the tomb. The mausoleum of Henry III. has been splendid in the extreme, but is now greatly defaced and mutilated. The effigy of Henry V., stretched on his tomb, is headless; the head, which was of solid silver, having been stolen. In Edward the Confessor's Chapel, are kept the chairs in which the kings and queens of England are crowned, and in the choir of Westminster Abbey, this ceremony always takes place. Henry the Seventh's Chapel is said to be the most highly finished piece of gothic architecture in the world. It costs two hundred and eighty thousand pounds. His own tomb, erected by himself, cost seventy-five thousand dollars of our own money, and was six years in building. Here also is the tomb of Queen Elizabeth, and a magnificent monument to the memory of Mary, Queen of Scots, and a curious effigy of Margaret Tudor, mother of Henry VII. The cloisters are well worth a visit. They are tenantless, of course, and gloom and dampness, and sad recollections press upon you as you wander within their silent walls. The celebrated Doomsday Book of William the Conqueror, is kept in the Chapter House. This we were anxious to see, but the door was closed. Here is Clement the Seventh's Golden Bull, confirming the title of Defender of the Faith on Henry the Eighth, for his defence of the faith against Luther: also, the original *wills* of Kings Richard the II., Henry IV., Henry VII., and Henry VIII.

We attended once the church, of which Rev. James Hamilton, author of "Life in Earnest," is pastor. He was not at home, but in his stead, we had the pleasure of hearing the Rev. Mr. Bonar, of Scotland, biographer of McCheyne. His sermon was remarkably practical and impressive, one I can never forget.

The hymns they sang were so old fashioned in poetic style, as to carry us back a hundred years or more, and were quite a novelty. One ran thus:

We, with our fathers, sinned have,
And of iniquity
Too long we have the workers been;
We have done wickedly.

The wonders great, which thou, O Lord,
Didst work in Egypt land,
Our fathers, tho' they saw, yet them
They did not understand.

Rev. Dr. Cummings we also had the pleasure of hearing. He is very popular among the Dissenters. We went early in order to obtain a seat; the pews were, many of them, quite empty, but the sexton told us to stand up in the aisle till after singing and the *first prayer*, when he would give us a seat. Odd as it seemed, we had to obey orders. The people crowded in till service commenced, while the pews were still not half filled, but the three aisles were full of persons, waiting according to direction, till after the *first prayer*. I was so tired of standing, and so curious to see the end of this novel treatment of strangers, that the hymn and prayer seemed unusually long, and in my anxiety to know what was to be done with the crowd in the aisles, they failed of producing the good effect they might have done under other circumstances.

At length the time arrived for disposing of us, when to my astonishment, the sexton *turned down a seat* in the aisle, and a hundred or more strangers, like ourselves, were accommodated in this fashion. The recent movements in the Papal Church, as affecting the interests of the Church of England, were the theme of discourse, upon which, Mr. Cummings was quite eloquent. We also attended Surrey Chapel, where eccentric Rowland Hill was so long stationed. This is a very plain old Church, and the present incumbent was not at home. As I sat within the walls which had so long echoed to the voice of that singular man, I could not but recall some of his eccentricities. I wondered which aisle poor Mrs. Hill came up so late on Sunday morning, after sermon commenced, and how she must have felt when her husband called the attention of the congregation to her tardiness, and attributed the circumstance to the fact, that she had just received a new bonnet and other articles of dress on the previous evening, which she was anxious to display to the greatest advantage, quite to the dismay and consternation of the poor wife.

On one occasion, not more than three years before his death, it is said, "he was preaching to one of the most crowded congregations that ever assembled to hear him. In the middle of his discourse, he observed a great commotion in the gallery, (he was always greatly annoyed at any noise in the chapel;) for a time he took no notice of it, but finding it increasing, he paused in his sermon, and looking in the direction in which the confusion prevailed, he exclaimed: 'What's the matter there? The devil seems to have got among you.' A plain, country-looking man immediately started to his feet, and addressing Mr. Hill, in reply, said: 'No sir, it arn't the devil as is a doing on it; it's a lady wot's fainted; and she is a very fat un, sir, as don't seem likely to come to again in a hurry.'

"Oh, that's it, is it," observed Mr. Hill, drawing his hand across his chin, "then I beg the lady's pardon—and the *devil's* too."

By some means or other, Mr. Hill always had a full house. The following anecdote is told of him, and it is positively affirmed as true. "Passing through a small town in the provinces, principally occupied by journeymen mechanics and apprentices, he intimated to the Dissenting Minister of the place, his intention of preaching in his chapel in the course of an hour. The Minister readily assented, but said he would have to preach to empty pews, as there was not only no time to give the people notice, but they could not, at the hour specified, conveniently leave their employment, even if they were duly informed that he intended to preach. 'Ah, we'll take the chance of that,' said Mr. Hill. He accordingly sent the bell-man round the place, with an intimation that Mr. Rowland Hill, from London, was to preach at the Dissenting Meeting House, at a particular hour, and that before leaving the pulpit he *would make a pair of shoes* before the whole congregation. The droll intimation had the desired effect. Curiosity to see the shoes made in the pulpit overcame all considerations of commerce and profit. The place was crowded. At the end of the service he said, 'Now, my friends, I proposed to make a pair of shoes before leaving the pulpit. It now becomes my duty to redeem my promise.' And so saying, he bowed down, and taking in his hand a pair of boots, which he had brought with him for the purpose, he exhibited them to the congregation saying, 'You all see that this is a pair of boots.' There was no audible reply, but every countenance seemed to answer in the affirmative. 'Well, then,' resumed Rowland Hill, pulling a pen-knife out of his pocket, and first cutting off the leg of one and then of the other about two inches above the soles, he exhibited his quondam boots to the gaze of the astonished congregation, exclaiming, 'There, you see, I have my pair of shoes already.'"

In spite of his odd and unheard-of ways, he was eminently successful as a preacher. His very oddities awakened attention, and his solemn and powerful reasonings and appeals, though made in the most familiar way, led many a man to turn his thoughts from time to eternity, and seek a preparation for another world.

LETTER NO. XXXI.

London, July, 1850.

If the palaces of London and its suburbs do not, in general, compare favorably with those of the Continent in size and architectural magnificence and beauty, there is certainly one feature in this great metropolis, which calls forth the wonder and admiration of all travelers. I mean her *parks* and *squares*. Never have I seen such ample provision made for the health and pleasure of any people. As I wandered about through the shady avenues and retired walks of Hyde Park, situated in the very heart of London, yet sheltered from its dust and removed from its din, and literally threaded its paths for miles, or sat down when weary, on seats scattered about, I fell into a musing mood. I watched the bright smiling faces of childhood as they glided by, and heard the wild laugh of many happy beings, whose hearts seemed tuned to melody by the freshness and beauty of the landscape, or the carol of the birds that sang so sweetly about us, and saw the gleam of pleasure that lighted up the pale countenances of the invalids, who were rolling by in their chairs, and breathing the pure air of heaven, and even the elastic step of the poorer classes, who seemed animated with unwonted gladness, as they wandered about free as the air they breathed, in this Eden of a place, and I felt, as I never did before, the propriety, the necessity, and the humanity of providing such Elysiums in our crowded cities. Here the rich and the poor, the grave and the gay, the listless and lazy, and weary and forlorn and heart-stricken, especially babies and children, can flee from the noise and turmoil, and dust and danger of the thoroughfares, and from the closeness of their suffocating rooms, and refresh their weary souls and their gasping bodies with a look at the beautiful and a breath of heaven's pure air. Why not provide in cities for the health and comfort, and recreation, and I may add morality, of the masses, as sacredly and bountifully as for intellectual improvement, and to increase commercial facilities, and encourage the industrial arts! Why not have *a country* in the city, where the rich can take an hour's pleasant drive, without riding miles on pavement through the mean, dirty suburbs of the town, to *reach* the fresh green fields and groves — where the man of business shutting up his store and leaving his cares behind, can, in a few minute's walk, find himself in Paradise, (as a park like Hyde Park, or Regent's, or St. James', really must seem to a weary and care-worn mortal;) where children that pine for fresh air and flowers, and space to run and give strength to their little limbs, can do so, unharmed and unlimited, and every body can go to obtain a fair look occasionally at the heavens and the green earth, such as they cannot have in town: where boys can go to "fly their kites" and "have fun" without scaring the horses, and getting into the calaboose in consequence, and where the poor who are destitute of so many comforts, can at least find *one* luxury, God intended all should enjoy, good fresh air!

I thought of our own beautiful city, St. Louis, stretching far and wide its limits to fulfil its noble destiny, almost entirely unprovided for, too sadly forgotten and neglected in this respect, while it is marching on northward and southward, and westward, and the time to secure the advantages of delightful promenades, is winging itself away forever. I felt more than words can express, the importance and great utility, and gain of such healthful resorts in our city, and I wished most fervently, that the Lord or somebody else, would put it into the hearts of some of our millionaires, Messrs. A— B— C— D— &c., to give or to sell on the most favorable terms, tracts of land *now* for these purposes. For more than two hundred years has Hyde Park been the fashionable resort of London. If you wish to see all the world, go there in the afternoon; if you wish to get out of the world and be *alone* with nature and nature's God, undisturbed by aught, save the melody of the birds, the sighing of the breeze and the rippling of the waters at your feet, go early in the morning. At all hours of the day, from six till nine at night it is open for the use of the people. The Queen also provides a band of music to play every Saturday afternoon, when thousands crowd around, standing or sitting, to enjoy the feast, and doubtless many aching hearts and ruffled spirits go home soothed and comforted, or softened and subdued into harmony with the world around them. There are five entrances to Hyde Park. We entered by Hyde Park Corner, the great gate which adjoins Apsley House, the residence of the Duke of Wellington. Opposite the arch of entrance, the "Ladies of England" have raised a colossal statue of Achilles, by Wesmacott, in honor of the Duke and his associates in the great continental war. It is cast from artillery taken in various battles, and stands on a large granite base. A broad foot-path leads from Hyde Park to Kensington Gardens, which are three miles in circumference, and are thought to be the most beautiful promenade in Europe.

Regent's Park contains between three and four hundred acres, and is beautifully laid out in gardens, lawns, walks, ponds, &c. Every kind of aquatic bird, almost, is sailing about in the water, to the great delight and amusement of the children, who watch them for hours, throwing in occasionally a crumb of bread or cake for their benefit. In this park are the Zoological gardens, where you can spend a day in the most delightful manner imaginable. Nothing can be more entertaining and instructive to children, than a ramble in this beautiful place. Every variety of quadruped, bird and fish, is here to be found, living *in style* in separate houses, according to his nature and habits. Many of the animals have romantic little cottages, embosomed in trees and surrounded by a white paling; and it was quite amusing to see a lama or a giraffe, standing quietly in his door and looking out upon the world around, seeming to say as he chewed his cud, "I am Lord of all I survey." We spent the morning in making calls. We called on several noted families — the Bruin family, from the Polar regions (white) — the Porcupines — Elephants — Reptiles — Monkeys and their family connexions, the Baboons and the Ourang Outangs, who really have the power to make themselves very entertaining, if not agreeable. The Lions, Tigers, Leopards, Panthers, &c., had distinct stone dwellings, surrounded completely with iron work, allowing them some space to walk about, but perfectly secure. Printed notices were posted in various places, that the tortoises would dine at twelve o'clock, and the hippopotamus would be fed at one. So we wandered about hither and thither, through beautiful lanes and shady walks and among stone and brick houses, wonderfully amused at finding such an enchanting little village of wild cats, elephants, snakes and lambs, living in perfect harmony and elegant style, and actually, by the neatness and beauty, and order of their settlement, putting man to blush for many of his.

Quite a crowd of visitors assembled to see the tortoises eat their dinner. One old fellow of enormous size and about a hundred years old, they said, crawled along to a fine large cabbage, which disappeared in a very short time. There was a general rush to the mansion of the hippopotamus, at one o'clock. The history of his brute-ship is quite interesting. "He is the only living animal of his species, that has been brought to England in modern times, if ever. Many attempts have been made to bring them alive, but have failed. This one is a present from the Viceroy of Egypt, to the Zoological Society of London. It was found in the Island of Obaysh, one thousand and eight hundred miles from Cairo. The value of the animal is enhanced by the fact, that an offer of twenty-five thousand dollars from an American agent at Alexandria, could not induce any speculator to obtain one from the White Nile and deliver it at that place." An Arab takes care of and sleeps near this one. The animal is a very ugly looking creature of India ink color, something like a hog, but his legs are so short, you can scarcely see that he has any as he waddles about. He is only a year old. The deer, antelopes, gazelles and other harmless, but frisky animals, have large enclosures, encircled by pickets so high and sharp as to forbid escape, and houses suitable for shelter in rain and cold.

The reptiles live in a very pretty stone cottage, delightfully situated and surrounded with shrubbery, &c. So tasteful is their residence, that I fancied I should like to live in it myself; but as soon as I entered, I changed my mind. A sight of thousands of snakes, squirming and crawling, and eating and snapping and staring at you, is certainly calculated to make you feel forcibly the antipathy that exists between the serpent and mankind, in striking fulfilment of the curse pronounced. On each side of the halls are compartments of iron or wood-work, with glass fronts, reaching from the floor of their divisions, which is three feet, perhaps, from the floor of the building to the ceiling above Here is a nest of rattlesnakes, performing various gyrations for their own amusement as well as ours; and there is a huge, parti-colored fellow, taking a nap on a nice bed of moss, prepared for his accommodation. In another place is a family of lizards, entertaining themselves in snaky style. Here is a monstrous black snake, trying experiments on the trunk of a tree in his apartment, and showing off his capabilities, as he crawls and twines about its branches, while the younger members of the family amuse themselves at the foot of the tree.

But the greatest of all curiosities in tho tribo is the boa constrictor, a foot or more in circumference, wound around a tree with his spiteful eyes glaring frightfully about. In other places, you see every variety almost of the reptile species, of all sizes and colors, some panting with their mouths wide open, and others darting out their venomous tongues with a rapidity truly astonishing. Curious as was the exhibition here, I could not but rejoice when I was safe out of the walls, fearing that by some accident or other, those awful creatures should get loose and make climbing poles of us.

I cannot conceive of any amusement so entertaining, healthful and instructive for parents and children, as a visit, for a day, occasionally, to this wonderful garden. The grounds of themselves are as beautifully and fancifully laid out as you can imagine, and shady knolls and winding-paths, losing themselves in deep thickets, and animals from all zones and of all species, and of every habit, and ponds of fish, and beds of flowers, and pretty cottages, nestled amid trees and shrubs, afford a variety of scenery and mental recreation, which is quite enchanting. And then, there is an excellent Cafe provided for the rest and refreshment of weary pilgrims, where coffee and tea, and cakes and fruits, and sweets of all kinds that can be named, are placed before you with irresistible charms, especially if you are very hungry.

Such a provision for the enjoyment and recreation of the people is an honor to its founder, Sir Humphrey Davy, and a blessing to the British nation. If I had been a believer in a *fairy land*, I should certainly have thought, as I wandered for miles about the Zoological Garden, that I had at length found the enchanted place. St. James, Green and Victoria Parks have also their charms, and I am told that there are more than *seventy* squares in London, some of which, though quite small, are very pretty. But I am spinning out such a yarn about the Parks, that I shall have no room to speak of the British Museum, which, I think, is certainly one of London's greatest wonders. The Museum is free on certain days, from ten to four; but seven hours do not afford scarce a glimpse at the world of curiosities collected here.

There are five Galleries of Natural History, containing rare and beautiful specimens of almost every animal we have ever read or heard of. The collection of birds is immense and of great value, and the variety of bird's eggs is a great curiosity, from the size of a pea to a baby's head, and of all colors and shades. The shells, too, are numberless and beautiful.

In the gallery of portraits, besides kings and queens, and warriors of great renown, you may see Sir Isaac Newton,

Archbishop Cranmer, Voltaire, Martin Luther, Alexander Pope, Richard Baxter, and so on. There is also one Mary Davis, aged seventy-four, out of whose head grew two horns, one of which is represented in the portrait. In another room, amid hosts of other things, are wasps' and hornnets' nests of various kinds. A wasp's nest, from India, was a marvelous sight; it was as large as a water-pail. And I saw a few spiders I shall never forget.

The rooms filled with minerals, fossils and corals, would have detained me many hours, had I had more leisure. They are elegant specimens. In one room is a fossil human skeleton.

Thirteen immense rooms are filled with antiquities. We saw the specimens sent from Nineveh by Layard to London, so beautifully described in his works of Nineveh. The *winged bull* had not arrived, but is soon expected. In one room are eleven bas-reliefs, formerly parts of the famous mausoleum at Halicarnassus, one of the seven wonders of the world, built three hundred and fifty-seven years before Christ. In the Elgin saloon, nearly all the articles were brought from Athens by Lord Elgin, and bought by Parliament for $175,000

In the Egyptian rooms are mummies enough to fill a common grave yard, to say nothing of embalmed snakes, dogs, bulls, &c., innumerable; and in the Bronze and Etruscan rooms are statuary and vases of every description, some of them in a great state of perfection, and very tasteful productions of ancient art.

The Library is immense and contains many rare literary antiquities, but unfortunately we did not gain admittance, not having made application to the proper person for a ticket.

We visited the Vernon Gallery, a collection of paintings and sculpture by British artists, and the National Gallery containing many of the productions of Rubens, Rembrandt, Nicholas Poussin, Titian, Correggio, Raphael, Paul Veronese, Annibale Caracci, Tintoretto, Guercino, Gaspar Poussin, Vandyck, Domenichino, Guido Reni, Copley, Reynolds, Hogarth and many others of world-wide fame. We had a feast.

LETTER NO. XXXII.

LONDON, July, 1850.

The manufacturing cities of England are a great curiosity to an American, who has seen only a few factories in a few manufacturing villages in his own country. I opened my eyes wide with amazement, and lifted up both hands, as we whizzed along the railway and caught our first glimpse of Manchester, which seemed like a *city of chimneys*. Oh, what a place for smook, and bustle, and work! There are more than one hundred and sixty thousand inhabitants, and almost all are busy in mills, or work shops, or foundries, or warehouses, that for immensity and variety perfectly bewilder and astound you. We visited, among others, the largest Calico Print Works, Bradshow's Printing and Engraving establishment, and the Irwell Silk Mill. In the last the work is confined to narrow ribbons and trimmings. One hundred and fifty hands are in the spinning room, and four thousand and two hundred shuttles are running. By *law*, no children under eleven years of age, are allowed to work in the factory. They work ten hours. The rooms were clean and well ventilated, and the girls were fair and looked healthy and happy. Their wages vary from three to ten shillings per week, (from seventy-five cents to two dollars and a half.) They are allowed to sing hymns and popular songs. They sang two songs for us, greatly to our delight. I assure you, it was a beautiful sight to see so many young, neat and busy girls together, and to hear them sing so sweetly while their hands were employed. The silk, in its natural state, is all either white or yellow; only one pound in ninety comes white. The white silk is brought from China, and the yellow from the East Indies. It is not known how to account for the difference in color of the cocoons. The Superintendent informed us, that *one* silk worm thread, is equal in strength to one hundred spider's threads, and that a thread of sewing-silk, as prepared for use, contains about ten silk worm threads.

At Derby, we visited the Porcelain Works, and saw many articles of the famous Derbyshire china made — such as pitchers, cups and saucers, &c. The processes of shaping, painting, baking, &c., are very curious. All kinds of marble, spars and petrifactions, are to be found here. The Derby Grammar School, is said to be one of the most ancient foundations in the kingdom. We strolled about the *Arboretum*, with which I was delighted. This is an enclosure containing eleven acres of land, nobly donated by Joseph Strutt, Esq., to the city of Derby, for a promenade and retreat, especially for the working classes. He not only gave the land, but employed J. C. Loudon, a man of great taste and judgement, to lay it out and fit it up at his expense. The cost of buildings and improvements is estimated at fifty thousand dollars. We saw many children here frolicking about, while their mothers or nurses were knitting or sewing under the shade of the trees.

We paid a visit to Matlock-Bath, a beautifully wild and romantic place, and explored quite thoroughly the mines in the neighborhood. No sooner had I expressed a desire to visit the mines, than five donkeys, all saddled and bridled, were driven up to the door, for my ladyship to ride on; but I preferred climbing the crags to riding on such mean looking animals. The mines were formerly quite celebrated, but are now mostly abandoned; they contain fine stalactites and spars. The museums in the town are full of beautiful specimens of spars and fossils, wrought into vases and various ornamental designs, which can be purchased. The petrifying wells are very curious. Here a great variety of things may be seen in process of petrifaction. Baskets, eggs, &c., are among the deposits, upon which the water is slowly, but constantly dripping, and in the course of a year they are completely petrified. The scenery about Matlock is wild and enchanting.

Birmingham, renowned for its commerce and manufactures, is nearly in the centre of England. It is quite a mean smoky looking city, but contains nearly two hundred thousand inhabitants. We were recommended to a hotel called the "*Hen and Chickens*," but I remonstrated against stopping at a tavern with such a *name*, till assured it was a very excellent place. The English certainly have an odd taste in naming their inns. The names of themselves, I should suppose, would scare people away, instead of attracting travelers. One, I remember, is called "The Cat and the Cucumber." They have also some queer customs, especially that of feeing servants. You are sometimes assailed by a half dozen servants asking for a fee. In one hotel, where we had requested servants' fees to be included in our bill, and had actually been charged for service two dollars for two days, we were followed to the carriage by a man, saying "Please remember boots." It seemed the two dollars had not covered this man's claim. We were almost afraid to have the dog that lay upon the steps look kindly upon us, lest it should be an extra charge.

The only wages servants receive in most hotels, is what they receive from travelers. While waiting for supper, which we had ordered at a country inn, a servant girl appeared in the parlor and said "Madam, will you please walk into the other room and *make the tea?*" I followed her in a state of wonder at such a request in a hotel, when she pointed out the tea caddies, black and green, wishing me to measure out and put in to the tea-pot what I pleased. I did so, and returned to the parlor, until we were called to tea. I was quite amused one day at the evident dilemma a gentlemen traveler was in, who stopped where we were. He had ordered supper, and a table in the parlor was set for him. The servant requested him to come and *make his tea.* Whether he should empty the tea caddy altogether or in part, seemed a question that caused some deliberation. He finally settled the matter, but from the quantity he measured out, I doubt whether he shut his eyes in sleep for a week afterward.

We hoped to have seen the Rev. John Angell James, who preaches here, but were disappointed; he was not in town.

The Papier Mache establishment of Jennens & Bettredge is well worth a visit. A person unacquainted with this process, and ushered into the splendid show rooms of this company, and told that the beautiful specimens of art before him were made of brown paper, would naturally doubt the truth or possibility of the fact. The tables are made of fifty or more sheets of coarse wrapping paper, pasted together and pressed till dry. Then there are rooms for painting, varnishing, polishing and finishing, till the most perfect gems of beauty, that can be conceived of, are spread before your eyes. Some of their specimens, for delicacy and beauty, I have never seen surpassed. We visited here one of the largest cut glass factories and a steel pen factory. A steel pen undergoes thirty-two processes before it is ready for use.

From Birmingham we went to Stratford on Avon. Passed the Park where Shakspeare stole the deer, and saw the gate on which he posted the verses, so obnoxious to Sir Lucy, and which resulted finally in his leaving Stratford in somewhat of a hurry, and seeking his fortune in London. Little did he think as he scribbled away, that his destiny hung on these lines. You remember them:

> " A Parliament member, a Justice of Peace
> At home a poor scarecrow, in London an asse;
> If Lucy is Lowsie, as some volke miscall it,
> Synge Lowsie Lucy whatever befall it, &c."

It was nearly dark when we reached Stratford. We stopped at the " Red Horse" inn, the best in the little village, and immediately paid a visit to Shakspeare's birth place. Strange as the old house looks in these times, I dare say when Shakspeare's father purchased it, two hundred years ago, for forty pounds, "with its two gardens and two orchards with their appurtenances," it was quite a respectable house, with its dormer windows and gable roof. We could not but laugh at the great fireplaces, especially in the kitchen, with its stone seats in the corner, where Shakspeare in his boyhood sat, doubtless, many days, looking up the chimney at the blue sky above, and out upon his parents and then into the fire. The floor is composed of flag stones, broken into all shapes; the roof above showed the huge bare timbers on which the upper story rests. We went up stairs into the room where he was born, and looked out of the windows he looked out of, and sat down in the chair he sat in; (*perhaps*, for I have no great faith in relics.) At any rate, I felt I stood a better chance of imbibing the inspiration of the old bard, when I crept into the chimney corner and sat on the stone block, for I was sure he had sat there. The chamber is a very pleasant, cheerful room, just such a bright, sunny place as would stir up any body's thoughts and glad feelings, and we sat down in every corner and in every chair, and puzzled our brains over the walls, which are so completely crossed and recrossed by writing, that scarcely an inch of the original wall appears. Byron's and Walter Scott's names are written in several places at different dates, and in fact, the autographs on the walls of hundreds of great man I had heard or read of, were as great curiosities to my eyes almost as the house itself. Then we were called upon to put *our* names in the great book, as big as a family bible, which has been used since 1815, where every body that visits the place records the fact, now that the walls and window frames of the house are covered. We found many recent insertions of the names of our own countrymen, among whom were added a few days before, those of Abbott Lawrence, our Ambassador to England, and several of our ship-companions, who had already paid their respects to Shakspeare's memory. From the house we went to Shakspeare's grave. It is in the chancel of the village church. In a niche on one side is a half length effigy of Shakspeare, said to be the best and only portrait of him, now to be relied upon. The graves of the Shakspeare family lie in a row in front of the altar. The marble slabs that cover them are concealed by a matting, which we removed and read the inscriptions. Shakspeare's runs thus:

"Good friend, for Jesus' sake forbeare
To digg the dyst encloased heare;
Blest be the man, that spares the stones;
And curst be he that moves my bones."

Tradition says, that " his wife and daughter did earnestly desire to be laid in the same grave with him, " but that "not one, for fear of the curse above said, dare touch his grave stone." The inscription on the stone of Shakspeare's daughter, runs thus:

"Witty above her sexe, but that's not all,
Wise to salvation was good Mistres Hall.
Something of Shakspeare was in that; but this
Wholly of him with whom she is now in bliss.

Then, passenger, ha'snt ne're a teare
To weep with her, that wept with all?
That wept, yet set herself to chere
Them up with comfort's cordiall.
Her love shall live, her mercy spread
When thou ha'st ne're a teare to shed."

Not far from the church is the Grammar school-house, where Shakspeare acquired his 'small Latin and less Greek.' From Stratford we went to Leamington, the most beautiful spa in the kingdom. We went to the pump-room and baths, and drank the water, which was enough to make a well man sick. Invalid ladies we saw drawn about the spacious streets in small carriages, by handsomely dressed *men*, a curious sight. We took the railroad from Leamington to Kenilworth, and from there went in an omnibus two miles to Kenilworth Castle. What hosts of recollections crowded upon us, as we strolled about among these stately ruins, and looked up to its crumbling battlements, mantled with ivy, and actually grey with age. Little is left but its massive walls — a perfect shell — but enough to give you an idea of the magnificence of the feudal ages, and to impress the mind deeply with a sense of the instability of all earthly things and the vanity of all human splendor. How did all the honor and fame and wealth and pageantry of earth float away into nothingness before my mental vision, as I stood gazing about, contrasting the silence and desolation of this beautiful spot now with the scenes of courtly festivity, which in the Earl of Leicester's time, took place within its walls, when the proud and haughty Elizabeth was a guest here in her last visit of seventeen days! I know not how long I had been absorbed in melancholy musings, when a merry laugh fell on my ear and I turned around; who should I see but Mrs. ———, with a smiling face and almost flying feet hastening up the court-yard to greet me. It was a joyous meeting with an old American friend. She had seen us, as we passed in the omnibus through the town of Kenilworth, and had come on the wings of the wind to meet us. So we traversed the court-yard and tilt-yard and parks together. We went up into the room, which it is said Elizabeth occupied in her last visit, and looked out upon the moat, now grown over, upon the waving fields and forests beyond, and stepped into the banqueting Hall, or rather, stood on its threshold, and gazed up the turret where Amy Robsart was concealed. We asked questions, which nobody answered, and started inquiries, which echo, in mockery repeated. Every one of all the gay crowds, that year after year, has glided in and out of this splendid castle, making its walls ring with merriment, has pased beyond the bounds of time, and is to the world now, as if he had never been!

LETTER NO. XXXIII.

CHATSWORTH INN, Aug. 5, 1850.

We spent one day in Sheffield, so famous for the manufacture of cutlery. It is pleasantly nestled at the foot of a range of hills, and contains nearly seventy thousand inhabitants. We visited the celebrated establishment of Rogers & Sons, also an electro plate factory; and saw casters, cake baskets, spoons, and every variety of articles, undergoing the process of plating. Spoons, forks, &c., of the new style — *electro-plating on German silver* — are used here every where in hotels and private houses. They look as well, and do not cost half so much as silver, and wear for years without looking defaced.

From Sheffield, we took a private carriage with Mr. S—, of St. Louis, and rode sixteen miles to Chatsworth, the magnificent mansion of the Duke of Devonshire. The day was delightful, the air balmy, and though in August, everything in England is as fresh and green as with us in June. The country in this region is beautiful. Part of our ride was over a moor, covered with heath in full bloom — a small pink flower. At our right, lay the scenery inmortalized by Scott in Ivanhoe and in Peveril of the Peak. It was Saturday, and we settled ourselves for a few days at Chatsworth Inn, a quiet, delightful place, a few rods from the great entrance to the Duke's park. After an early tea, we took a ramble through the grounds, which are open to the public till quite dark. Oh, what walks, what lawns, what groves! What herds of deer, of every variety of shade, springing from the bushes and dashing away at full speed! In the shade of the beach and chestnut, stood a group of cows of rare size and beauty. Away in the distance, were browsing a flock of sheep; before us was a sheet of water filled with water *fowls, sailing* about to their heart's content. Yonder was hedged in a perfect forest of several acres, filled with game of all kinds, wild with tangled brush and old, lofty trees, that seemed to have weathered ages, with its game keeper and lodge, which no one dares to enter, but over whose hedge we ventured to peep. And then such beautiful fountains, rising like mist or wreath of snow above the luxuriant foliage around! Never did I see so beautiful a picture of quiet, rural beauty as Chatsworth. Everything is just right. Nothing can be added, and nothing altered; not a tree too many, nor one too few, and all where they ought to be. The roads wind about, till lost in the distance, white as the whitest gravel can make them, creeping through the green grass. They are swept every day, and not a dead limb or an unsighly object meets your whole vision. Every tree even is perfect in its shape and of its kind; the grass is like velvet, cropped close by the two thousand deer and one thousand cows that roam over it. And the sweet little cottages that peep out upon you, each unlike and more beautiful than its neighbor, covered with honeysuckle or ivy, or wreathed with roses, looked as if they might be the abode of industry, refinement, love and peace. So entranced was I with the vision of this landscape of beauty, which stretched away as far as the eye could reach, (for the circumference of the Duke's park is fifteen miles) that, for the moment, I yielded to the belief, that I had at last found a place into which sin and sorrow had never stalked. But who lives in all these beautiful cottages, scattered about, thought I; surely not the poor, they are too elegant and tasteful, and surely not the rich, for what business have they in the Duke's Park. We stopped a man to inquire, and were told the cottages were all owned and built by the Duke, and the occupants were all his tenants — and "his Grace," the man said, "was a *real* nobleman — so kind to his people and so benevolent to the poor." In one cottage, picturesque and beautiful, lives the old and infirm gamekeeper, too old for service, to whom the Duke has given the use of the cottage and settled on him a certain number of pounds per annum for life. Every voice here speaks in the Duke's praise. He spends but about six weeks during the year at Chatsworth, and fortunately he is here now. This is but one of several of his vast domains.

But I have said nothing as yet of Chatsworth House. It is a square pile, massive, and richly ornamented with fluted columns and pilasters; it has been built at different periods, yet all in good taste, and wears quite a modern air. The last addition is in Grecian style. The masonry is of a rich buff color — a soft sandstone — and it is all surrounded with an open balustrade, and adorned with urns, vases and statues. With the rich dark green hills behind, and the terraces, extending twelve hundred feet in front, with its gardens and fountains, and a lawn, stretching away before all, through which winds a small river like a stream of silver, and a beautiful cascade on the right, with a jet d'eau, said to be the most magnificent in Europe, attaining the height of two hundred and sixty-seven feet, and the hunting tower perched on a peak at the left, embowered in trees, from which a red flag always floats when the Duke is here, Chatsworth, to my eyes, presents the most imposing and magnificent spectacle of taste, art and primeval beauty combined, that I have ever beheld.

Chatsworth is open to visitors from eleven in the morning till five, P. M. In our first ramble, we were too late to gain admittance that day, so we wandered on, over an elegant bridge with three arches, thrown across the lovely stream that meanders through the park, to a small tower, shaded with venerable trees and built on an eminence, surrounded by a moat. We ascended a flight of steps to the Bower of Mary, Queen of Scots, so called from the fact, that the unhappy and beautiful princess used to spend many of the hours of her confinement here, when, for thirteen years, Chatsworth was her prison. Espying a noble looking structure to the left of Chatsworth House, apparently a church, with its great tower and huge clock, we concluded to enter it, as it seemed open, and take a nearer view of the place where we should probably attend worship the next day, and perhaps see the Duke of Devonshire himself, the Lady Carlisle, his sister, and the Earl of Burlington, the Duke's heir apparent, and family, who are all here now. On arriving at the entrance and receiving permission of a man standing there, to enter, we walked in, and to our great astonishment as well as amusement, found ourselves in the Duke's *stable*, with a hundred horses perhaps, instead of the Duke's *chapel*. On our return to the Inn we met the Duke and Lady Carlisle, who were just returning from a drive in the park. The Coachman, postillion and footman, looked like black and yellow butterflies, in their gay striped livery; the Duke himself and his sister, were plainly and simply dressed. The Duke is sixty-two years of age. In his younger days he was Lord Chamberlain to George the Fourth, and was then, I imagine from portraits taken of him at that time, quite a handsome man.

The next day we attended the old church, which we found at length, embowered in trees, so trimmed as to form a row of arches around the church yard. It was a communion season, and the Duke partook of the sacrament. There were, perhaps, seventy people at church.

The next morning we rose early, and in order to heighten the modern beauty of Chatsworth, by a contrast with the antique, we drove, before breakfast, five miles to Haddon Hall in company with a gentleman from Natchez and our friend from St Louis. It was a beautiful drive, through a rich country, on the east side of the river Nye. Haddon Hall is not a ruin, but has been deserted these fifty years, on account of its rudeness and antiquity. It is kept in perfect order, and a family live near who keep the keys, and for a fee show it to strangers. I had not a correct idea, previous to my visit here, of the mode of living two or three hundred years ago. Their style was even more rude than I had supposed. The banqueting hall is no better than a rough farmer's kitchen, and the dining table, from which royalty itself was served, is an old rough oak table, no better than a butcher's meat bench. A gallery runs across one end of the hall, to which, we were told, the ladies retired after dinner, where they were privileged to look down and witness the antics, and enjoy the merriment of their uproarious lords when full of wine.

The large pewter platters on which the meat was served, are nearly three feet in diameter, and at the cooking utensils and queer old fashioned boots, and curious articles, worn by the old nobility of England, we, rude scions from the American wilderness, laughed till we cried. The dancing hall is the only good and really comfortable room in the place. The window panes are about six inches by four. The workmanship of the doors is so rude as to make any body laugh. The room Queen Elizabeth occupied, when a visiter here, contains her bed, just as she used it. The counterpane is of white satin, flowered over with gold and silver tinsel and colors, wrought into marvelous looking animals, and was once a beauty, no doubt, but somewhat the worse for wear. George the Fourth was the last person who slept in this bed. The bedstead is six feet long and sixteen feet high! The canopy was the work of the Vernon family, who once owned this seat. Several of the rooms are covered with tapestry, wrought by the Vernons, who must certainly have been quite industrious. We were shown the door by which Miss Dorothy Vernon eloped with Sir John Manners, and by this *bad manners* the place passed into the hands of the Rutland family. The bust of the old Lady Manners, taken at ninety-three years of age, stands in the dancing saloon. The last male heir of the Vernon family, Sir John Vernon, was called the King of the Peak, on account of his hospitality and magnificent mode of living. So much for the times!

Next to the porter's lodge was the chaplain's room. I pitied the poor fellow who enjoyed, or rather endured, this honor. He had not as comfortable a room in his stone cell, as many of our State's prisoners. No part of this building is of latter date than the sixteenth century.

After breakfast we paid another visit to the Park. We went first to the "Kitchen Gardens;" they cover twelve acres and are exceedingly beautiful. I must say, that the celebrated Mr. J. Paxton is the presiding genius of Chatsworth, and that to his exquisite taste and ability, Chatsworth owes its peculiar charms. And moreover, I ought to add, that it is said the income of the Duke of Devonshire, is one thousand pounds per day, or five thousand dollars, and that Mr. Paxton has unlimited power to carry out every thought and plan. So great is the celebrity of these gardens, grounds and conservatory, and the fame of Mr. Paxton, that even foreigners come here to receive instructions in horticulture. Every quarter of the globe has been ransacked by parties, sent out by his Grace, the Duke, to collect plants and obtain varieties. We waited at the garden gate some time before we gained admittance. To every eight persons was allowed one guide. I expected to be ushered into a magnificent cabbage plat, and to see turnips as big as my head, and cucumbers half a yard long; but did not really anticipate much pleasure from my visit to the *Kitchen gardens*, as they are called, so that when I had actually entered, and found myself surrounded by the most rare and elegant flowers, and fruits of the choicest and most exquisite kinds, I could not refrain from expressions of admiration and delight. The show-house, for flowering plants, is filled with splendid specimens. One house contains an African lily, whose leaves are five feet in diameter, and about fifteen feet in circumference; the blossom is one foot in diameter, when fully open. So hot is the temperature necessary for this exotic, that I felt as if I was half cooked, when I emerged into the open air. Another plant, called the sacred Brahman plant, from the East Indies, is a wonderful specimen. It is valued at two thousand guineas. One green house is devoted to New Holland plants, and beautiful heaths. One house is devoted to one tree, the "Amherstia Nobilis," said to be the most beautiful tree in the world, and the only specimen in European gardens. Then comes the geranium house, with its infinite variety, and the orchidaceous house, containing the greatest private collection of air-plants in the country. Then we went into the cherry house, the peach house and the strawberry house, and several pineries and graperies. The peach house contains the finest Royal George peach tree in the kingdom. It is trained to the walls of the green house, and extends from tip of branch to branch, seventy-two feet. Seventy dozen peaches were raised on this one tree one year. Lace netting is stretched underneath, a foot or two from the ground, to receive the ripe fruit as it falls. Pine apples are growing in all stages. Melon vines are trained up to the wall in a perpendicular position, and wherever there is a melon, it is laid on a little shelf, built up by its side, to grow and ripen. Currants are trained up to a stake, by one stalk, to the height of four feet before it begins to branch out. The body of some of the currant bushes is an inch an a half in diameter. Gooseberries are trained in the same way. The graperies produce the year round. The conservatory, near the house, built of glass, three hundred feet long and seventy-two feet high, designed and arranged by Paxton, *has* been a wonder, but the glass palace for the World's Fair, in process of erection, designed and superintended by the same person, will throw this entirely into the shade. I have not time even to name the rare productions of all climates which are gathered here. The water works are very extensive and beautiful. More than six thousand feet of piping is laid, of various sizes, to supply the jets. One curious looking dead tree particularly attracted our attention. It was not very large, and its branches were very peculiar —stiff and crooked, not a leaf on them. While gazing at it, in wonder, we were surprised by a perfect shower bath from this mysterious tree, and we all took to our heels. It was in fact only a curious jet, which our guide had slipped away to play upon us, and then returned to enjoy our surprise. In some parts of the premises, every thing that can produce the wildest scenery has been brought together and huddled into the most elegant and tasteful confusion possible. We climbed up by a rugged, winding path to the *hunting tower*, from which the country can be overlooked for miles. This was erected, it is said, for the ladies, that they might here look down upon and enjoy the diversion of stag-hunting, without its perils or its fatigues.

At 12 o'clock, we, with a hundred or more visitors that had collected, were ushered into Chatsworth House, each party with a separate guide. We were led through the Green Hall, the State Rooms, one hundred and ninety feet in length, the Chapel, Library, Sculpture and Painting Galleries, &c. Although a vast collection is not found here, there are, nevertheless, many productions of the greatest artists. And every thing is arranged in such admirable taste and order, that the finest effect is produced. The mosaic floors are of oak, curiously and beautifully inlaid and polished. The walls, in one room, are covered with buff leather, stamped in figures and embossed in gold. In some they are fitted up with Gobelin tapestries, from the cartoons of Raphael. The Chapel is wainscoated with the finest cedar. The ceilings are ornamented with elegant paintings, and as everything is fresh and kept in perfect preservation, all appears to advantage.

The tables are exquisite productions of art, and the mirrors, ornaments and curiosities are all of the most splendid style. Although the Duke spends but six weeks in the year here, one hundred and fifty persons are attached to the establishment, (besides those who occupy the cottages) and are here the year round. The Duke is not married; it is said he would lose his estates should he marry. After spending several hours, examining paintings, &c., we resumed our rambles in the Park. We explored almost every avenue, and startled the deer from every glade. We met the game keeper, who, after selecting a choice fawn with his eye, picked him off the herd with his rifle; at which the whole flock, nearly one thousand in number, plunged into the stream and swam across, sending forth such an unearthly yell as I never heard before.

And now, gentle readers, all, both great and small, having conducted you to the most beautiful place in all my travels, taking it altogether; beautiful in natural scenery, and the embellishments of taste and art, I most take my leave. I could not part from you in a more delightful spot—away from the world, its noise, bustle, dust, beggars and troubles;

and though Solomon "in all his glory" has declared, that "the eye is never satisfied with seeing, nor the ear with hearing," yet, I must beg leave to differ from the wisest man that ever lived, and say, that mine *is*, and I am afraid *your* patience and long suffering with my long "yarns" are well nigh exhausted, and so I must say, *Farewell.*

www.ingramcontent.com/pod-product-compliance
Lightning Source LLC
LaVergne TN
LVHW010251110826
845151LV00004B/1443
* 9 7 8 1 4 2 5 5 2 4 4 4 9 *